SHAKESPEARE
AND
SOUTH AFRICA

SHAKESPEARE
AND
SOUTH AFRICA

DAVID JOHNSON

CLARENDON PRESS · OXFORD
1996

Oxford University Press, Walton Street, Oxford OX2 6DP

Oxford New York
Athens Auckland Bangkok Bombay
Calcutta Cape Town Dar es Salaam Delhi
Florence Hong Kong Istanbul Karachi
Kuala Lumpur Madras Madrid Melbourne
Mexico City Nairobi Paris Singapore
Taipei Tokyo Toronto
and associated companies in
Berlin Ibadan

Oxford is a trade mark of Oxford University Press

Published in the United States
by Oxford University Press Inc., New York

British Library Cataloguing in Publication Data
Data available

Library of Congress Cataloging in Publication Data
Johnson, David.
Shakespeare and South Africa / David Johnson.
Based on the author's thesis.
Includes bibliographical references and index.
1. Shakespeare, William, 1564–1616—Study and teaching—South
Africa.   2. Shakespeare, William, 1564–1616—Appreciation—South
Africa.   3. English drama—Study and teaching—South Africa.
4. English drama—Appreciation—South Africa.   5. Education—South
Africa—History.   6. Criticism—South Africa—History.   I. Title.
PR2971.S6J64   1996
822.3'3—dc20   95–36180
ISBN 0–19–818315–1

1 3 5 7 9 10 8 6 4 2

Typeset by Graphicraft Typesetters Ltd, Hong Kong
Printed in Great Britain
on acid-free paper by
Biddles Ltd,
Guildford and King's Lynn

FOR

My parents

Acknowledgements

My principal intellectual debt is to Jonathan Dollimore, who provided excellent supervision for the thesis on which the book is based. Jason Freeman at Oxford University Press has been a superb editor, patient, encouraging, and unfailingly professional.

I am very grateful to the following sponsors for funding my research: the Africa Educational Trust, the Centre for Scientific Development, the Overseas Research Scholarships, and the University of Natal. Librarians at the following libraries were enormously helpful: the South African Library and University of Cape Town Special Collections in Cape Town, the National English Literary Museum in Grahamstown, the UNISA Library in Pretoria, and the Sussex University Library in Brighton.

Special thanks to Nic Visser and Shane Moran, who read and commented in detail on the final drafts; also to all the following people, who gave time and consideration to my work: Des Bailey, Vivian Bickford Smith, Laura Chrisman, Gill Clark, Leon de Kock, Fenuala Dowling, Saul Dubow, Sally Eberhardt, Garth Fourie, Rosibel Gomez, Peter Kallaway, Rochelle Kapp, Conor McCarthy, David McFarlane, Craig McKenzie, Graham MacPhee, Celia Maud, Robert Morrell, Sharda Naidoo, Graham Pechey, Prem Podar, Ciraj Rassool, Rory Ryan, Corinne Sandwith, Alan Sinfield, Kelwyn Sole, Elaine Unterhalter, Norman Vance, Clive van Onselen, and Lyndall van Onselen. A shorter version of Chapter 2 appeared as 'Starting Positions: The Social Function of Literature in the Cape', *Journal of Southern African Studies*, 19/4 (Dec. 1993), 615–33, and of Chapter 3 as 'Aspects of a Liberal Education: Late Nineteenth-Century Attitudes to Race, from Cambridge to the Cape Colony', *History Workshop Journal*, 36 (1993), 162–82.

Contents

Introduction

Shakespeare

My central concern is to relate the political mission of English studies in South Africa over the past 200 years first to its historical context, and second to current cultural, political, and theoretical debates reflecting on its future.

The range and variety of English studies in contemporary South Africa can best be conveyed by juxtaposing two very different versions of Shakespeare I encountered in 1989. The first Shakespeare was firmly entrenched at Athlone Teachers Training College in Paarl, where students were protesting against apartheid education policy, the state of emergency, and elections for the discredited tricameral parliament. This Shakespeare is described in prescriptive detail in the college's English examination paper from the previous year as follows:

It sounds absurd to ask why one should read Shakespeare, but the unfortunate fact is that very few grown-up people read him at all. And most boys and girls read him not because they want to, but because public examinations demand that they should.

Everybody agrees to put Shakespeare on a pedestal, which is the last place he would care to choose for himself. The truth about him is that he is the greatest living writer that we have ever had, for the simple reason that he knew more about humanity than anyone else of whom we know. Other men may have known more, but they could not express their knowledge, and it isn't much good having knowledge or sympathy if you can't express them.

Again, if you are amongst those who are bored by Shakespeare, you must remember that the reason for your boredom lies in your own dullness, not Shakespeare's. If a man has interested all types of people for several hundred years it is probable that if he fails to interest you, there is something radically wrong with you. You may prefer authors like Zane Grey, Edgar Rice Burroughs or Barbara Cartland just as some of your ignorant ancestors preferred the Zane Greys and Edgar Rice Burroughs of their time, whose works are deservedly forgotten.

There is perhaps only one infallible test of genius: that is time. Those whose work does not merit immortality don't achieve it. You may reply that you find the atmosphere of the immortals too rarefied for you, but after the initial effort to arouse yourself, you will hug yourself with delight at having got out of the ruck. So persevere with Shakespeare, not for the sake of passing an examination but in order to increase your delight in life.

But you need not necessarily persevere in the same way that ended so disastrously last time. The best way of dealing with Shakespeare is to go to the theatre and see his plays acted. As he wrote for the stage, it is after all, only natural that they should be most successful in their proper place. If you can't see them acted by other people, you should act them yourself. Failing that, you will have to fall back on reading them—but read them fast to begin with, and don't worry if you fail to understand isolated words or similes. The first business is to get down to the development of the characters. You may well find them too wordy, for instance. Whenever you find some definite cause for your dislike, stop and analyse the reason—this wordiness, for example.

Think for a moment of the conditions under which Shakespeare worked. His audiences were composed of people who were in love with words; they were exactly like children who have just found the joy of being able to speak. Words meant much more to them than they do to us. I am not making excuses for Shakespeare's shortcomings. I am merely trying to show you that many things that we are inclined to regard as faults, were not faults at all.

It is worth remembering that Shakespeare was an actor who knew what the public wanted, let them have it, and made a considerable sum of money doing so.

After reading the passage carefully, the students had to answer the following questions:

1. Why does the author of the passage consider Shakespeare to be the greatest writer we have ever had?
2. What, according to the writer, is the reason, if the writing of Shakespeare does not interest you?
3. Why does the writer feel that the works of writers like Grey and Rice Burroughs are quite rightly already forgotten?
4. What is the final test of whether a book is great or not?
5. The writer mentions something that one may dislike in Shakespeare's works.
   5.1. What is this?
   5.2. Give a reason for this apparent fault in his writing?

6. Quote a sentence from the passage to prove that the writer realizes that Shakespeare was not perfect.
7. Why does the writer think that the most effective way to get to appreciate Shakespeare's work, is to go to the theatre?

This is the only Shakespeare the overwhelming majority of South African students ever encounter. The comprehension test sets out explicitly the assumptions underwriting the literature component of South African school and college English syllabuses: that Shakespeare was an extraordinary genius ('the greatest living writer'; 'he knew more about humanity'; 'interested all types of people for several hundred years'; will 'increase your delight in life'; and 'made a considerable sum of money' giving the public what it wanted); and that students should accordingly prostrate themselves before his great works ('your boredom lies in your own dullness, not Shakespeare's'; 'things that we are inclined to regard as faults, were not faults at all'). This Shakespeare, reproduced in the violently unstable educational context of post-1976 South Africa, might indeed be more properly connected to the date 1876, since he faithfully recalls the figure institutionalized in English teaching in the second half of the nineteenth century.

At the same time, I came across a second Shakespeare on the shelves of the University of Cape Town library in an article written by South African critic Rob Nixon for the US literary journal *Critical Inquiry*. In 'Caribbean and African Appropriations of *The Tempest*', Nixon takes full advantage of excellent research facilities and, more importantly, of the intellectual possibilities opened up by contemporary Western Shakespeare critics. Starting from the related premises that cultural value is 'an unstable social process rather than a static and, in literary terms, merely textual attribute',[1] and that audiences have the capacity to determine the meaning of literary texts in ways 'responsive to indigenous interests and needs' (229), he contrasts the Eurocentric interpretations of the play by Octave Mannoni and Philip Mason, and the sympathetic identification with Caliban by George Lamming, Aimé Césaire, and Roberto Fernandez Retamar. He concludes:

Between the late fifties and the early seventies *The Tempest* was valued and competed for both by those (in the 'master'-culture's terms) traditionally possessed of discrimination and those traditionally discriminated against. On the one hand, a broad evaluative agreement existed between the two sets of feuding cultures, the colonizers and the colonized both regarding the play highly. On the other hand, the two groups brought utterly different social ambitions to bear on the play. Writers and intellectuals from the colonies appropriated *The Tempest* in a way that was outlandish in the original sense of the word. They reaffirmed the play's importance from outside its central tradition not passively or obsequiously, but through what may best be described as a series of insurrectional endorsements. For in that turbulent and intensely interactive phase of Caribbean and African history, *The Tempest* came to serve as a Trojan horse, whereby cultures barred from the citadel of 'universal' Western values could win entry and assail those global pretensions from within.   (577–8)

This Shakespeare differs in fundamental ways from the one taught in Paarl. In the first place, the context in which Shakespeare appears is different: he is presented to a much smaller audience, not for a mass education system in crisis, but for the consumption of a relatively small élite of mainly First World university students in stable educational institutions. Further differences relate to Shakespeare's status as a figure of unquestioned authority: 'he' is not the 'greatest living writer', but rather a corpus of texts forged over a long period by a variety of cultural institutions to become 'the gold standard of literature' (560). Secondly, the colonial audience's relation to Shakespeare is not framed in authoritarian terms: instead of being berated for showing insufficient respect for the Bard, the colonial writers' 'repeated, reinforcing, transgressive appropriations of *The Tempest*' are affirmed as worthy components of 'the grander counterhegemonic nationalist and black internationalist endeavors of the period' (558). Seeing Shakespeare as a text rewritten by different audiences to suit their own interests enables the creation of an oppositional Shakespeare, a figure in Césaire's argument opposed to the colonizer Prospero's 'cold reason' (quoted in Nixon, 571), and in sympathy with the colonized Caliban's struggle against Western totalitarianism.

What these two Shakespeares—the conservative Paarl Shakespeare, and the radical Columbia Shakespeare—point to is a third figure implicit in Nixon's argument, namely

'Shakespeare'. 'Shakespeare' is a body of texts produced, disseminated, contested, institutionalized, performed, and criticized over a long period of time by a wide variety of social agents, and it is a small part of the history of this 'Shakespeare' I relate here. I am interested in the central, symptomatic role played by Shakespeare (I will dispense with the scare quotes, unless the constructed nature of Shakespeare is specifically being discussed) in South African English studies, and survey all South African literary criticism, and particularly Shakespeare criticism, produced from the beginning of the nineteenth century to the present. This includes critical texts written for both university and school consumption. English criticism for the different periods is summarized, with particular attention paid to those metropolitan critics who were cited by South African critics and those who were ignored. Metropolitan constructions of Shakespeare continue to exert a defining influence on the versions of the Bard deployed in former colonies: A. C. Bradley is as much part of the South African Shakespeare landscape as any critic writing from the geographical space of South Africa. As regards the place of English studies in South African schools, I look at educational journals, syllabuses, examination papers, set-work books and recommended reading-lists, school editions of Shakespeare plays, and study aids.

This focus is narrowed in several ways. First, the education departments have similar syllabuses, and, in order to avoid repetition, I concentrate for the most part on the Western Cape. This still allows me to look at how English studies proceeds within the range of institutions functioning in South Africa, since all forms—universities, teacher training colleges, and high schools—for each of the state-defined race groups, are represented in this area. Specific initiatives in English teaching and Shakespeare production outside the Western Cape are, however, also surveyed. For example, in Chapter 5 I look at the work of three energetic critics at the University of Natal (Pietermaritzburg), Geoffrey Durrant, D. R. C. Marsh, and Christina van Heyningen, and in Chapter 6 I refer to the efforts of the Shakespeare Society of Southern Africa based in Grahamstown. Inevitably, much interesting work is not covered; as far as possible, I refer to it in the notes.

The second way in which the research area is limited is by treating Shakespeare as representative of English studies, and 'Shakespeare' is further narrowed by concentrating on the most frequently studied plays, particularly *Hamlet*, *Othello*, and *The Tempest*. Again, this focus is not exclusive, and arguments about Shakespeare's other works, and indeed other literary figures contending for a place in South African English syllabuses, are followed where they shed light on my main concerns.

Finally, since my interest lies primarily with criticism and education, I look at publishing and dramatic productions only where they relate directly to the educational reproduction of Shakespeare and English literary culture. In Chapter 5, for example, I note the establishment of Maynardville Open-Air Theatre in Wynberg, where Shakespeare productions have played a central role in supporting Shakespeare in schools, and in Chapter 6 I describe the very high stakes involved for publishers competing for the contracts to provide the set literature texts for pupils studying under a unified post-apartheid education system.

. . . And South Africa

If there are many 'Shakespeares', there are also many 'South Africas'. And, furthermore, there are many ways in which the relationship between 'Shakespeare' and 'South Africa' might be conceptualized. My principal methodological assumption is that there is a connection between ideas and history. The classic formulation of this assumption is set out by Karl Marx and Friedrich Engels in *The German Ideology*, where they assert that '[t]he production of ideas, of conceptions, of consciousness, is at first directly interwoven with the material activity and the material intercourse of men'.[2] The production of the ideas associated with the study of Shakespeare is thus taken to be interwoven with the material accumulation of capital and the functioning of the racist state in South Africa.

That such an approach might lead to crude generalization and simplistic homologizing is a methodological risk Edward Said insists is worth taking:

Thus it seems to me that one thing to be tried—out of sheer critical obstinacy—is precisely that kind of generalization, *that* kind of political portrayal, *that* kind of overview condemned by the present dominant culture to appear inappropriate and doomed from the start. It is my conviction that culture works very effectively to make invisible and even 'impossible' the actual *affiliations* that exist between the world of ideas and scholarship, on the one hand, and the world of brute politics, corporate and state power, and military force on the other.[3]

Said does not acknowledge any debt to Marx here,[4] but proceeds to explore the 'actual affiliations' between Reaganism and the American left criticism of Fredric Jameson and others. In this study I search for the connections between the 'brute politics' described in histories of South Africa and the Shakespeares functioning within its borders, from the time of Lord Charles Somerset and Thomas Pringle, to the decade of P. W. Botha and Professor J. M. Coetzee.

Four kinds of writing are employed in trying to do justice to the subtleties of the relation plotted between texts and contexts. The first two might be drawn out from Marx's famous formulation in *The Eighteenth Brumaire of Louis Bonaparte* that '[m]en make their own history, but not of their own free will; not under circumstances they themselves have chosen but under the given and inherited circumstances with which they are directly confronted'.[5] To extend the first part of the formulation, 'men make their own history', I follow the line of figures who taught English literature and had it institutionalized at the core of the educational systems in England and later in South Africa. This involves summarizing, for example, the cultural analysis of Matthew Arnold, the literary criticism of A. C. Bradley, and the reports of government commissions investigating educational reform in England and South Africa. The assumption is that the conscious and willed personal action of men is sophisticated enough to explain this particular history.

In pursuing the second part of the formulation, 'not under circumstances they themselves have chosen', narratives about 'men' would be replaced by ones about the 'circumstances' that produced 'the men'. This involves detailing economic and political histories which analyse the emergence of the modern South African state, paying particular attention to how impersonal factors, which could be theorized as 'class', 'ideology', 'discourse', or 'episteme', have determined the acts of figures prominent in the evolution of South African English studies. To this end, extensive use is made of recent revisionist South African historical writing, in the areas both of education histories and of more general political–economic–social histories. The assumption here is that the most decisive explanatory terms and narratives are those about the circumstances determining English studies, and that an 'internal history' of the subject in South Africa is doomed to banality and myopia without the contextualizing of external forces.

The choice made between 'men' or 'circumstances', however, does not automatically commit the project to a particular political position. Both alternatives can in their own ways challenge the dominant assumptions about historical change, but they can also both shore them up. It is as easy for the former to proceed with the subtext that great men have determined the nature and practice of English studies, and that the most students can hope for is a more benevolent patriarchy to direct the discipline in the future, as it is for the latter to be underpinned by the assumption that particular cultural practices (like the teaching of English) are functions of structural forces impervious to individual and collective acts of resistance in struggles for educational empowerment. A solution therefore might be to assume a discursive form that retains some kind of creative tension between these parallel alternatives: both tell a great deal about English studies in South Africa, and their juxtaposition in a continuous yet fragile narrative might destabilize their respective assumptions. For example, the details of Roderick Noble's regime in the South African College's English Department, and the dramatic transformations in the social and economic polity of the Cape in the late nineteenth century might profitably be read against each other.

The question then arises as to what other forms of writing might profitably be employed. An obvious one is that diverse body of work which is grouped under the heading 'critical theory'. Closely associated in its early years with radical student challenges to universities in Western Europe in the late 1960s and early 1970s, critical theory has since been increasingly institutionalized. However, as Raymond Williams argues, it retains the potential to interrogate dominant forms of cultural production: '[T]heory is at its most significant when it is concerned most precisely with the *relations* between the many and diverse human activities which have been historically and theoretically grouped in these ways, and especially when it explores these relations as at once dynamic and specific within describably whole historical situations which are also, as practice, changing and, in the present, changeable'.[6] Williams's argument here for a practice of cultural theory that seeks to describe the relations between different human activities is very close to Said's insistence above on the need for criticism in the Western academies to identify the 'actual *affiliations*' connecting the world of ideas and scholarship and the world of politics. Critical theory, as conceived by Williams and Said, therefore has the capacity to generate a vocabulary for writing about these relations or affiliations, and to reflect on how they might be changed. There are of course theorists who would reject the analytical categories used by Marx, Said, and Williams, questioning among other things the implications of 'men' making history, and the hierarchies assumed between the political and the textual.[7] I return to these salient objections.

From the vast body of theory, there are two areas which I have already invoked that receive particularly extended attention: the Marxist tradition, and the more recent work of colonial discourse theorists like Said and Gayatri Spivak. In writing a material history and at the same time reflecting at some length on literary theory, I hope to bridge the received division between those who largely theorize about colonial history writing (Said, Spivak, Homi Bhabha, Robert Young, and Aijaz Ahmad) and those who write social histories of colonial subjects (in the South African context, this would include figures like Tim Couzens, Brian Willan, Bill Nasson, and Shula Marks).[8] History might thus be read, in Jonathan Dollimore's phrase, through 'theoretical lenses',[9] but at the same time, theory might itself be read historically. This involves drawing on contemporary theory to read historical texts, while using those texts to try and map, however tentatively, the historical roots of current theoretical preoccupations.

Finally, textual analysis, the form of writing most

conventionally associated with English studies, is also used. The close reading of selected texts, has, not without good cause, come to be identified with the most conservative strand of English studies. Performed in isolation, and upon a narrowly defined range of specifically literary texts, textual analysis has been perhaps the exemplary critical practice containing potentially radical challenges to a traditionally conservative discipline. Even Marxist and feminist readings of canonical works (or canonical critics) run the risk of simply contributing to the authority of those works, and in the process confirming the legitimacy of the 'decent pluralism'[10] ruling English studies. However, *in combination with other critical discourses*, textual analysis has the capacity to focus arguments in a manner that lends indispensable support to the more general arguments pursued. Texts are read, in Walter Benjamin's famous phrase, 'against the grain',[11] with an eye to exclusions and silences.

In the pages that follow, these different types of writing coexist in what I hope to be some kind of creative tension. Whatever advantages such a strategy might have, and I believe they would be substantial, it too would operate within definite discursive limits, since exclusion is axiomatic in every kind of discourse, in every kind of beginning and method. However, I hope that the contours of exclusion forged in the arguments below are sufficiently porous to admit fruitful dialogue, while at the same time are resistant to easy reinscription within the conservative assumptions and themes of dominant historiography.

Contemporary Debates

The second promise is to relate the history of English studies in South Africa to contemporary political, theoretical, and cultural debates. This too requires further explanation.

Each chapter of the book covers a certain time period and is organized in terms of a particular contemporary issue or debate. Chapter 1 surveys the literary criticism produced in lectures and literary journals at the Cape of Good Hope in the first half of the nineteenth century, connecting it to contemporaneous developments in England. Recent debates in South Africa on the role of art and culture, notably Albie Sachs's arguments in *Spring is Rebellious*, provide the focus for organizing this early material in terms of the different social functions conceived for imaginative literature. Four positions are identified: the missionary position (Shakespeare as substitute for the Bible); the utilitarian position (Shakespeare as body of facts to be tabulated and assessed for potential use-value); the romantic position (Shakespeare as source of transcendental truths); and the imperial position (Shakespeare as preeminent symbol of Englishness).

Chapter 2 looks at the second half of the nineteenth century, surveying South African and English criticism, as well as school editions of Shakespeare. The material is organized in terms of an extended reflection on the connections between colonial racism and liberal humanism, between the imperial project and the invention of English studies. Part of a common world-view in the 1880s, the question I pose is: to what extent do the racist assumptions axiomatic in the founding moment of English studies persist today?

Chapter 3 is based on the many tributes produced in England and South Africa in 1916 to mark the tercentenary of Shakespeare's death. The tribute by Sol Plaatje in Israel Gollancz's *A Book of Homage to Shakespeare* occupies particular prominence, providing a basis for exploring different ways in which the relationship between colonial subject and metropolitan culture has been expressed. Four possible constructions of Plaatje are suggested: by Frantz Fanon and other anti-imperialist writers; by Marx and Western Marxists; by social historians; and by Western colonial discourse theorists like Said and Homi Bhabha.

Chapter 4 surveys the criticism and school editions of Shakespeare in England and South Africa in the 1930s. Current arguments concerning the relationship of designated 'minority groups' to English studies provide the basis for exploring how South African women, black South Africans, and white male critics writing in the Cape searched for a critical voice. I argue that in the 1930s there was a decisive change in the critical persona assumed by literary scholars, from the voice of the Victorian gentleman scholar occupying the centre of the discipline to the voice of the professional critic writing from its margins. What I emphasize, however, are the limits of assuming such a marginal voice, both in terms of changing the assumptions and procedures of the discipline, and in terms of the (negligible) influence such voices have on the teaching of English at schools.

Chapter 5 surveys the criticism and school editions of Shakespeare produced in South Africa in the 1950s. (As the amount of material is far greater, the attention to contemporaneous English criticism is not as detailed.) The opposition constructed during this period and subsequently between Shakespeare and apartheid is examined, with a version of and reflection on Marx's dialectical method structuring the discussion. Three versions of the relation between Shakespeare and apartheid are considered: the one of opposition imagined by white liberal critics; the one of compatibility assumed by school Shakespeare syllabuses and editions of the plays; and the more ambivalent relation expressed in the criticism of the political journals of the Communist Party of South Africa, and the Non-European Unity Movement.

Chapter 6 covers the period from 1976 to the present, and focuses on travelling theory, exploring the passage of post-1968 radical literary theory from the West to English departments in South Africa. In particular, I consider the impact of such theory on Shakespeare studies, questioning the assumption that the presence of a Western 'radical Shakespeare' in South Africa would automatically undermine existing power structures. Recent political and critical developments are incorporated into this chapter, with particular attention paid to efforts to keep Shakespeare alive in South Africa (Martin Orkin's *Shakespeare against Apartheid* and the new journal *Shakespeare in Southern Africa*).

In the Afterword, noting the profound changes in South Africa while this study was in process (1989–1994), I reflect very briefly on positions available in relation to English studies in the 'new South Africa'.

1

The Social Function of Literature:
1800–1850

Introduction

Two related concerns structure my discussion here of the
public lectures and literary journals at the Cape in the first
half of the nineteenth century. The first is to reflect on the
origins in South African culture of arguments about literary
value, and the second is to understand how these arguments
prepare the way for the institutionalization of English literature[1] as a subject in school and college curricula at the Cape
Colony.

The early literary journals in the Cape constitute among
other things the beginning of attempts to contain and regulate
the (possibly subversive) effects of imaginative literature. The
writers and critics who controlled literary and critical production in the Cape in different ways sought to secure the interests of their constituencies. That these anxieties about literature
continue to preoccupy South African cultural thinkers is evident in recent disagreements in left culture. The debate occasioned by Albie Sachs's recently declared desire to ban the
slogan 'Culture is a weapon of struggle'[2] for five years is based
on the same assumption that literature matters enormously,
that it has the potential either to serve or to challenge ruling
blocs and their orthodoxies. There are of course no simple
continuities from the positions of the 1820s to those of the
1990s; none the less, contesting the social function of literature is central in both contexts, and at the very least this survey of the earlier period reveals that contemporary arguments
have a long and complicated history.

As regards the preparatory function of these arguments
in enabling the emergence of English studies, there were a

number of specific events in the early nineteenth century that might be identified as signalling the beginnings of English studies in South Africa: the production of *Hamlet* by soldiers of the garrison at Port Elizabeth in 1799; the opening of the first English-medium school at Gaika's Kraal in the same year; the essay on Wordsworth in the first edition of Thomas Pringle and John Fairbairn's *South African Journal* in 1824; or the first classes in English by Edward Conduitt Judge at the South African College in 1829. These events, however, preceded the teaching of English literature in its recognizably modern form, and in themselves offer little insight into the ideologies underpinning the discipline in its early years. The arguments in favour of teaching English literature—proposed in the second half of the century by the likes of Matthew Arnold—were put together from an uneasy synthesis of earlier views on literature, and it is these constituent arguments that are examined here.

These two concerns are connected in that the arguments about the social function of literature are for the most part the same arguments subsequently fused to justify the teaching of literature in a major educational project. I therefore deal with them as one, abstracting four overlapping positions on the social function of literature implicit in the writings of this period. They are: the missionary position, which sees literature as a proselytizing aid and occasional substitute for the scriptures; the utilitarian position, which sees it as something of limited use-value in the emergent capitalist social order; the romantic position, which sees it as a repository of profound spiritual truths; and the imperial position, which sees it as a means of constructing and securing British identity. I lay these positions out in some detail, and suggest in conclusion how they might relate to current arguments about literature in South Africa.

The Missionary Position

The settler economy in the first half of the nineteenth century was based on an enclave of merchants in Cape Town, wine and wheat farming in the Western Cape, and cattle farming in the interior.[3] Unlike other African colonies, the Cape had a relatively large white community (22,000 in 1800) which administered the economy and state apparatuses. This community was made up of four distinct groupings: British administrators and officers; British settlers and professionals; Boer settlers of Dutch, French, and German descent; and the missionaries largely from Britain. In the first half of the century, the balance of power between white and black communities in South Africa was such that it was possible for the majority of Africans to survive independently of the settler economy. It was only after the devastating military defeats inflicted upon the Xhosa in the 1850–3 Frontier Wars, and more particularly after the discovery of minerals in the 1870s, that Africans were drawn in substantial numbers into the settler economy and social polity.

The first mission school was set up in 1799 by Dr Johannes van der Kemp of the London Missionary Society at Gaika's Kraal.[4] The school was abandoned a year later, but the missionaries were not easily discouraged and the number of schools increased rapidly in the next fifty years. The overall impact of Christian educational initiatives was modest, for by mid-century only a very small number of Africans had enrolled at the mission schools (4,000 of the 9,811 pupils at school in the Cape in 1853[5]). Those few at schools were inducted into the white social polity as teachers and ministers for the missionary societies, or as clerks and minor officials for business and government.

The missionaries in South Africa came from the predominantly Evangelical missionary societies that had been established in England in the late eighteenth century. They were drawn for the most part from the labouring, artisan, and peasant classes in Britain, and extended their own personal biographies of modest social advancement to Africa: through literacy, Christianity, and industry, the African would ascend to the same (English) state of grace. Their principal aim was to win converts, an aim which overlapped with their professed desire to relieve material deprivation.[6] The core premiss of the movement was that all people are equal before God, and actual inequalities were but the result of environment, climate, or lack of opportunity. Missionary endeavour could overcome these disadvantages and liberate the full human potential in individuals of all races and classes. William Shaw, an early missionary among the Xhosa in the Eastern Cape, summarizes this position: the Xhosa 'probably possess as much capacity for mental improvement as the people of any other nation; and no one who had ever seen them would ever question their physical ability for being trained to any of the arts or habits of the most civilised society, were they placed in circumstances that favoured such a development of their powers and faculties'.[7] An important part of the appeal of Christianity for the Khoikhoi was its millenarianism; missionaries often emphasized that God was on the side of the oppressed and that damning judgement awaited false Christians like the Boers. These lessons for Africans were the colonial versions of similar efforts to incorporate the working classes in England into a Christian universe based on individual salvation and obedience to the Almighty, and similar strategies for conversion were employed in both contexts.

Schooling was the corner-stone of Christian initiatives, and functional literacy which would enable converts to read the Bible, the goal. Charity schools—set up by the Society for the Propagation of Christian Knowledge for the poor in England, and by the Society for the Propagation of the Gospel for the poor abroad—sought to convey the required level of knowledge, instilling habits of industry, sobriety, and deference in their pupils in the process. These schools subsequently introduced the monitorial systems perfected by Lancaster (for the Dissenters) and Bell (for the Church of England). These systems, which were used alike in schools at home and in the colonies, involved senior pupils in the teaching of the younger ones by means of rote learning, and in an atmosphere of strict rules of reward and punishment.

In England, by the first half of the nineteenth century there were a number of readers in print which carried excerpts from English classics for pupils to memorize or use for elocution training. These textbooks for teaching literature included both elocution anthologies and general anthologies for schools, with sections of prose and poetry. Where the selected passages did not deal directly with religious themes, three strategies were used to contain the potential subversiveness of literature:

framing the selection with stern moral commentaries; combining the fictional account with factual detail; and treating literature as a vehicle for memory training. The conservatism implicit in these procedures is articulated in F. C. Cook's collection *Poetry for Schools*, where the compiler expresses the hope that by exposing 'the children of the peasantry and artisans' to his selection, they might be inoculated against the influence of the 'socialist infidel'.[8]

In South Africa, the Bible was the only text generally available to teachers, and educators in the Cape were preserved from similar anxieties by the simple fact that their teaching resources did not include potentially threatening tales. No such alternatives were available, as Jane Sales explains: 'The ability to read meant the ability to read the Bible. Nothing else was available.'[9] Even at the South African College, which opened in 1829 in Cape Town with 100 students, the Bible was the most frequently used textbook, and most of the teachers were ministers of religion more than prepared to make extensive use of it. The first Professor of Dutch and English Literatures, Revd Edward Conduitt Judge, complained bitterly about the lack of textbooks in his first report of 1829, but, as a fervent Evangelical himself, saw some advantage in this: '[T]he book which I have thus put into their hands, is recommended by its own paramount importance, and by the neglect with which it has been treated in systems of education'.[10] Confronted with large classes, a demanding syllabus, and the shortage of books, Judge devised a system of teaching where he divided English classes into three parts: part 1 studied logic and composition; part 2 studied Roman history, the Old Testament, reading, grammar, parsing, and spelling; and part 3 studied the New Testament and reading. Although the Subscribers supporting the South African College wanted it to be a secular, non-sectarian place of learning, their intentions were thus substantially undermined by the personnel they employed, particularly for the teaching of English. The opposition of the College to the teaching of religion led Judge to resign from his post in 1830 and set up his own private grammar school, but his successors, John Pears and J. C. Adamson, were also deeply religious, perceiving their role as English teachers to be closely tied to their duty to spread the

Word. Adamson in particular took his pastoral obligations very seriously, ministering to the poor of all races.

The religious inclination of these early Cape intellectuals was also reflected in their literary criticism, with the arguments of English Evangelical magazines repeated in the Cape's more general equivalents. Broadly, two conceptions of the social function of imaginative literature were held by the missionary critics, the first being one of deep suspicion and antipathy. This view is expressed in a letter from 'A Well Wisher to the Youth of this Colony' to the editor of the *Cape of Good Hope Literary Gazette*, a magazine 'Devoted Exclusively to Literature, Criticism, Science, and the Advancement of Useful Knowledge'. The Well Wisher warns against the diabolical dangers of reading imaginative literature instead of the Bible or factual material:

There may be persons who cannot perceive any harm in a novel or romance; but experience teaches us that there is a tendency in novel-reading to affect and deteriorate the mind; and no determined novel reader ever arrives at that state of intellectual knowledge, which we find those possess whose reading has been confined to sober facts.[11]

He then quotes at some length the views of an unidentified 'celebrated writer':

My principal objection to novel reading, is *its immoral tendency.* . . . In making this assertion, however, I am taking the New Testament as the standard of morality; and by this standard, although there will be comparison in the shades of guilt, few will escape condemnation. . . . What are we to say of works which are polluted by luscious description of sensual pleasures, lascivious innuendoes and infidel bon mots; and which, almost uniformly, make love a passion wholly irresistible? What are we to say of works which justify not only the inordinate desire of the corrupted mind, but pride, vanity, revenge, ambition, and hatred; of works, which, in some instances, become the apologists of drunkenness, gambling, duelling, swearing, lying, and suicide?   (391–2)

To the fear that imaginative literature serves the 'socialist infidel' might therefore be added the fear that it undermines the Church's control of sexuality. Shakespeare too was seen to carry these threats, and certain Evangelical critics in England discouraged the reading of his plays (seeing performances of

Religion

them was of course entirely forbidden): one reviewer in the *Eclectic* insisted that it would have been better for English morality had Shakespeare never been born, and another in the *Christian Observer* objected to his plays on the grounds that they were neither Christian nor moral, and tended to excite the passions.[12]

This desire to control imaginative literature by censorship was not, however, the only position encouraged by missionary critics. There were others less fearful, who recognized the didactic potential of fiction and sought to harness it for their own ends. This second conception is expressed, for example, in an article entitled 'Fiction' in the short-lived *Cape Town Mirror*, which makes the reasonable point that even Jesus used stories to convey the Word:

The greatest of teachers, who perfectly knew every chamber in, and avenue to, the human heart, saw fit to embody the lessons of infinite wisdom and goodness in the form of concise fictitious narratives; compositions so beautiful, so impressive, so plain, so profound, so universally interesting and instructive, that, as even infidels have admitted, nothing of equal excellence has ever before or since been invented.[13]

Indeed, our desire for stories is not a sign of delinquency; it is something implanted in us by 'the beneficent framer of our mental constitution' (107), and as such something to be nurtured. The writings of Shakespeare and Scott are held up as incontrovertible support for the view that creative writing has an instructive function.

This second conception of literature is given its fullest expression in South Africa in two lectures delivered by Nathaniel James Merriman on behalf of the 'General Institute' of Grahamstown. In the first lecture, entitled 'On the Study of Shakespeare', Merriman's central argument is that

the faculties which we bring into exercise in studying Shakespeare . . . are the self same faculties which we are required to use in a far higher pursuit—I mean, in studying that one Divine Book which is given for the study of mankind.[14]

Shakespeare's only blemish—his 'coarse and abominable language'[15]—can be overcome by recourse to Bowdler's *Family Shakespeare*.

In this sanitized form, his magnificent wisdom, acknowledged by critics from Milton to Sir James Stephens, can be the 'instructor of every Englishman' (3). Like the Bible, Shakespeare is 'eminently the property of us all', and can nurture the finer aspects of the English character:

And those who know the influence of language in the formation of character, will easily see how the best parts of the English character have been ministered to by Shakespeare's rich and noble usage of words. (3)

Merriman then quotes a number of passages from *Hamlet* in order to demonstrate that Hamlet's character strikes 'a responsive chord . . . in the bosom . . . of every thoughtful Englishman' (7).

Furthermore, Shakespeare's characters function as moral examples to audiences. For example, Merriman argues that there is a 'lesson to be learned in watching the refined susceptibility of Hamlet's nature, making him a being gazed at in admiration,—one to be instructed by—but *never, never* to be envied or imitated' (8). Caliban is held up as a particularly accurate portrait, but, for Merriman, even more impressive than Caliban's verisimilitude is the 'great moral purpose for which Shakespeare employs him' (9). In the relationship between Caliban and Trinculo and Stephano, Merriman sees a parable warning the white man of the temptations which are offered by the colonial experience:

The Bard continues, skilfully to show us the hideous aspect which the low-lived and selfish vices of European civilisation assume when placed as they are by his master hand side by side with this poor savage. Here we have in Caliban the embodiment of more hatred and more treachery than any will impute to the worst tribe of wild Kaffirs—more ingratitude and folly than they will charge upon the deluded Hottentot (though Caliban like them, excuses himself on the plea of having been cheated out of his land) here is more grovelling and unreclaimable barbarism than we usually ascribe to the Bushman, yet when he is purposely brought into comparison or contrast with the dissolute seaman and the drunken butler, Trinculo and Stephano, with what a wonderful moral and poetic force does the loathsomeness of civilized vice exhibit itself to our eyes. Caliban in some contrasts rises to the dignity of moral, and certainly to the superiority of intellectual power. (9)

Merriman suggests that Trinculo and Stephano's counterparts, as well as Caliban's, are to be found in South Africa, and that even more honest likenesses abound in Western Australia, 'where the natives . . . are generally thought to approach as near to Caliban as any part of the human species' (9).

Not only is Shakespeare pre-eminent in his ability to nurture patriotism, and in his understanding of human nature, but his grasp of history as displayed in the history plays is also unequalled. Merriman in this lecture establishes this point by quoting long passages from *Macbeth* and *Richard II*, and then asserting that they reveal 'poetry and history in their best combination' (13). As authority for this judgement, he quotes Dr Arnold, who observes that 'the genius which conceived the incomprehensible character of Hamlet could alone be able to describe with intutive (*sic*) truth the character of Scipio or of Cromwell'; he further insists that if we fail to study imaginative literature, we lose access to 'a whole region of truth and reality' (14).

In the second lecture, *Shakespeare as Bearing on English History*, Merriman elaborates his view that Shakespeare is the pre-eminent guide to the historical past. Critical of historians who confine themselves to facts, Merriman quotes with approval Coleridge's view that

though 'the personages, events and dates, are subjected to the transmuting processes of a great Poet's imagination, it is so done as not to darken or distort, or falsify historic truth, but rather so as to array the whole with a living light'.[16]

For history to be arrayed 'with a living light', it should for Merriman reveal the workings of Divine Providence, and this too is the high function of dramatic art: dramatists should display 'the laws of the moral universe not didactically in set discourse but in action' (5). Shakespeare fulfils this dual function in his plays where he portrays God's hand in the affairs of men:

I confess I had been used to regard wicked rulers as a curse to a land and as a judgment sent from the Almighty, and good and virtuous rulers as the reverse of this. I am sure Scripture so represents them, and I am equally sure that the pen of Shakespeare does not go about to contradict this, but to exhibit its truth before us in action.   (7)

However, this more generous view of literature's potential for good does not extend to all writers. Shakespeare might be used to further the Lord's mission, but others most certainly cannot. Though he approves of Coleridge, Merriman is extremely hostile towards Byron.[17] He refers to the 'diseased and unhappy mind of Byron', quoting the American critic Reed, who contrasts Byron's inability to create 'a single healthful impersonation of humanity' with 'Shakespeare's genuine morality so loyal to the best moral instincts, never making vice attractive nor tempting us to look fondly on the proud and sinful temper'.[18] He concludes:

Shakespeare, it is true, never tarries to sermonise, nay, never betrays a consciousness that he is saying a word to auditors or readers in his own person, yet everywhere sets up the most unmistakeable finger-posts pointing to the moral government and the retributive justice of God in the affairs of men.   (16)

For Merriman then, only certain literature (Shakespeare) has the capacity to fulfil a worthy social function; other literature (Byron) revives the fears of the Well Wisher, and must be censored.

The Utilitarian Position

In the first decades of the nineteenth century, two distinct generations of colonial officials can be identified at the Cape Colony. The first was associated with the rule of the Tory governor Sir Charles Somerset. Before Somerset's arrival at the Cape, there were only desultory efforts on the part of the colonial authorities to establish English-medium schools.[19] In 1807, under pressure from the new government, the School Commission restarted and subsidized a purely English school, and ensured the teaching of English at the Dutch-medium girls' school and at the Latin school. In 1812 the existing 'Church Clerk' schools were brought under government control and subsidy by the governor, Sir John Cradock, and the teaching of English was awarded with a £15 increase in salary. The following year, at the initiative of the English Colonial Chaplain, a free public school run according to the systems of Bell and Lancaster was established for the children of the poor.

However, in 1822, in 'the speedy and masterful manner peculiar to him',[20] Somerset introduced a far more determined policy of Anglicization. He issued a proclamation substituting English for Dutch as the language of the Colony, and he authorized the employment at public expense of teachers whose mission would be to facilitate 'the acquisition of English by all classes of society' (15). His successor, Richard Bourke, set forth the conditions of employment for English teachers in the Colony: an ability to teach English grammar; familiarity with the system of Bell or Lancaster; willingness to submit to state inspection; and having sufficient knowledge of Dutch. In addition to enforcing the English language, the governors of the period deliberately undermined religious instruction in the schools carried out under the auspices of the Dutch Reformed Church by insisting upon the use of non-Calvinist texts in the schools.

Somerset's Anglicization programme met with limited success, attracting pupils in the predominantly English Eastern Cape, and remaining empty in the Western Cape. This failure led to renewed efforts to expand the education system on the part of the second generation of administrators. These men are described by historian E. G. Pells as 'a small group of altruistic individuals who happened to find themselves together in this out of the way corner of the globe during the years 1836 to 1839'.[21] They included Sir John Herschel, John Fairbairn, and Sir John Napier, and together introduced a number of measures to rationalize the Colony's Education system: the appointment of the first Superintendent-General of Education (James Rose Innes) in 1839; the division of the system into first-class (secondary), second-class (primary), and aided mission schools; the creation of a teacher training college; the introduction of a modern (as opposed to classical) curriculum; the enforcing of non-denominational religious instruction; and the teaching of English as a subject, but not necessarily as the medium of instruction.

The shift in the Cape Colony from the autocratic, patrician rule of Somerset to the rule of reason initiated by Herschel and his friends was not unique. In other parts of the Empire, there were similar changes in the nature of British colonial governance. For example, Gauri Viswanathan describes how in India the British administrators in the early part of the nineteenth century 'gravitated intuitively toward a classical approach to the study of language and literature as an end in itself, resisting implicitly utilitarian pressures to enlist literary study as a medium of modern knowledge'.[22] However, as the Indian colonial governors in the tradition of Somerset, like Lord Thomas Macauley, lost power and influence, so '[b]y mid-century a pedagogy of Christian morality gradually yielded to a pedagogy of worldly knowledge geared to the various occupations of life' (145).

To return to the Cape, Herschel and his group's collective confidence in their capacity to undertake major tasks of social engineering in this manner derived from a deep faith in the dynamic potential of rational thought placed at the service of societies no longer under the control of a derelict aristocracy. John Stuart Mill's conviction that 'mankind will not always consent to allow fat elderly gentlemen to fill the first place, without insisting upon his doing something to deserve it'[23] is echoed in an article by John Fairbairn 'On Literary and Scientific Societies' in the first edition of the *South African Journal*. Fairbairn (identified as 'N') praises extravagantly the achievements of the recently formed societies in England dedicated to increasing knowledge of the physical sciences, contrasting the intellectual conservatism of Oxbridge with the creative energy of these neo-Baconian societies:

To this order of things the New Societies gave a fatal and final shock. The accumulation of facts, which was their first object, overthrew in a moment the baseless fabrics of the Theorists; and active minds once thrown loose from their philosophic superstitions, combined with eagerness to multiply these facts, and to aid each other in classifying and reasoning them. . . . The man who could not speculate could observe, an indifferent observer could report, and the union of all these was not only effected, but provided for through all the classes of society, and through all the civilised countries of the world.[24]

Drawn from England's rising middle class and dispatched to the colonies, these 'altruistic individuals' confronted by 'a fat elderly gentleman' in the person of Somerset not surprisingly reproduced arguments that had been used by their metropolitan equivalents in their struggles against inherited privilege: that individual abilities rather than birth should determine access to power; that the accumulation of facts was a necessary first stage in any intellectual undertaking; that the application of reason to such facts guaranteed that knowledge thus gathered would be usefully deployed; and that the collective good—understood as the maximizing of pleasure and the minimizing of pain—was best served if those with the greatest reasoning powers were free to exercise them.[25]

As a result, utilitarian ideas underpinned the education reforms in the Cape during this period. They are most clearly explained in a letter Sir John Herschel wrote to the Revd James Adamson in 1835, where Herschel holds up England and its institutions as the model for schooling in the Cape:

In fact I cannot but think that what is good education in a highly civilised and peopled country is also good education in a colony and considering how much below the standard of *good* is the *best* usually afforded in England, I cannot regard that ... a bit too good for the Cape. In education as in coinage to lower the standard is suicidal.[26]

As regards what should be taught, Herschel places great store upon providing pupils with knowledge 'which possession goes to constitute our idea of a well informed gentleman', which is of 'obvious utility in every station of life', and which facilitates the 'exercise and development of the reasoning faculties' (41–2). Conceived in this way, education is the most effective means of overcoming the incidental disadvantages of industrial capitalism, of rescuing the working people from their own ignorance and torpor: the great object of education is 'to civilise the mass of a community and to spread [a] universal standard of intellectual attainment as well as moral feeling' (46–7). If all were educated in the same fashion, the sharp differences between opposed social classes would disappear:

A practical equality of moral and intellectual culture could it be established, so far from having tendencies inimical to a due subordination of stations and wealth would operate as a powerful correction of some of their worst evils, by smoothing the intercourse between distant ranks, and facilitating that perfect interfusion of classes which is essential to the harmony of society where free institutions prevail.   (47)

Like Somerset, Herschel is eager to encourage the teaching of English, but is less dogmatic. He values English as a means of communication and as a means of instilling a love of England in the subject peoples of distant lands:

entire ignorance [of English] ought to operate as a bar to admission. Considering also that this *is* and for centuries to come will *remain* a British possession—that communications with Britain are constant and increasing—British settlers flowing in yearly—British institutions multiplying—and British habits gaining ground I should conceive that *Caeteris paribus,* so far as can be done without sacrificing what is more important, a preference should be given to the English language as the medium of oral communication; and in the choice of Elementary books.   (45)

Although he never spells out 'what is more important' than the promotion of the English language, Herschel presumably refers in these passages to the ultimate protection of British rule in the Cape. In other words, be prepared to concede the priority of teaching the English language in schools if British interests can be secured in the process. But until then, ignorance of English will function as a 'bar to admission', a check on upward mobility within Cape society.

Herschel's oblique willingness to sacrifice English was certainly not shared by the majority of English officials at the Cape during this period, but the value of such strategic concession was also divined by Robert Niven of the Glasgow Missionary Society. Niven wrote to the Chief Commissioner of British Kaffraria in 1848, acutely identifying the place of language policy in maintaining British hegemony:

His Excellency's wish to supersede the vernacular tongue, by a foreign, the language of the conquered, by that of the conqueror, to make the euphoneous (*sic*) vehicle of the pathos patriotism and poetry which move the affections and feed the imagination of the Caffre, give way to one, which in the judgement of the nation is a cold complex uncouth impracticable species of the Babel genus, will be a work of time. English is taught at all Stations, it is believed. Methodically at some, and grows in favour, all the more that the capacity to read and speak it, is regarded as a *learned* acquirement, as much as the Latin tongue was in Europe, centuries ago. This fact combined with the increase of English Settlers, english institutions, and an english administration, must soon realise His Excellency's design without a tittle of constraint, or of a *purposed* extinction. The last, it is feared, would be fatal to the desirable ascendancy of our tongue, unless it were enforced with the *sensible* machinery of Prussia—and then the issue would not be worth the agency put in motion on its behalf.[27]

Besides instancing the tension between missionary and colonial bureaucrat, between the Commissioner's desire to colour the map red in bold strokes and Niven's preference for more subtle shading, Niven's letter reveals a keen insight into what makes for successful missionary work, whether it be for converts to Christianity or English. Only when an English administration and settler institutions are securely in place, only when the 'Caffre' can no longer survive outside the settler economy and polity, will there be any success in teaching English. And, further, such success will be greatly enhanced by avoiding the Prussian methods of coercion.

It would be mistaken, however, to see the shift from Somerset to Herschel as one of uncomplicated progress, as the latter's meritocratic, egalitarian intentions with regard to education policy were also premised on hierarchies and exclusions. This is perhaps best demonstrated by pointing to the arguments of Herschel's equivalent in England, Dr James Kay-Shuttleworth, who was the chief educational policy-maker within the British government in the 1840s. State educators in Britain during this period subscribed to this body of beliefs, conceiving themselves as 'experts' uniquely equipped to devise a schooling system for the working classes that would both help them and serve the common good. Kay-Shuttleworth resolutely exonerated industrial capitalism from responsibility for the plight of the poor: 'A system, which promotes the advance of civilisation, and diffuses it over the world ... cannot be inconsistent with the happiness of the *great mass of the people.*'[28] The fault lay rather with working people themselves, and educational experts like Kay-Shuttleworth sought to rescue them from poverty and depravity by providing via schooling a form of surrogate parenting that would integrate working-class children into society. According to historian Richard Johnson, this entailed an emphasis not only upon 'shaping the child as a rational and moral being, [but also upon] ways of combining literary education with an induction into labour for boys and into domestic duties for girls'.[29]

Kay-Shuttleworth saw the colonies as a space for testing out ways of educating and controlling the working class in England, and in 1847 sent a circular to Earl Grey, the Secretary of State for the Colonies, setting out what he considered to be the appropriate forms of education for the colonies:

> Nor will a wise Colonial Government neglect any means which affords even a remote prospect of gradually creating a native middle class among the negro population, and thus, ultimately, of completing the institutions of freedom, by rearing a body of men interested in the protection of property and with intelligence enough to take part in that humbler machinery of local affairs which minister to social order. . . . The objects of education for the coloured races of the colonial dependencies of Great Britain may be thus described. To inculcate the principles and promote the influence of Christianity, by such instruction as can be given in elementary schools. To accustom the children of these races to habits of self-control and moral discipline. To diffuse a grammatical knowledge of the English language, as the most important agent of civilization, for the coloured population of the colonies.[30]

He repeats with very little adjustment the policy with regard to working-class education in England. The opening paragraph insists on the nexus of a native middle class, institutions of freedom, protection of property, and social order, and the education system seeks to secure these connections. The aim accordingly is to teach Christian forbearance and moral discipline; to equip the lower orders with practical skills of some utility in the expanding capitalist economies; and to constitute the school as a substitute Christian family rescuing the unfortunate children of the poor (black or white) from the corrupting influences of the home. Herschel's arguments for an education system seeking to reconcile the 'distant ranks' of society therefore coexist with Kay-Shuttleworth's ideas for an education in the Cape based on vocational training for certain of those 'distant ranks'.

Official documents governing colonial education at this time reflected the increased status of science in England, with 'scientific' appraisals of the negro's educability replacing the assimilationist Christian ideals which characterized administrative documents of the 1820s and 1830s. An opposition emerged between missionaries, who tended to rely on a religious discourse to defend the abilities of Africans, and officials and state educationalists, who drew on a scientific discourse to establish a racial hierarchy with certain definite limits set on African intellectual potential. The missionaries failed to refute the arguments of science, moderating their aspirations with regard to converting Africans into black Englishmen and aiming instead at overseeing them in a relationship of trusteeship.[31] This meant in effect a different type of education: rather than receiving a literary education for potential equals, Africans increasingly received a vocational training which equipped them for lower forms of service. Generally, then, although only a very small proportion of Africans received a Western education, those that did were subjected to a three-pronged programme of indoctrination, made up of instruction in Christianity, the English language, and vocational skills, all contained within an organizational structure consciously modelled on the Victorian middle-class family.

Lovedale Seminary, which was started by the Glasgow Missionary Society in 1841, combined this complex of concerns: the curriculum included elementary reading lessons in Xhosa; primary education in the three Rs and geography, also in Xhosa; needlework for the girls and practical training in agriculture for the boys; courses in English for those Africans becoming teachers and missionaries; instruction in the classics for the sons of missionaries; and a special course for the daughters of missionaries. However, Lovedale also experienced the effects of the shift towards more racist perceptions of Africans in the 1840s, with James Stewart introducing a different educational dispensation when he replaced William Govan as principal in the 1850s. Whereas Govan had provided an education that sought to integrate Africans into colonial society on a basis of equality, and included Latin and Greek in Lovedale's curriculum to this end, Stewart favoured a separate curriculum for Africans, with English replacing

Latin and Greek, and vocational training enjoying a greater prominence. These changes were symptoms of the wider transition from assimilation to trusteeship in English relations with their African subjects.[32]

As was the case with the criticism of missionary critics, the literary criticism associated with the utilitarian position expresses anxieties about the subversive qualities of certain kinds of literature. Herschel, in the letter to Adamson cited above, reflects on the powerful influence of literature, and sets out his criteria for deciding what literature should be taught:

In what I have said I would not be understood as advocating a merely utilitarian course of instruction. Something must be conceded to ornament and elegance. The influence of a tincture of Elegant Literature early imbibed, on the tastes and habits in after life is far too important to be lost sight of.[33]

Although, he argues, it would be a 'very erroneous system which would banish [the study of poetry] as superfluous', the selection of poems should be 'cautiously made, and with reference to the matter as well as to the language' (47). He provides the following examples:

It is not easy to say on what defensible grounds the feeble pastorals of Virgil or the sickly loveletters and wild extravagances of Ovid are generally selected as the avenues by which the temple of the Latin Muse is approached, when there is quite as easy language for the beginner, joined with pleasing narrative and far loftier and more poetical diction to be found in the Aeneid, made the vehicle for the soundest good sense or the noblest sentiments and the most sterling wit in Horace. (47–8)

Unable to justify the place of poetry in the curriculum in strictly utilitarian terms, unable to dismiss it because of its status as a central part of the inherited classical tradition, and uneasy about its subversive potential, Herschel opts for the strategy of selective censorship: only certain types of literatures are allowed, with writing about sex banished, prose favoured over poetry, and morally uplifting literature encouraged.

A second reason for exclusion applied by utilitarian critics in determining the suitability of a particular text was faithfulness to reality. Literary realism was installed as a key criterion, as the report on 'Literature, Science and Art' in the first edition of the *Cape of Good Hope Literary Magazine* insists: 'All that is required is truth to nature.'[34] And Shakespeare is seen as exemplary in representing social reality accurately: Iago is 'portrayed in true, and natural colors' and 'Goneril and Regan are true to nature' (106–7). The effect of such realistic fiction being read is entirely to the good of the social whole: 'no work of fiction, which contains faithful representations of society of any grade or age, can be read without improvement' (108).

A related means of containing imaginative literature was to reduce it to a body of scientific facts. In the early nineteenth century, there was in England an enormous amount of scholarship directed to uncovering facts about Shakespeare's plays and his life.[35] An example of such criticism that appeared in the Cape is 'On the Sources of Shakespeare's Plots', an anonymous twenty-one-page defence of Shakespeare's creative originality. Taking on critics alleging that 'Bill was an adapter',[36] the writer surveys in scrupulous detail the original sources of Shakespeare's plays, and concludes (in tortured syntax) that attention to the facts of their composition reveals more clearly than ever the scale of his creative achievement:

But, because he did occasionally adopt a practice, which has been adopted by dramatists of all ages—the reproduction, in dramatic form, of events, fabulous or authentic, with which his audiences were familiar—some critics, who thought they did good service to the cause of literature, by attempting to bring Shakespeare down to the level of their own vulgar comprehension, and who delighted to display the great dramatist to their readers as an inspired barbarian, who, if he *did* know something intuitively about the stage, couldn't write Latin, and speak French as *they* could—(another popular fallacy which modern commentators are labouring to dispel)—these critics, we repeat, have endeavoured to persuade the general reader— who is content to recognise great thoughts and sublime imaginings, irresistible pathos, and genuine humor, in the works of his author, and cares little whence they came or how they were produced—that Shakespeare was devoid of original thought and powers of invention. Therefore it is, that we owe thanks to Mr Collier and to the members of the Shakespeare Society, for exposing delusions . . . and for thus restoring to the immortal poet a part of the glory, of which these detractors had sought to rob him.   (591–2)

Conceived in these terms, literature—a carefully selected and censored corpus of texts reducible to certain facts—is then seen as having the potential to play an extremely positive social function.

The Romantic Position

Although the journals of the 1820s and the 1830s in the Cape were dominated by writers inclined to favour utilitarian arguments, there were at least two contributions expressing support for the romantic position. The first was a two-part article by Fairbairn 'On the Writings of Wordsworth' in the *South African Journal*, and the second a short unsigned article on 'Poetry' in the *Cape of Good Hope Literary Gazette*.

Whereas Merriman wanted to ban Byron, and Herschel Ovid, the anonymous authors of these two pieces extend the range of approved literature to include writers offensive to missionary and utilitarian alike. Indeed, they celebrate what they see as the unique powers of contemporary poets like Wordsworth and Byron, emphasizing their superiority in terms of both what and how they write. In the first piece on Wordsworth, the poet's exceptional personal status is stressed:

The genuine poet, indeed, is stirred more than other men by the same objects, but the specific affection is not different; he does not love what they dislike, nor admire what they despise. His mental processes go on more rapidly, and yet with more stateliness and elegance than those of the crowd; but they are conducted by the same principles of association. Fancies he may have . . . but they are not current money with the merchant, and ought not to be presented in the market of real life.[37]

In part 2, the focus shifts to Wordsworth's poetry, and Fairbairn sets out to establish first its literary qualities, and then the 'moral qualities and the character of the Author's genius'.[38] His conclusions with regard to the former are extremely generous: his style displays considerable '*excursive power*' (110); his observations of humanity and nature are 'pencilled out with the same fidelity and precision [and are] admirable for their beauty, strength and novelty' (110); and 'his own genuine style . . . is purer mother English, and richer in native idioms than that of any other poet of this age, with the exception of Lord Byron' (114).

In his concluding assessment of Wordsworth's character, Fairbairn extends the claims for these poets to the realm of the religious:

> To conclude,—the principal features of his character, taking all his systems and theories at one view, are—profound wisdom chiefly of the heart, and grandeur of imagination. . . . His works are not given so much to quicken and beguile the temporal part of our nature, as to incite and support the eternal.   (117)

In thus giving the secular truths produced by poetic geniuses the stamp of the eternal, the supreme position of Christian truths assumed by missionary critics is threatened.

The romantic position, however, does not only challenge the missionary; it also undermines the claims of the utilitarian. In the short piece 'Poetry', the unnamed author confronts the hegemony of scientific discourses:

> At the same time, we wish it to be distinctly understood, that we are desirous of cultivating a most friendly intercourse with the Poets, and do most earnestly request their constant aid and correspondence. Poetry is a magnificent and exalted art. It is a nobler result of the intellectual power of man, than the profoundest science, or most subtle and erudite research. It is the proud and peculiar privilege of the Poet to *delight*! Instruction he frequently aims at (if he be of the right stamp,) but to excite refined and pleasurable sensations is particularly his object—failing in which, he fails completely. Poetry, it must not be forgotten, has in many countries been a chief instrument of civilisation. It has not only preceded science in the history of human progress, but it has in many countries preceded the knowledge of the mechanical arts. Even the mediocre effusions of the humbler poets, have been highly beneficial in the promotion of national improvement.[39]

Starting out as a conciliatory and even patronizing gesture towards poets—we, the sensible and practical, wish to have intercourse with you, the creative and spiritual—the argument then shifts in the next few sentences to elevate poetry above all other forms of writing. Not only is it nobler than science, but it also precedes it in the progress towards civilization.

Like the utilitarian notion cited above that literature has the capacity to produce social cohesion, the concluding claim here that poetry promotes national improvement elevates poetry to a position of extraordinary authority.

Despite this articulate plea on behalf of the unacknowledged legislators, seeing poetry as the ultimate guide continued to be a minority position in the Cape's cultural circles in the 1830s. The 'Poetry' article, for example, jars with the general tenor of the journal, which was earnestly committed to the 'Advancement of Useful Knowledge', and as a rule only included material of a more obviously scientific nature. However, although the pages of the *Gazette* never reflected any further support for the romantic position, it would seem that it gradually became more popular in the Cape because by 1847 the claims of literature were seen to supersede those of science in public debates held at the South African Library. The above-mentioned report on 'Literature, Science and Art' in the *Cape of Good Hope Literary Magazine* records general support for Mr Porter's contention that 'if England were driven to choose between her great men, she would be worse off, without her Shakespeares (*sic*) and her Scotts, than without her Newtons, and her Davys'.[40] Dr Adamson's arguments in favour of the study of science, on the other hand, were dismissed as unworthy of him, as doing 'no credit to a man of such sound learning, and deep erudition' (105).

The Imperial Position; or, Thinking of England

There was a fourth position on the social function of literature implicit in the prior three, the imperial position. Of particular importance was the connection between the romantic elevation of the poet genius, and the constitution of the nation. There are two dimensions to this, one looking outward to the Empire, and one looking inward.[41] As regards the imperial capabilities of English literature, they are well summed up by an essay in the *Cape of Good Hope Literary Gazette* entitled 'The English Language':

We learn from the daily and other Periodical Journals of Europe and America, of the great progress of the English Language. In the French and German Courts, English Tutors and Governesses are especially employed, whilst the perusal of English publications is sought after with avidity. In Germany, Clubs have been formed for the express purpose of promoting English conversation and the diffusion of English Literature. The truth is, much of this progress may be attributed to Sir Walter Scott. He has rendered ours, an almost universal language.[42]

English literature was taken as a symbol of English political and economic advance: Scott, in this argument, and not British traders, is responsible for the global spread of English language and culture.

In addition to standing in for the economic, military, and political conquests of British imperialism, English literature also played an important internal role in cementing the unity of the English nation. A version of this view was current in the eighteenth century in the work of Lord Kames. Kames argues:

The Fine Arts have ever been encouraged by wise Princes, not simply for private amusement, but for their beneficial influence in society. By uniting distant ranks in the same elegant pleasures, they promote benevolence: by cherishing love of order, they enforce submission to government: and by inspiring a delicacy of feeling, they make regular government a double blessing.[43]

The belief that the fine arts might unite distant ranks and ultimately enforce submission to government is repeated in the article 'Popular Literature' from the *Cape Town Mirror*, where the unidentified writer praises the efforts in England of the 'Society for the Diffusion of Useful Knowledge' for making literature cheaply available to a wide audience. The argument is that better periodicals and books would, by 'a kind of natural and intrinsic buoyancy',[44] supersede inferior competition, and that literature, like education, is primarily useful because it has the capacity to soothe antagonisms between different classes in society:

[F]or the first time, a common literature for all ranks of English society has been called into existence. The effect has been morally as well as socially beneficial,—creating sympathies and mutual kindness, where otherwise alienation—or, at the best, utter indifference, would have existed. Like those light and airswung bridges of rope, on which Peruvian travellers cross in safety over the tremendous abysses of their mountains, this universal literature extends its slight but tenacious bonds over the fearful chasms in the social system of England, and messages of peace and good-will pass to and fro between them. (3)

Less anxious than Herschel about the capacity of literature to pervert and distract, more convinced of the workings of the hidden hand, this writer thus uses a metaphor drawn from distant lands to dramatize the fantasy that literature secures communication between opposed classes and ultimately guarantees social cohesion.

In the Cape, literature therefore unsurprisingly played an important role in efforts to unite the local *English* community. This was perhaps most evident in the dramatic productions of Shakespeare's plays. In 1829 the first civilian theatre company was formed in Cape Town, and it provided for the homesick settler populace several Shakespeare productions in its first year of opening, including *Othello* (twice), *Richard III* (twice), and *Romeo and Juliet*.[45] The invariable pattern for an evening's entertainment was: a Shakespeare play, a melodrama, and a rendering of 'God Save the King'. In 1831, for example, the programme for one series of performances combined *The Merchant of Venice* and a locally scripted satire entitled *Jack at the Cape; or, All Alive among the Hottentots*.

A central part of the pleasure these performances afforded the English settlers can be located in their strong associations with 'home', since each item on the programme bolstered their collective identity as Englishmen Abroad. The Shakespeare play announced their continuing cultural proximity to London. The satire affirmed their Englishness by constituting the other inhabitants in the Colony as functions of the imperial English subject: the black population, 'the Hottentots', are the savage other to the English colonizer, 'Jack', and the Afrikaner community are simply effaced. (Bear in mind that three years after English theatre-goers enjoyed *Jack at the Cape*, the most celebrated event in Christian National education, the Great Trek, commenced, with disenchanted Afrikaners quite literally effacing themselves from the Anglophile landscape of the Cape.) Singing 'God Save the King' then represents an appropriate climax to the evening's entertainment.

Climax?

That these positions and the discourses associated were in no way mutually exclusive is clear from even a superficial glance at the work of some of the principal figures discussed above: Merriman, the missionary, quotes extensively, and with approval, the ideas of Schlegel and Coleridge; and Herschel, the utilitarian, insists upon the value of poetry. Two further examples illustrate how the boundaries between these four positions were blurred in the writings of the Cape's literary figures.[46]

In the report on 'Literature, Science and Art' in the fourth edition of the *Cape of Good Hope Literary Magazine*, the claims for literature are taken further, where the reviewer praises Lady Georgiana Fulleston's new novel *Grantly Manor* not only for its likeness to reality—'we have seldom met with a book more *Shakesperian* (sic) in its illustrations of human nature'[47]— but also for its capacity to instruct and entertain. He concludes: 'we would conscientiously recommend it . . . as a book which might be read with pleasure, and thought of afterwards with advantage' (465). Here once again a version of the synthesis of utilitarian and romantic is effected by insisting that there are indeed books which satisfy the requirements of both discourses, books that instruct and inspire.

The second example is James Adamson's lecture entitled *Modern Literature*, which in twenty-one pages surveys the history of world literature. Adamson's sympathy for science is referred to above, and here his utilitarian inclinations are again in evidence: he insists that the judging of literature should include in it 'a reference to some acknowledged form of utility or excellence'.[48] At the same time, however, he follows Schlegel's romantic definition of literature as being 'the most interesting monument of [man's] capacity which he can conceive or create' (4). But ultimately he subordinates these other two discourses to the authority of Christian faith, with the intellect—both scientific and cultural—directed to understanding the ways of the Almighty:

It is good that Christianity is an object of philosophic enquiry. . . . Philosophy may thus occupy its highest domain in the mystery of

Redemption, and expatiate, most nobly and richly, on such relations as are presented in Justification through Faith, or Renewal by Grace. (14–16)

Adamson's synthesis of these three discourses therefore runs counter to the general increase in sympathy for the romantic position by favouring the missionary.

However, although these positions do come together in this period, it is only later that they combine to defend the *teaching* of English literature. The arguments put forward by missionary, utilitarian, romantic, and imperialist in support of English literature, and specifically of Shakespeare, are subsumed in the second half of the nineteenth century within a rhetoric defending instruction in English literature as a fundamental component of England's education system.

It would be a mistake, however, to assume that in being subsumed within larger policy formulations, these four positions disappear; they continue to appear in arguments about literature in recoded forms. A glance at recent debates about the social function of literature in South Africa make this clear. In the first place, it is the missionary's puritanical fear of literature—expressed by F. C. Cook and the Well Wisher to the Youth of the Colony—has until recently driven the South African Censorship Board, who have tried to police writing bearing the mark of the 'socialist infidel' and the 'apologist for sensual pleasure'. Though the level of vigilance has moderated significantly since 1990, 'subversive texts' continue to be scrutinized. Secondly, the convictions of the utilitarian—that it is impossible to read good literature 'without improvement'—underlie South African high-school English syllabuses. For second-language students particularly, for whom 'knowing English' means memorizing facts about plot and character in literary texts, the shadow of the utilitarian is especially deep.

Also interesting is the prominence of the romantic position, and its reworked relation with the imperial position. The early romantic dissent of the *South African Journal* emphasized the elevated status of the poet and the capacity of the poet to protect the nation. For Fairbairn, the 'genuine poet' is an exceptional individual in touch with truths beyond the grasp of

lesser mortals, and should be free to give expression to creative gifts. For the anonymous author of the piece entitled
'Poetry', even the efforts of 'the humbler poets, have been
highly beneficial in the promotion of national improvement'.
And in the article 'Popular Literature', the vulnerable nation
is secured by literature in that 'literature extends its slight but
tenacious bonds over the fearful chasms in the social system
of England'.

A recent version of this argument is contained in Albie
Sachs's paper 'Preparing ourselves for Freedom'. Sachs holds
up South African musicians like Abdullah Ibrahim and Miriam
Makeba as exemplary instances of what the artist might be:
'Their music conveys genuine confidence because it springs
from inside the personality and experience of each of them.'[49]
Like Fairbairn, Sachs insists that the artist should be free to
create, unfettered by bureaucratic fiats. Giving artists the freedom to express their talents will enrich political struggles,
and ultimately contribute to a national culture that transcends
existing divisions: 'The dance, the cuisine, the poetry, the dress,
the songs and riddles and folk-tales, belong to each group,
but also belong to all of us' (25). In the same way that early
nineteenth-century English critics constructed a canon of great
writers—Shakespeare, Scott, Wordsworth—as their contribution to the constitution of 'England', so Sachs constructs a
canon of great artists—Ibrahim, Makeba—as his contribution
to constituting (the new) 'South Africa'.

In his choice of artists, and in his vision of quite what the
South African nation is or could be, Sachs appears to challenge existing aesthetic and political orthodoxies. But what he
ultimately embraces is the conservative late romantic / imperial commitment to a necessary connection between canonical
artists and the nation. For the 'radical' critic like Sachs, difficult questions remain: what about the artists and the narratives denied admission to the canon, or with diminished status
within the hierarchies of the canon? And, more importantly,
what about those people (migrant workers, children, prisoners)
systemically denied full status within the nation?

Humanism and Racism: 1850–1900

Introduction

The relation between Western thought and colonial racism has received much attention in recent years. Liam O'Dowd asks, '[D]oes the fundamental political and intellectual ambiguity persist which links western humanism and progress to colonial racism and exploitation?'[1] Robert Young glosses Frantz Fanon's arguments, and has no hesitation in asserting the connection: 'Every time a literary critic claims a universal, ethical, moral, or emotional instance in a piece of English literature, he or she colludes in the violence of the colonial legacy in which the European value or truth is defined as the universal one.'[2]

These writers take different routes in responding to the question: O'Dowd discusses Irish history and politics, and Young French philosophy of the 1960s. The route I follow in this chapter is to reflect firstly on how the connection between liberal humanism and racism is formulated in the writings of certain key thinkers of the late nineteenth century in Britain and the Cape Colony: Matthew Arnold, Langham Dale, and James Cameron. And secondly, I relate their formulations to one of the central liberal humanist educational projects initiated during this period, namely English studies.

Matthew Arnold: An English Liberal

Matthew Arnold's views on democracy, the state, and education have been the subject of much commentary and critique, and it is therefore necessary here to repeat only certain key arguments.[3] Arnold believes that the primary role of the state is to represent its subjects. He asserts: '[The state] is the

collective action of the nation itself, and the nation is responsible for it. . . . Nothing can free us from this responsibility.'[4]
Furthermore, different sections of the citizenry have the right
to represent themselves. With regard to the voting rights of
the agricultural worker, for example, he argues that 'it is well
for any great class and description of men in society to be able
to say for itself what it wants, and not to have other classes,
acting for it as its proctors, and supposed to understand its
wants and to provide for them. They do not really understand its wants, they do not really provide for them.'[5]

This suggested method of representation does not, however, on its own guarantee the containment of all resentments
and conflicts in society. The innate human instincts for expansion and liberty cause tensions, particularly as a result of the
growth in trade, which operates on similar principles to those
regulating civic liberty: '[T]he development of trade, like that
of liberty, is due to the working in men of the natural instinct
of expansion' (143). Not everyone benefits equally in seeking
to give expression to their natural desires for expansion:

And perhaps these capitalists have had time to make their fortunes;
but meanwhile they have not made the fortunes of the clusters of
men and women whom they have called into being to produce for
them, and whom they have, as I said, as good as begotten. . . . And
so there arise periods of depression of trade, there arise complaints
of over-production, uneasiness and distress at our centres of manufacturing industry. People then begin, even although their instinct
for expansion, so far as liberty is concerned, may have received
every satisfaction, they begin to discover, like those unionist work-
men whose words Mr John Morley quotes, that 'free political institutions do not guarantee the well-being of the toiling class'. (146)

Compounding these tensions is the denial of beauty in society: 'Man's instinct for beauty [and] for intellect and knowledge has been maltreated and starved' (147).

Expressing doubts about the capacity of 'the hidden hand'
to regulate these tensions, Arnold contends that the traditional English antipathy to government intervention in the
affairs of individuals should be moderated:

[T]he action of a diligent, an impartial, and a national government,
while it can do little to better the condition, already fortunate enough,

of the highest and richest class of people, can really do much, by institution and regulation, to better that of the middle and lower classes.[6]

The principal agency through which the state should intervene for Arnold in order to contain these tensions is the education system. He argues that schools protect society in a similar way to prisons:

And so, too, in schools the State has another interest besides the encouragement of reading, writing and arithmetic—*the protection of society*. It has an interest in them so far as they keep children out of the streets, so far as they teach them . . . an orderly, decent and human behaviour.[7]

The highest forms of knowledge, to be conveyed where possible by means of the education system, are contained in Great Literature. In numerous essays—most elaborately in 'The Function of Criticism at the Present Time' (1864) and 'The Study of Poetry' (1880)—Arnold repeats the romantic view that literature should occupy a central place in the nation's intellectual life. The literary critic in this projected schema accordingly assumes the crucial function of determining what and how literature should be read, occupying a position at the centre of the nation's social polity. The extent of the influence literary critics were able to exert on affairs of state is uncertain. They were, however, able to enforce the study of literature in the schools, though they did so by resorting to modes of instruction generally associated with utilitarianism. Arnold remarks:

I find that of the specific subjects English literature, as it is too ambitiously called—in truth the learning by heart and reciting of a hundred lines or two of standard English poetry—continues to be by far the most popular. I rejoice to find it so. . . . The acquisition of good poetry is a discipline which works deeper than any other in the range of work of our schools. . . . Hence its extreme importance to all of us; but in our elementary schools its importance seems to me to be at present quite extraordinary.[8]

Arnold's theory of the state and of the social function of teaching of English literature, however, does not extend to colonial subjects. Some idea of Arnold's view on African subjects of the Empire can be gained from his essay *An Eton Boy* (1882). The essay consists of the letters and diary of Arthur

Mynors, an old Etonian who died of dysentery in 1879 while fighting in the Zulu War. Arnold's warm approval of all Mynors stood for suggests that their views on race, if not identical, were at least similar. Arnold holds the boy up as one of England's finest: 'unsullied, brave, true, kind, respectful, grateful, uncensorious, uncomplaining'.[9] He quotes from the funeral tribute of the adjutant: 'The old school may well grieve so fine a character . . . who never said an unkind word of anyone' (44). And then concludes himself in terms of supreme adulation: '[T]his natural and charming boy, too, has virtues, he and others like him, which are of the very part and tradition of England; which have gone to make "the ancient and inbred integrity, piety, good-nature, and good-humour of the English people," and which can no more perish than that ideal' (45).

Constructed by Arnold as representing the apex of England's cultural pyramid, Mynors, in his diary, provides some sense of his relation to those 'at the other extreme' of the pyramid, the Africans. Mynors, who never said an unkind word of anyone, describes the Zulus as 'awful looking beasts' (32), as 'scarcely human beings; naked and their skins like leather; awful beasts to look at and very hideous' (32), and as 'the most hideous creatures I ever saw, more like wild animals' (41). He writes of their land, 'if only inhabited, it would be one of the most charming countries in the world' (36).

Arnold's failure to censure Mynors' racist views might be attributed to a reluctance to speak ill of the dead. The effect of his silence, however, is to endorse tacitly Arthur's thoughts on Africa and Africans. For Mynors, Africans at their most positive could function as fierce enemies confirming the martial valour of the English, and he accordingly depicts them in crude stereotypes. In his warm approval of Mynors, Arnold endorses the crude racism reflected in the diary which consigns Africans to a subhuman space beyond the boundaries of the British nation state.[10]

Langham Dale: A Colonial Administrator

In his special report to the House of Assembly of the Cape Colony in 1889, the Superintendent-General of Education, Sir

Langham Dale, insists upon the differences between Britain and the Cape on issues of education policy.[11] There is in Dale's report no echo of Arnold's arguments that the state should intervene on behalf of the lower classes; that society is best served if all classes represent their own interests; or that capitalism might at times lead to unjust differences in wealth and opportunity. Rather, Dale elevates the interests of the colonists above all these other considerations:

The first duty of the Government has been assumed to be to recognise the position of the European colonists as holding the paramount influence, social and political; and to see that the sons and daughters of the colonists, and of those who come hither to throw in their lot with them, should have at least such an education as their peers in Europe enjoy, with such local modifications as will fit them to maintain their unquestioned superiority and supremacy in this land. Tradition, religion, custom, all demand this as essential to the stability of the Government and the material progress of this colony and the neighbouring States.[12]

Having established that white settlers should as far as possible have a European education, Dale moves on to consider what kind of education the black populace should receive:

[T]he desire to rise in the social scale is natural, and the lower grades of employment in handicrafts and menial offices must be constantly recruited from below. And this is just the channel for employment which should be kept open for the coloured races. For social order, as well as for their own elevation from savageism, these races should get elementary instruction and be trained to the manual industries of civilised life. Society, indeed, puts a marked line of demarcation between the two great groups: European and African aborigines. No legislation, no opinions about identity of origin, no religious sentiment about the effacement of the distinctions of white and black, can delete the line. (71)

Dale relates the education of the Cape's black population directly to the colonial state's labour needs: 'I do not consider it my business to force education on all the aborigines; it would mean ruin to South Africa. If I could produce 60,000 educated Tembus or Fingoes tomorrow, what would you do with them?' (85). Africans, unlike the 'toiling classes' in England, are not citizens, but Dale does offer a route for them to advance: 'The

only available agencies for transforming the native savage
into a citizen, capable of understanding his duties and fulfilling them, are the school, the workshop, and the Christian
Church' (87).

Before playing a prominent role in transforming the Cape's
education system, Dale had from 1847 to 1859 been the English lecturer at the South African College, and in subsequent
years continued writing pieces for local magazines on literary
matters, including discussions of philology and portraits of
poets. He wrote two pieces that shed light on how he understood the place of literature in Cape society.

In *The Philosophy of Method*, he draws together into uneasy
synthesis three of the positions outlined in the previous chapter: the utilitarian desire to accumulate facts; the Christian
faith in good deeds; and the romantic belief in the power of
Great Literature. He first distinguishes two principal types of
philosophical enquiry: 'the old method of speculative inquir-
ies, and the modern of scientific research; in the former, the
philosopher starts with an authoritative system of doctrines
or theories, and sets to work to reconcile the conclusions of
experience with those theories: in the latter, the enquirer
ascertains facts, and from the assembled facts leads up by
accurate generalization to the laws which regulate them'.[13]

In the next two sections, Dale demonstrates his commitment to the modern method by arguing that the South African universities should dedicate themselves to adding to the
'traditional stock of knowledge' (22), particularly in the areas
of geography and African languages. Further, the Cape should
follow the example of the agricultural university of Illinois,
with all efforts made to establish 'experimental and practical
teaching' (32). Although he refuses the charge of 'narrow
utilitarianism' (29), at this stage his credentials as a champion
of English literature look rather thin.

In the final section, there is a shift in his argument away
from crude positivism to more romantic notions of literature.
He reiterates his conception of philosophy—'an energy and
striving after higher development . . . piling fact upon fact, and
thus adding to the edifice of universal knowledge' (34)—but
then adds to this grim quest the uplifting element of culture:
'Life may appear an unlit path to those whose higher powers

are undeveloped; but culture will . . . spiritualize our experience' (35). The rewards for attaining a state of culture include 'a
thrilling delight in catching the influence of the word-painting
of the poet' (35), and Dale exhorts his readers to be resolute
in their search for it: 'Seek it in Nature; seek it in the garden;
in the studio; in pictures, in books; in the graces and amen-
ities of social life; in the voiceless communings that each one
holds with his monitor; in the philanthropic atmosphere of
Christian practice; in going about doing good' (36). Dale the
positivist, racist bureaucrat thus ends up appealing to poetry
and Christian practice to supplement the areas of social existence that the more prosaic ideologies fail to contain or explain.

In 'Imagination: An Essay', Dale's religious devotion and
his commitment to empiricist theories of knowledge are
again in evidence: '[A]n external object acts upon the mind; I
grasp its aspect; I perceive it'.[14] But in this essay, the romantic
arguments about literary value are far more to the fore.
Dale admits that the effects of literature on an audience are
contradictory, might indeed even be dangerous:

[T]he habitual novel-readers and theatre-goers, although their appreciation of the representations may be vivid, and Shylock and
Macbeth may awaken in them the intensest contempt and indigna-
tion at the miser's hard-hearted covetousness, or the blankest horror
at the foul deed which took the royal guest's life at the beck of
ambition, are least likely to come under the due influence of the
active principles of benevolence, patriotism, and the defensive affections; are least likely to regulate their conduct in harmony with the
moral emotions. . . . [The spectacle] may harden the mind in a contrary course. (159)

But the supreme value of poetry—'[t]he deeper and more
complex parts of human nature can be exhibited by means of
words alone' (301)—leads him overlook this risk, and to insist
on a central place for the teaching of literature in the education of youth. He summarizes what kind of literature should
be taught:

It is impracticable to define the limits which should be observed in
admitting works of imagination into a course of study. . . . Those
surely cannot be excluded, without serious loss, which stimulate
honourable desires, as love of knowledge, love of esteem, love of

action, and emulation; nor again those which awaken into activity the pure affections—candour, benevolence, truth of purpose, and patriotism; nor those which tend to cherish, regulate, and chasten the domestic affections, the cultivation of which makes the homes of our race to be proverbially the homes of chastity and happiness.   (300)

The writers Dale cites for this noble mission include Shakespeare, Milton, Shelley, Dante, and Homer. What is remarkable about these passages is the potential influence imputed to 'works of imagination': it is as if the full range of social contradictions of late nineteenth-century Britain—economic, political, and domestic—are all to be resolved by the application of appropriate literature to young minds.

James Cameron: Passage to Africa

An article by another lecturer at the South African College, James Cameron's 'Classical Studies and the Relation to Colonial Education',[15] provides an opportunity to examine a variety of arguments about education policy in England and the Cape. Cameron engages closely with arguments carried out in English literary journals and seeks to contribute to them, and his numerous quotations from contemporaneous articles by English scholars function as imprimaturs of intellectual authority placed to impress his readers. What emerges from a careful reading of Cameron's sources is that he *selects* a very specific position from a wide range of possibilities available in metropolitan writing, thus reproducing for the Cape a particular understanding of the relation between humanist education projects and colonial racism.

Cameron's argument, briefly put, is that a classical education represents by far the best alternative for the youth of the Cape Colony, and the sources he quotes all emphatically confirm this view.[16] A look at three of the sources Cameron relies upon, however, demonstrates the extent to which his conclusions are selected rather than pre-ordained by the metropolitan authorities he cites.

From Professor J. G. Greenwood's address on the opening of Owens College in Manchester, 'On the Languages and

Literatures of Greece and Rome', Cameron quotes the following passage:

It is a rich inheritance that we have received, and if we would hand it down not impoverished, but strengthened, it must be by duly appreciating the relations that we bear to it. They who have no past have no future. It is as wise for races as it is for individuals to wish their 'days to be bound each to each in natural piety'; and an indispensable condition to our contributing anything to other generations, either in science, literature or politics, is that we forbear to look on what we have as the fruits of our own toil, but reverently and gratefully own our debts to other and earlier nations.[17]

This of course confirms Cameron's argument, but he leaves out important qualifications Greenwood adds to his love of the classics.

In the first place, Greenwood's support for the classics was tempered by a keen sense of the need to encourage the teaching of practical sciences. He argues here that some equilibrium should be maintained, as 'a too exclusive study of literature, unbalanced by the sterner discipline of the exact sciences, is apt to lead to a vagueness of thought';[18] and further, study of the sciences is necessary in 'counteracting the mischievous effects of an exclusive devotion to classics' (35). Indeed, Greenwood's colleague at Owens College Henry Roscoe recalls that, in the early years, 'I saw that the only chance of making a successful college in Manchester was to give importance to scientific studies, and in this Greenwood fully agreed.'[19]

A second prominent aspect of Greenwood's address that Cameron does not take up is the former's insistence on the need to read the classics in their historical context. Greenwood argues that there should be 'a careful attempt to fix the relations between the people and their literature',[20] and this applies not only to Greek and Roman literature, but also to that of the nineteenth century: 'If he has never observed the close relation in which our greatest writers have stood to the times they have lived in, he will assuredly fail to read aright many of the best authors among the ancients' (30). Cameron concedes that the methods of teaching Greek and Latin could be improved, with the excessive emphasis on the rules of grammar moderated. This does not, however, lead him to endorse Greenwood's more historical approach; rather it leads him to repeat with more force the value of the mental discipline involved in learning the principles of the classical languages before translating them into English.

A third difference between Cameron and Greenwood lies in how they understand the ultimate ideal of a liberal education. In his concluding paragraph, Cameron writes in general terms that a sound liberal education might enable one 'to bring the utmost culture to bear upon the duties of daily life' (303), whereas Greenwood is much more clear about the need for education to instil an ethic of service. The student acquiring the 'weapons [of a liberal education must] use them most worthily for himself, and most beneficially by the entire community' (23). He repeats this theme at length in a later essay, 'On Some Relations of Culture to Practical Life', where he argues that higher education encouraging a life of service should function as an antidote to the excesses of industrialism and its attendant competitive brutality: 'assuredly trained talent has no *jus divinum* of its own, apart from the services which it can, and therefore is bound to, render to the common good'.[21] He concedes that balancing the needs of the individual and the society is not easy, but insists that one cannot be sacrificed at the expense of the other. Greenwood concludes:

I have endeavoured to demonstrate the principle that, in the choice of studies, men have to consider the needs of the community as well as those of the individual; and further that, if we allow self-seeking to be the prime motive-power, we shall not only overlook the due action of the principle of social benevolence, or rather of social justice, but also directly weaken and stunt our intellectual growth.   (14–15)

Cameron's gesture to 'the duties of daily life' thus effectively mutes Greenwood's commitment to an education in service.

A second authority invoked by Cameron is E. E. Bowen, the author of the essay 'On Teaching by Means of Grammar', from F. W. Farrar's collection *Essays on a Liberal Education*. Cameron quotes Bowen to support his contention that the method of learning the grammars of classical languages is uniquely able to teach mental discipline. Learning the grammar of any other language can never be a substitute. And yet in the same collection there is another essay, by J. W. Hales, which puts in a strong plea for the teaching of English grammar, and which Cameron refers to only in summary. Hales argues that there is much to be learnt from studying 'the subtle, delicate, vigorous expressiveness of the sentence'.[22] He proposes the following: 'that the linguistic studies of all our schools should begin with English, should then proceed with the dead languages in the case of boys who are likely to have leisure to study them to any profit, and in other cases should proceed with English and living languages' (302).

On the basis of these two cases, Cameron seems to display an inclination towards the more conservative opinions from the range of possible positions articulated within metropolitan discussions: in his use of both Greenwood's lecture and *Essays on a Liberal Education*, Cameron silences arguments that might have strengthened the case for a less élitist system of education. This is not to impute a conscious right-wing procedure of censorship in place in the colonies—for Cameron, the excerpts he quotes simply make the most sense of the challenges facing colonial educators—but rather to note the existence of a tendency which in effect operates as successfully as any conscious censorship. Although Cameron's thoughts on classical education do not directly deal with the teaching of Africans, he supports the more conservative thread of an educational ethos that systemically excludes Africans, and he does so at a time when there *were* more liberal variants current within the metropolitan mind.

There is a third authority quoted by Cameron, however, in which this pattern is not followed. The following passage from William George Clark's essay 'General Education and Classical Studies', in *Cambridge Essays*, is cited by Cameron:

If that be 'useful' which trains a man's reason, cultivates his taste, enlarges his capacities for acquiring and digesting varied knowledge,—which helps him to distinguish truth from falsehood, right from wrong, beauty from foulness,—which makes him, in the best sense, a wiser and, consequently, a better man,—if that be 'useful', then I maintain that a liberal education which proposes to itself these high aims, is as useful to a youth destined to stand behind a shop-counter, or sit on an office stool, as it is to the heir of broad lands and a feudal coronet.[23]

Clark thus supports Cameron's conclusion about the weak moral fibre of the settler community: 'The temptations to indolence, to flippancy, to indulgence in every form, are very great [and] the intellectual and moral tone among us is not high' (302). Classical education will insure against further degeneration; for the 'supine and weak-kneed' of Cape Town then, a bracing dose of Shakespeare, Greek, and Latin.

Coming at the end of Cameron's essay, Clark's contribution on the 'usefulness' of Latin and Greek enjoys particular prominence, but, in this case, the passage Cameron includes is rather less reactionary than some of Clark's arguments that he leaves out. For example, Clark has an extremely uncharitable view of childhood and an accordingly authoritarian conception of schooling. While at home, children tend to be docile and obedient, but,

once removed to school, the turbulence of boyhood asserts itself in a bitter hatred of all indoor occupation, and an incessant longing for muscular exertion. When a missionary catches a young savage, he does not conceive his business to be to supply him with the food he loves, and to leave him to rove about in nudity, picking off the white babies of the settlement with little poisoned arrows, but to train him, against his will, to a civilised acquiescence in beef and broad-cloth, buttons and good behaviour. An English boy is a young savage in his way, and a judicious application of force is not only not useless, but even necessary, not only not cruelty, but kindness.[24]

For Clark, the primary purpose of education is to tame and subdue boyhood exuberance, and therefore 'it is no valid objection to any subject to affirm that it is dry and distasteful, but on the contrary, a strong recommendation' (294). It is at this point that he brings in Latin:

The question now arises whether, besides the Latin grammar, we can find any other subject equally dry, and by consequence as powerfully tonic to the juvenile mind, which recommends deserving, in lieu, thereof, to form the basis of education by its more general applicability and greater fertility in after results. (294)

Considering the alternatives, he strongly recommends that Sanskrit be introduced as widely as possible, but rejects English because, in studying it, its familiarity would 'mislead the boy's mind' (295).

In this case, the most reactionary ideas from the metropolis are not automatically taken up by the colonial writer. Clark's most bizarre and brutal ideas on education are passed over by Cameron in favour of his less contentious arguments. What this points to is that the most extreme forms of racism arise not only in the colonies at points of contact between settler and native, but also in London: the conjunction of colonial racism and Western education is nowhere more apparent than in Clark's analogy of the 'young savage' and the schoolboy. The pages of *Cambridge Essays* therefore are as likely to generate racist mythologies as are those of the *Cape Monthly Magazine*, with the important difference that because of the greater cultural capital accruing to them, arguments produced in Cambridge have a wider impact.

Above Politics

Martin Legassick in his influential paper 'The Frontier Tradition in South African Historiography' rejects the long-dominant view that racism arose at the point of colonial encounter: 'The [racist] ideas were there from the beginning. . . . There is no reason to suppose they were more prevalent on the frontier.'[25] These texts—especially Clark's essay—confirm Legassick's view that an opposition of liberal humanist metropole and racist colony cannot be sustained, and also that the ways in which declarations of universal humanism and colonial racism connect resist easy geographical categorization. There are, none the less, certain distinctions that can be drawn in terms of the differences between metropole and colony.

In describing the role of the state, the writer in London appears more liberal than his Cape Town contemporary. Whereas Dale writes quite brutally about the imperative to privilege white settlers and transform the black population into cheap labour, Arnold argues that the state should represent its subjects, defends the right of the 'toiling classes' to act on their own behalf, and criticizes the material inequalities occasioned by capitalism.

As regards education policy, a similar contrast can be noted. Dale and Cameron in their different ways are principally concerned with attaining the best possible education for the white colonists, seeking to produce efficient businessmen, professionals, and administrators. When writing about black education, the emphasis is firmly on the incorporation of black subjects into the settler economy at its lowest level via technical education. There is no mention of education functioning either to heal and contain social tensions (Arnold's concern) or to create a class dedicated to service (Greenwood's emphasis).

The pattern of enlightened metropolitan–reactionary colonial does not continue on quite the same lines when comparing their respective attitudes to race.[26] For metropolitan thinkers like Clark and Arnold, the notions of 'African' and 'citizen' are mutually exclusive. Arthur Mynor's views on the Zulu nation and Clark's image of the young savage both attest to the limits of their intellectual horizons: Africans function as worthy enemies for British armies, but never (unlike English workers) warrant inclusion in the British social polity. For Dale, on the other hand, contact with black people and above all the pressure to find a means of recruiting cheap labour resulted in a somewhat more pragmatic racism, where space is left for the step up to be made from savage to citizen.

The area of greatest agreement, however, is in their ideas about literature. All the writers discussed here are deeply indebted to the positions outlined in Chapter 1: Arnold, Dale, and Cameron, each in a different way, combine the missionary, utilitarian, romantic, and imperial positions in order to defend the study of approved literatures. What differences there are between them arise principally as a result of a time-lag between London and the Cape: both Dale, with his more prominent utilitarianism, and Cameron, with his insistence on the classics, put forward arguments increasingly residual within metropolitan culture at the same time. None the less, they *all* champion some form of high literary culture, both in abstract terms, and in terms of encouraging the mass teaching of literature: Arnold repeatedly stresses the 'quite extraordinary' importance of teaching English literature, and even the fact-obsessed Dale is unequivocal in his enthusiasm for poetry, 'the word-painting of the poet'.

At least as important though, is their common perception of high culture as existing *above* politics. At a theoretical level, there is consensus that certain texts, notably Shakespeare, are timeless and universal achievements impervious to the contingencies of the political. The fusion of the romantic and the imperial positions on the social function of literature—that the work of great writers forges national unity—by the time of Matthew Arnold therefore enjoyed wide sanction in the minds of state educationalists. It is this consensus which then enables instruction in Shakespeare on a mass scale. While other knowledges—religious, economic, sociological—might be contested in terms of their political interests and consequences, English literature had been fixed by the immense intellectual labour of Arnold and his kind as neutral, as transcending the 'narrowly political'.

In the official culture of veneration for Shakespeare, what then happened to the racist ideas of Arthur Mynors? The founding fathers of English studies gave full expression to their sentiments of universal humanism: English literature is a noble achievement and all should be given the opportunity to pleasure and benefit from its greatness. This narrative, this version of what English studies is about, has been remarkably resilient, and it excludes any overt traces of racism. In recording the insertion of English literature in the education systems of Britain and the Cape in the remainder of this chapter, I therefore try to highlight those traces by showing the defining (if suppressed) presence of colonial racism in the establishment and functioning of English studies.

Shakespeare in English Education

During the second half of the nineteenth century, the British economy came under serious threat from the competing economies of Germany and the USA.[27] These countries initially protected their internal economies against British goods, and then by heavy expenditure on superior technology, new marketing strategies, new products, *and* technical education, they succeeded by 1860 in overtaking Britain's control of world markets. By 1910 Germany was the chief supplier of manufactured goods to the whole of Europe, and this fact, together with the effects of the Great Depression of 1873–96, meant that the basis of Britain's economic survival had shifted fundamentally. Britain by and large avoided modernizing and competing, firstly because the existence of the Empire enabled Britain to export on a far larger scale to its satellite economies, and secondly because the decline of the industrial sector was disguised by the growth of the City as the commercial and financial centre of world trade.

The impressive progress made by Germany led to demands from within the British ruling class for a centrally planned science-based education system on the German model, designed to help Britain catch up with its competitors. There were only limited initiatives to this end because ultimately, as Kevin Brehony concludes, ' "[i]mperial" rather than "industrial" needs were perceived as the most urgent at the turn of the century'.[28] This meant that pressure groups seeking more technical instruction remained marginal, and that the demands for education along traditional lines prevailed.

The class deciding education policy in this period was therefore made up of three fractions Raymond Williams in *The Long Revolution* identifies as the public educators, the industrial trainers, and the old humanists.[29] Their concerns regarding education were expressed in different terms: for the public educator, education was conceived in utilitarian terms, with all subjects translated into a body of facts for the pupils to memorize; for the industrial trainer, education was to provide a stable and controllable work-force, and too much schooling might even threaten to undermine this end; for the old humanist a classical education was a *sine qua non* for the traditional élites, giving them the mental discipline to be good rulers. What these three fractions of course ultimately still shared was a commitment to defending the existing distribution of wealth and power.

The education system that evolved under their guiding influence was strictly hierarchical. There were effectively three grades of schools: first-grade schools for sons of the aristocracy and professional classes, continuing until they were 18, and with a strong emphasis on classics; second-grade schools for the middle classes, keeping boys until 16, preparing them for the Army or Civil Service, and with a curriculum based on 'a thorough knowledge of those subjects which can be turned into practical use in business, English, arithmetic, the rudiments of mathematics';[30] and third-grade schools for the working classes, designed to keep pupils until the age of 14, and comprising instruction in the three Rs. Some mobility was built into the system: it *was* possible for the children of labourers to receive a secondary education. The overwhelming force of the system, however, was towards teaching people their place, as the Cross Report of 1888 made clear: 'Care must be taken lest in attempting to raise too much the standard of education the country might defeat the object for which education was given, namely, that manual labour in which so many children must be occupied afterwards.'[31]

The introduction of English literature was justified in similar terms, with the regulating of upward mobility and exercise of social control emphasized at least as much as spiritual improvement. In the evidence collected in the Taunton Report of 1867, for example, Indian Civil Service examiner W. G. Dasent argues that access to knowledge of English literature should be restricted: the upper classes should enjoy the privilege of studying English literature, but the class 'just above the National schools, which includes the superior artizan, the foreman of works, and the lower shopkeeper'[32] should have their English studies confined to 'the rudiments of English' (528).

The Earl of Harrowby, on the other hand, enters a plea for the English classics to be accorded the same esteem as the ancient ones, and argues that they be taught to a wider range of students. He concerns himself specifically with those attending national schools, expressing the key question facing the Commission thus:

I take the problem as of an ordinary boy from ordinary classes going into an ordinary career in life, and over whom you have control only till the age of 13, 14 or 15. Well then, I say, what is the best use to make over those years during which you have control over him? (534)

The solution for the Earl is:

I do believe it will be of the most infinite moral advantage to our nation if our youth of every class were accustomed to read our best books in literature from their earliest days, proportioned of course to their age and their condition in various ways; but if they were accustomed to read the most interesting and profitable books in English literature, I believe the moral as well as intellectual effect would be enormous.   (534)

With the traditional division of the classics for the upper classes and religion for the lower failing to secure consensus, a new subject of study was needed during this period, and the argument set out above was invoked with increasing frequency.

The Taunton Report did not lead directly to legislation introducing English literature, but by the 1870s, literature none the less formed part of the curriculum. English as a subject was divided into three components: reading, writing and 'English' (grammar). R. D. Altick summarizes the syllabus:

    I. Narrative monosyllables
    II. One of the narratives next in order after monosyllables in an elementary book used in the school
    III. A short paragraph from an elementary reading book used in the school
    IV. A short paragraph from a more advanced reading book used in the school
    V. A few lines of poetry from a reading book used in the first class of the school
    VI. A short ordinary paragraph in a newspaper, or other modern narrative
    VII. (added in 1882)   A passage from Shakespeare or Milton or some other standard author, or from a history of England.[33]

Pressure to teach English literature in the secondary schools increased with the establishment of the public examinations. Similar examinations had been in place for some years in India,[34] but it was only in 1849 that a Royal Charter was issued allowing the University of London to award degrees on examination to students from institutions approved by the Privy Council from all over the Empire (colleges from Malta, Canada, and Ceylon, but none from South Africa, were approved). In 1858 the Charter was replaced, and anyone paying fees and with a matriculation certificate was allowed to sit the examinations. The new Charter was strongly criticized by the existing colleges, who argued that crude preparation for examination would supersede continuous and systematic study. In 1859 English language and literature was introduced for the first time as a subject at London University, for both the matriculation certificate and BA degree. The almost simultaneous passing of the new charter and the introduction of English meant that from the beginning methods of teaching English were designed to facilitate cramming for examinations, with students striving to memorize hundreds of facts concerning Shakespeare's life, works, and favourite bedtime reading.

Ian Michael distinguishes four skills that were normally tested in these papers: to analyse passages in the style of analysing Latin poetry; to summarize plots; to discuss characterization in detail; and to paraphrase. As this selection from the BA examination for Honours in 1860 shows, the questions function largely as prompts for vast blocks of memorized knowledge to be regurgitated:

1. Quote any passage in 'Hamlet' that best explains his character.
2. Explain 'action' (the great secret, according to Demosthenes and Bacon, of effective oratory) from Hamlet's remarks on the players.
3. What qualities in Shakespeare seem to you, from a comparison of 'Hamlet', 'Macbeth', and 'King John' most remarkable?
4. What authors seem to have been favourites with Bacon, Shakespeare, and Milton respectively?[35]

Not surprisingly, the system was not dissimilar for the Indian Civil Service Examinations, which began in 1855.[36] The number of examining bodies setting papers in English language and literature rose to seventeen by 1875; examinations in English were available to students wanting to enter not only the Civil Service, but also the military, the professions, and the universities. Their form is described by one of the examiners, W. G. Dasent, in his evidence collected in the Taunton Report:

I should take 40 or 50 passages, selected from what I call fair authors—Shakespeare, Milton, Pope, and some of the later writers, Sir Walter Scott and Tennyson. I have set this question over and over again. 'Here is a passage. State where it comes from, explain any peculiarities of English in it, and state the context as far as you are able to do so.' If you set 50 passages, if the candidates are at all instructed, you will find that they answer it in various degrees. I remember an Irishman answering 45 out of 50 right. I am sure I do not know how he did it.[37]

Further on, Dasent defends his method in favour of setting questions on a limited number of selected books:

If you give me a play of Shakespeare, I should take good care that I set my questions in such a way as to exhaust it. I can conceive nothing more trying than being really examined in a play of Shakespeare. It would be like the men who took up the whole Greek and Latin classics, and was floored in Phaedrus. You can crush a man in anything. (527)

Wanting to recruit only the most robust and manly types for the Empire, Dasent's reluctance to crush candidates with too many detailed questions about Shakespeare seems uncharacteristically sentimental.

The massive increase in students of English literature was reflected in the number of Shakespeare editions published (in 1887 there were over eighty Shakespeare editions in circulation). Many of these editions were produced for students sitting the types of examination promised by Dasent. Henry Roscoe BA (Gold Medallist), for example, edited an edition of *Othello* in 1883, which included the following preparatory questions:

2. What are usually considered to be the four grandest tragedies of Shakespeare?
3. From what source is the plot of *Othello* supposed to have been derived?
9. Give some instances of 'Double Comparatives' and 'Double Superlatives' which occur in Shakespeare. On what principle does Dr Abbott account for these?[38]

However, from the 1880s there was a shift away from testing knowledge of grammatical details and historical minutiae, and towards knowing the plot, undertaking analysis of the characters, and speculating on universal themes. To know Shakespeare, explains Lewis Maxy's 1892 edition of *Hamlet*, means students have to 'learn to love' his writings:

Until recently, Shakespeare's plays were taught like Caesar's *Commentaries* and Xenophon's *Anabasis* . . . As in the study of the ancient classics, so in the classic English, the main object—if indeed not the sole object—has been critical *notes, notes,* always *notes,* until, save for mechanical purposes, the text might have been omitted and not missed. Lately, however, with the enquiries into methods and principles of teaching, there has come the realization that this system is wrong,—and harmful as well; that the young student of Shakespeare is not to 'cram', for the examination purposes, data about the early editions, but that he is to learn to love the writings of the poet for their own sake.[39]

After the preface, the play is set forth with (not surprisingly) a minimum of explanatory notes; for each act, there are extremely detailed questions about the plot and characters, general observations about the play by famous critics, and a selection of familiar passages, presumably for memorizing; and at the end of the play, there are more demanding questions, like: 'If Shakespeare intended the tragedy of "Hamlet" to have a moral, what was the moral?' (196). Whereas the earlier facts-about-Shakespeare approach in no way encouraged students to reflect independently on what the plays might be about, this plot–character–theme approach allowed original thought *within strict limits*.

Furthermore, student encounters with Shakespeare were no longer simply examinations to be passed; they were love affairs to be relished. They were not, however, affairs to be undertaken by the faint-hearted. Shakespeare's plays were read as lessons in manliness, the competitive instinct, and respect for a stern moral order. An 1870 edition of *Hamlet* published for Rugby School, for example, emphasizes the virtue of physical courage:

[T]he real pervading cause for widespread melancholy at the end of the sixteenth century . . . was in reality the transition then in progress from an active out-of-door existence to a sedentary student life. . . . Their only chance to preserve a due balance between the bodily exercises of their fathers and the studious habits of their own time. Those who, like Sir Philip Sidney, succeeded in thus tempering their occupations, found life a wellspring of happiness. To them, pre-eminently belonged the 'mens sana in copore sano'.[40]

Hamlet's problem explained in a nutshell: not enough rugger. This edition covers the same areas as Maxy's—plot summaries, discussion of universal themes, and analysis of the characters' actions—but pupils reading this introduction were encouraged rather more directly in the habits of anti-intellectualism and Tory imperialism nurtured so steadfastly by the schools.[41]

Indeed, in its fusing of the aesthetic (Shakespeare) and the athletic (*mens sana*), this edition assimilates humanism and racism in a similar way to Arnold in his incorporation of Arthur Mynor's analysis of the Zulu War.

The imperialist themes of Shakespeare instruction are, not surprisingly, even more to the fore in editions of *The Tempest* produced at the time, with the play read in ways that contradicted flatly the humanist declarations of Arnold. The presentations of Caliban offered in the school editions of *The Tempest*, for example, suggest that Shakespeare's universal world has very definite limits. J. M. D. Meiklejohn in an 1880 edition quotes Dowden's description with approval: 'Caliban stands at the other extreme, with all the elements in him—appetites, intellect, even imagination, out of which man emerges into early civilisation, but with a moral nature that is still gross and malignant.'[42] And Revd D. Morris describes him as 'representative of the savage, uncouth and wild, and his name is merely an anagram of "cannibal"'.[43] Caliban is denied any humanity, or even the capacity to become human. Like Arthur Mynor's Zulus excluded from membership of the English nation, Caliban is placed firmly outside the moral order disclosed in Shakespeare's plays.

What these editions of *The Tempest* also reveal is the positioning of women in late nineteenth-century Britain. The ideology of education for working-class women is summarized by Anna Davin as 'listening to one's husband as well as to class superiors, being "a good tidy wife" and keeping the house clean and comfortable, as well as being generally industrious and content'.[44] For middle-class women, Carol Dyhouse notes an increased emphasis towards the end of the century on more practical training, with the impact of Social Darwinism diluting the 'blue-stocking' finishing-school ethos of girls' education, and underlining the 'importance of woman's role in furthering the progress of the race'.[45] Obedience to male authority is primary, and although Miranda does not quite promise to mother robust defenders of Empire, she remains an exemplary woman. In Morris's introduction, Prospero embodies 'the power of man over nature and especially of the power of a studious and cultivated mind', and Miranda is seen as 'a true woman . . . pure, modest, tender, artless' (4).

Prospero is the civilized Englishman exercising authority over his realm, and the docile Miranda wins an approved place in the social hierarchy that is read into the play: Meiklejohn quotes approvingly Mrs Jameson's description of her as more perfect than any other woman, 'even one of Shakespeare's own loveliest and sweetest creations' (5).

These versions of Shakespeare's plays are repeated in the criticism of major Shakespeare scholars of the period like A. C. Bradley. What has normally been emphasized about critics like Bradley is their role as intellectual pioneers, with their original thoughts on Shakespeare seen as filtering down through the system. While their power to influence all 'lower forms' of Shakespeare study is undoubted—the institutions they represent guarantee such influence—I would like to dwell not on their 'originality', but rather on the extent to which they reproduce in displaced form the anxieties and concerns of their class.[46]

Like the Shakespeare of Maxy's school edition, Bradley's Shakespeare has in his travels been routinely disconnected from his place of origin, and given his enormous influence it is important to reassert those connections. In the first place, Bradley shares with other late Victorian scholars a supreme confidence in his own inviolability as a unified and coherent subject. At the centre of the known universe, English historians entirely unself-conscious about their own construction followed the path to historical truth by accumulating facts about Britain's triumphant conquest of the globe.[47] Notwithstanding his idealist inclinations, a similar spirit underlies Bradley's enquiries: his known universe is Shakespeare's plays, and, starting 'directly from the facts',[48] he purports to construct his argument by taking into account at every point 'the whole of the facts' (36). In this lecture, 'The Substance of Tragedy', Bradley searches (successfully) for an 'ultimate truth' (39) contained in Shakespeare's tragedies. To see Shakespeare in these terms, to undertake such a quest, and to complete it with such conviction, all announce Bradley's belief in his role as intellectual guide and leader, as a kind of cultural correlative of Disraeli or Gladstone. Bradley controls and defines the terrain of Shakespeare studies in the same way that his political and economic counterparts control their empires.[49]

Secondly, having authorized the plays as an adequate basis for locating the ultimate truth about Shakespearean tragedy, Bradley singles out character and action as the most important keys to that truth: 'The centre of the tragedy, therefore, may be said with equal truth to lie in action issuing from character, or in character issuing in action' (12). In particular, the actions and character of the tragic heroes are central, for although they are exceptional, they 'are made of the stuff we find within ourselves and within the persons who surround them' (20). Bradley's focus on character, on the actions flowing from character, and on the meaning and consequences of the character's fatal flaw, is quite consistent with the dominant ideology for the middle classes of individual betterment. Encouraged to identify with the heroes, and to understand their defeats in terms of their personal psychology, the middle-class audience would have little difficulty in complying. Reared within a culture of competitiveness, individualism, and personal accountability, it would seem obvious that Hamlet's tragic end is caused by his own inadequacies and not by the corrupt society of Denmark, that the personal disappointments experienced by readers of Bradley are due to their own failings and not to the corrupt society of Victorian England.

The argument is more complicated than this because it must take into account Bradley's ideas about the context framing the actions of the hero, for although it is essential 'to recognise the connection between act and consequence', it is equally important to acknowledge that 'ultimate power in the tragic world is a moral order' (33). That which threatens the order is evil, and it is an evil which 'exhibits itself everywhere' (35), including within the souls of the characters themselves. The conclusion regarding the status of the moral order is crucial:

[T]he fact that the spectacle does not leave us rebellious or desperate is due to a more or less distinct perception that the tragic suffering and death arise from collision, not with a fate or blank power, but with a moral power, a power akin to all that we admire and revere in the characters themselves . . . the moral order acts not capriciously or like a human being, but from the necessity of its nature, or, if we prefer the phrase, by general laws,—a necessity or law which of course knows no exception and is as 'ruthless' as fate. (36)

The message is clear: the good in us coheres with the moral order, and to deny it in any way invites dire punishment. Shakespeare's heroes risked it, and look at what happened to them. Jonathan Dollimore explains the metaphysical basis of this schema: in his reading of Hegel, Bradley 'tends to concentrate upon the Hegelian theme of reconciliation rather than that of dialectical process [and] to conceive of absolute spirit not in historical but subjective terms (as a function of "character")'.[50] Bradley's identification of 'synthesis', 'moral order', and 'all that we admire and revere in the characters' accordingly produces a deeply conservative structure for reading the tragedies, which is all the more compelling for its borrowings from Hegel.

The imperial resonances of Bradley's schema originate in his own subject position, but they also extend to the moral frame in which he encloses the plays. The moral order Bradley sees defining Shakespeare's plays encloses the characters within a circumscribed boundary. Like Arnold's citizenry of the British nation state, the characters in Shakespeare's plays enjoy the ambiguous privilege of belonging within a powerful, centralized social order. And as Arnold's theory of citizenship and statehood was defined by its antithesis (most vividly figured in the absence of order epitomized by Arthur Mynor's savage Zulus), so Bradley's moral universe exists in unstable tension with a disorder both external and internal that constantly threatens to destroy it. As to the possible signified of Bradley's order-threatening evil, it is arguable that his deep anxieties about impending social chaos were produced by the increasingly apparent instabilities consequent upon the imperial adventure.

English at the Cape

Britain's increased economic dependence on the Empire in the late nineteenth century has already been noted. What should now be emphasized is the centrality of Southern Africa in this process. Being pushed out of American and Continental markets, British capitalists looked increasingly to the colonies to provide a high return on investments, and the Transvaal

gold-mines promised such returns.[51] D. M. Schreuder summarizes the stakes for the British state as follows:

The politics of Partition in Southern Africa were, accordingly, to
become a paradigm of the British world predicament in the later
nineteenth century. By the end of the era of the Scramble for Africa
and Asia, the Victorians could still, in several senses, continue to
think of themselves as the paramount power and culture. But that
ascendancy was increasingly rooted in a deep *dependency* on the
world beyond Europe; and it was a world in which the conditions
of trade, power and influence were progressively turning against
the British.[52]

With an economy based up until the 1870s primarily on its
function as a port, as a place of administration and government, and as a market and agent for the wheat and wine
farmers of the interior, Cape Town emerged as a city not
unlike London in its dependence on long-distance commercial activities rather than local production.[53] This position was
strengthened with the discovery of gold and diamonds towards the end of the century. In terms of labour, the needs of
the Western Cape's economy were therefore for domestic
servants, for clerks to occupy the lower rungs of the administration and government bureaucracies, for semi-skilled
workers in the building industry and docks, for a smaller
number of skilled artisans, and in the interior for farm
labourers. As in England, the onus of providing those needs
fell on the education system.

In the Cape, the class dictating education policy was also
made up of different fractions, and there were a number of
competing discourses defining their actions. First, there was
the discourse of 'Cape liberalism', which is now often made
to stand for the class as a whole,[54] and which included appeals
to both Christianity and a common humanity. Second, there
was a discourse of commercial utility and free trade, less vocal
than the liberal discourse, and seeking in education the means
to increase economic profitability. Third, there was a discourse
of racial hierarchies, most overt in the language of the
Afrikaner farming class, but also strongly present in the language of the urban English, directed against Afrikaners and
black people alike.[55] Although these discourses articulate

important differences within the ruling bloc between a professional and administrative fraction, an industrial and mercantile fraction, and a land-owning agricultural fraction, they should not be overstated, since they could be combined—as they are in Langham Dale's writings—without seriously questioning the Colony's mode of production and distribution.

The education system in the Cape developed along lines similar to those in England, with a three-tier hierarchy of schools enforced. The major adjustment in the Cape was the racial division of third-grade schools at the turn of the century.[56] The Cape's education system at this time was made up of the following levels: at the top of the ladder was the University of the Cape of Good Hope, an examining university, which had succeeded the Board of Public Examiners, and which from 1873 to 1918 awarded degrees in literature and science;[57] next, there were six colleges which prepared students for the university examinations and accordingly taught a curriculum determined by the examining university; the best category of schools, the first-class schools, were for the wealthy and taught a predominantly classical curriculum;[58] the second-class schools catered for those Ross describes as 'the superior ranks',[59] and were more likely to teach a more modern curriculum; and finally, catering for the poor of both races at this stage, were the third-class mission schools, which provided an imperfect elementary education.

In the years leading up to the Anglo-Boer War, the extreme Anglicization policies of Somerset had been moderated, but the Education Act of 1865 none the less legislated that in order to qualify for a state grant, the medium of instruction in both first- and second-class schools had to be English, with Dutch as a subject.[60] Third-class schools had to introduce English within the first twelve months of the students' tuition. The sustained pressure for Dutch to be recognized is acknowledged in the Barry Report, where Langham Dale sums up the official position: '[T]he teaching of Dutch is to be encouraged because it helps on the teaching of English. We have no sentiment about it: it is purely a business question.'[61]

Very few students reached the highest levels of the education ladder—in 1883 there were only thirty students studying at all the colleges for the BA degree—and those that did were all white men. Although there was no official barrier to black students and women, the first woman to obtain a BA degree from the university received one through private study in 1886, and the first black student only in the twentieth century.[62] Access to English studies in the Cape Colony, as in Britain, was therefore regulated in ways that excluded major categories of students. Student demographics in the Cape particularly demonstrate that for women and black South Africans, knowledge about the universal genius Shakespeare was only to be gained as an occasional guest of the white men's club. That white men were to be the principal benefi-ciaries of the available educational resources is made very clear in this letter from 'A Lady' to the *Cape Monthly Magazine* of 1875:

I have no sympathy with the 'woman's rights' movement; but I stoutly maintain that a girl's mind, at the outset, is composed of as good material as a boy's; and few will deny that for future needs it is quite as well worth the pains bestowed upon its cultivation. The happiness and prosperity of the next generation depends much upon the way girls are prepared for their destiny as the future mothers. Biography is rich in instances of most highly gifted men who were indebted chiefly to their mothers for becoming worthy of the fame they acquired; and without equal advantages how can the girls be-come fit companions intellectually for well-equipped, intelligent men?[63]

Once within the English class then, the language of universal humanity obtained, but entry was strictly circumscribed, and those outside the class remained subject to the racist and sex-ist categories of those privileged to study Shakespeare.

Within the educational institutions, and in the teaching of English literature, the pedagogical assumption was that the English teacher would offer classes of male students instruc-tion in Shakespeare, and, by extension, in the values of com-petitiveness, respect for order, and individual responsibility. This model was followed in South Africa, where the presence of a substantial (male) settler populace meant that the Civil Service was run by a white personnel. However, in the many instances where this was not the case, the practice of English teaching came under severe strain. One such case was in India, where the British recruited an élite of indigenous administrators from an early date. Viswanathan describes how as a result of religious opposition to Christian teaching in India, the British introduced examinations in English literature for those wanting to join the Civil Service. English literature, rather than the British East India Company, became the emblem of British imperialism, but this strategy failed in the long term to transcend a fundamental contradiction: '[E]conomic exploitation required the sanction of higher motives, but once colonial intervention took on a moral justification—that is, the improvement of a benighted people—the pressure to sustain the expectations of the people by an equalization of educational opportunities created new internal stress'.[64] Shakespeare announced those higher motives—individual improvement and governance by a benign moral order—but at the same time failed to guarantee material advance for the Indian student who had learnt the Bard's wisdom. This failure meant that 'the social control that literature as moral study was able to exert in England collapsed in India' (163).

As to what was taught in English classes in the Cape, the established pattern of trying to emulate the syllabuses and methods used in England continued. The status of English was unaffected by the modernization of the curriculum in the secondary schools, which saw the very gradual removal of Latin and Greek, the relegation of religion to one hour per week, and the introduction of singing, drawing, and needlework for girls and woodwork for boys. Ross's description of the syllabus in 1883 includes, under reading for standards 6 and 7, '[t]o read a passage from Shakespeare or Milton',[65] and this would continue to hold well into the next century. The curriculum for the secondary standards was entirely dominated by the matriculation examination set by the University of the Cape of Good Hope, which was still based on the forms developed by the University of London. The matriculation syllabus for the South African College for 1895, for example, includes similar components of Shakespeare and English grammar to those of London.

The English examinations for the University of the Cape of Good Hope between 1873 and 1902 were almost all set by James Cameron, H. M. Foot, and F. C. Kolbe, all of whom had studied at London University. Not surprisingly, the kinds of questions set reflected this, and answering them successfully normally involved recounting large amounts of historical and biographical information about the set texts. The following selection from the MA examination of 1897 gives a sense of what was asked:

3. Trace the growth, in the literature of the 16th century, of that patriotic spirit which culminates in the historical plays of Shake-speare: and show how English History and English Literature illustrate each other.

4. Marlowe is said to have invented and made the verse of the drama, and to have created the English tragic drama. Illustrate these statements, and remark on the claim for Marlowe that he was a worthy predecessor to Shakespeare.[66]

There were, however, less frequently, questions inviting some speculation about the plays. The 1887 BA examination, for example, posed the following questions about *Othello*:

2. Give Iago's own account of his hostility to Othello: and discuss carefully Coleridge's phrase 'the motiveless malignity of Iago'.

3. Refer to passages in the play which bring out the sweetness and purity of Desdemona's character, and show how these are enhanced by contrast with the other female characters.[67]

Romantic or missionary conceptions of literature are of course rather sorely absent in these examinations, which exemplify a utilitarian spirit quite at odds with notions of drinking freely at the pool of Art and Culture. Rather, they seek to encourage competition, to separate the fittest recruits from the rest, and to cement the ranks of the administrative and professional classes into a secure Anglophile unit. Indeed, if any distinction is to be made between the institutionalization of English literature teaching in England and the Cape, it would be that the functional aspect of the process is accorded greater import in the Cape, with the colonial élite displaying rather less inclination to dwell upon the spiritual in teaching and examining English literature.

Conclusion

Finally, how are the 'racist' and the 'humanist' tropes of nineteenth-century English studies coded in contemporary South

Africa? The following incident reveals that the arguments of the founding fathers of the discipline continue to exercise considerable force.

On 28 February 1990 four white school pupils at Dale College (named after Langham Dale) in King William's Town attacked and killed 70-year-old black vagrant Tom Ruiters. Members of the secret Frank Joubert Kaffir-Bashing Society, the boys had stolen out of their hostel that night armed with, among other weapons, a baseball bat, a truncheon, a hockey stick, and a knuckle-duster, intent on assaulting any black people they found on or near the school grounds. At the trial a year later, the four were found guilty of culpable homicide, and the group's leader received an effective eighteen-month jail sentence with the other three sentenced to community service.

The trial received a great deal of publicity, both in South Africa and abroad. Several explanations for the killing were put forward, with more than one concerned to deflect responsibility away from sensitive areas. The families of the boys were blamed: the court heard that Richard Bester (the leader of the gang) had seen his father assault black people, and further that the death of his mother from cancer had contributed to a traumatic childhood in which his racist father had been the only available role model.[68] All the boys were held to have come from 'broken families', leaving them with massive feelings of insecurity.

The school was blamed, with Bester's father asserting that the headmaster, Malcolm Andrew, should also have been on trial.[69] Not only had Andrew been the superintendent of Frank Joubert House, the hostel from where the attacks had been launched, but in a school assembly the previous year encouraged boys to take a two-by-four (a builder's plank) to vagrants damaging school property. He had also done all in his power to foster the masculinist and sport-obsessed ethos of the school.

The personal inadequacies of the convicted pupils were also emphasized. A psychologist interviewed in the *Weekend Argus* suggests that only well-rounded children cope with the pressures of boarding-school; for those less confident, like the members of the gang, the following suggestions:

It also helps to encourage the child to take up an artistic activity or hobby—to balance the academic and sporting sides which are stressed at school. When she does that, the hobby, like playing guitar, can be sustaining in negative situations, for example, if the child is cast out of her group or if she fails a spelling test or is not selected for the first rugby team.[70]

The press too were blamed, not for causing the tragedy, but for exaggerating its import. The mayor of King William's Town, Mr B. A. Radue, described the death of Ruiters as an 'unfortunate, isolated event', and continued that it had damaged the proud name of the school, which according to the headmaster had always been identified with the values of an English public school—'honour, decency and hard work'.[71] The head of the school's old boys' association, Buster Farrer, also criticized sensationalist newspaper reporting:

[Headlines] were twisted to make it look as if the school is a training centre for right wing activities. Ten percent of the pupils are black. We are progressive and looking to the future. It has happened and we must make sure it does not happen again.   (4)

There were attempts to locate responsibility more widely. In a letter to the *Cape Times*, Mike Bothma recalls incidents similar to the Dale killing from his own schooling experience, and argues:

I believe that the education system in this country in general, and the elitist boys boarding schools in particular, tend to create a culture of male-dominated physical aggression towards others which manifests itself in many different forms. It is not surprising, in our society of entrenched racial awareness, that one of these forms is the 'kaffir bashing' that is not confined to Dale College. Corporal punishment, the prefect 'skivvy' system, initiation and indeed maybe even rugby are all features of 'the system' that must share responsibility for the Dale College killing.[72]

Of these explanations there is one in particular I wish to explore, as it connects with the relation between liberal humanism and racism I have highlighted in the writings of Arnold, Dale, and Cameron. There are two articles suggesting that more culture and less sport in the Dale College curriculum might have averted the tragedy. In the British *Sunday*

Telegraph, English lecturer at nearby Fort Hare University, Charles Laggan, stresses the brutalizing effect of the exclusive emphasis on rugby at the school: 'I told Mr Andrew that there are rugger buggers and Botticellis at any school and a line must be found between the two. It was like talking to a block of granite.'[73] And in another article in the *Weekend Argus*, the activities of the Joubert Kaffir-Bashing Society are compared to the rather gentler nocturnal diversions of the pupils in the movie *Dead Poets Society*.[74]

The idea that the reading and teaching of English literature contributes to social harmony continues to be reworked in contemporary South Africa. For example, the Shakespeare Schools' Text Project, started in 1987 and funded by the Chairman's Fund of the Anglo American Corporation, seeks to promote the teaching of Shakespeare at all South African secondary schools, with particular attention to black schools. Prominent among the reasons justifying the project is director André Lemmer's argument that Shakespeare provides 'a bridge between past and present and between one culture and another'.[75] Again there is the suggestion that revised versions of nineteenth-century English literary education represent for contemporary South Africa a means of transcending social conflicts, *including* racial conflicts.

The implication is that the total English public school cultural package can be divided into different independent components, including an acceptable poetry-reading aspect and a violent and racist rugby-playing one. What for Arnold and Dale were quite compatible ideological strands in a common world-view are now separated out, with the racist impulse designated aberrant and excised from what is then recoded as an exemplary educational model. No connection is seen to exist between the material plunder of South Africa by English capitalists, the continuing racial subordination of the majority of the population, and the teaching of Shakespeare.

That this ideological reworking can be effective is demonstrable in many ways, not least by pointing to the fact that while the trial was in progress a report appeared that senior ANC official Steve Tshwete intended to enrol his children at Dale College. Tshwete is reported as saying: 'The students of Dale and KHS [Dale's sister school] are always well-disposed towards the traditions of the schools. I yearned to be a student there and share all those beautiful facilities.'[76]

In a recent essay, Alan Sinfield discusses the connection between literary culture and industrialism, arguing that they should not be seen simply in opposition to each other:

Poetry, literature, the spirit, nature, personal religion, personal and family relations and the arts are imagined as repudiations of mechanical, urban, industrial and commercial organization, working counter to those features of the modern world. But, actually, the two are correlatives: the *whole framework* belongs together and each part supposes the other. Poetry and the rest are constituted within the field of, in terms supplied by, capitalism. This binary formation, which is imagined, roughly, as 'human' values versus a dehumanizing 'modern condition', seems to denote a necessary distinction, so caught are we in its world view. But while we persist with those terms we will never rescue the 'human', because it is set up as the necessary and weaker term in the binary—it is the other of political economy that enables it to know itself, the resort of middle-class dissidents, the conscience of capitalism.[77]

I think a similar argument can be made about the opposition between humane literary culture and colonial racism, with one added difference. The opposition between the 'human' and 'the modern condition' is securely at the centre of Raymond Williams's 'culture and society' tradition, whereas, as I have shown, for late nineteenth-century writers there was no opposition between liberal humanism and colonial racism. They coexisted as compatible elements of a particular world-view. All the more reason to refuse the opposition at this time of quite extraordinary change in South Africa's history, to resist privileging and reinvesting in the one term without attending directly and explicitly to the connections between the 'human' and the 'racist'.

3

The Colonial Subject and Shakespeare:
1916

Introduction

Israel Gollancz's lavish collection commemorating the tercentenary of Shakespeare's death, *A Book of Homage to Shakespeare*,
includes 'A South African's Homage', which offers up the
following words of praise:

[Unlike cinema], Shakespeare's dramas . . . show that nobility and
valour, like depravity and cowardice, are not the monopoly of any
colour. Shakespeare lived over three hundred years ago, but he
appears to have had a keen grasp of human character. His description of things seems so inwardly correct that . . . we of the present
age have not equalled his acumen. It is hoped that with the maturity
of African literature, now still in its infancy, writers and translators
will consider giving to Africans the benefit of some at least of Shakespeare's work. That this could be done is suggested by the probabil-
ity that some of the stories on which his dramas are based find
equivalents in African folklore.[1]

The piece was written by Sol Plaatje,[2] a black South African
in London at the time petitioning the British government to
intervene in South Africa against racist legislation passed by
the Union government.

Plaatje's position in both political and cultural terms was
complicated, and this chapter is concerned with reflecting on
how he negotiated his relationship with the British state and
with Shakespeare. This reflection commences by briefly introducing Plaatje and his context, as well as other writers from
the colonies of his generation criticizing Shakespeare. I then
examine Shakespeare in his 1916 form, surveying both the
Shakespeare Tercentenary Celebrations in England and the
Cape Colony, and Shakespeare's deployment in the education

system of the Cape in 1916. The second part of the chapter focuses on how different thinkers have tried to make sense of Plaatje's relation with Shakespeare. I look at four groups: anti-imperialist writers from the colonies like Frantz Fanon and Albert Memmi, who rewrote their colonial past in the context of decolonization; Marxist theorists, including Marx himself, V. I. Lenin, and more recent figures in this tradition; social historians in the E. P. Thompson mould trying to recover unwritten histories of those who, like Plaatje, fell outside the Great-White-Men-Making-History pattern; and finally, literary theorists from First World universities bringing the vocabulary of current critical theory to bear in writing about matters colonial and neo-colonial.[3] What I emphasize in following this sequence is that each group of critics reads figures like Plaatje in terms of *their* particular contexts. Accordingly, these four versions should *not* be read as progressing from the crude and partial, to the sophisticated and judicious; rather, each version of Plaatje and Shakespeare should be read as revealing at least as much about these very distinct generations of writers who have reflected on the troubled relationship between colonial subjects and high Western culture.

The Colonial Subject, Sol Plaatje

Solomon Tshekisho Plaatje was born in 1876 and died in 1932. He was part of the generation of South African nationalist writers and political activists which included S. M. Molema, John Dube, and John Tengo Jabavu.[4] Plaatje received five years of formal schooling at a Lutheran mission school in the Northern Cape, and during his lifetime worked variously as a court interpreter (he spoke nine languages), journalist and newspaper editor, linguist, labour recruitment officer, pamphleteer, novelist, and politician. A founder member of the South African Native National Congress, he travelled to the United States, Canada, and Britain, meeting black leaders from those countries and waging an energetic propaganda campaign on behalf of black South Africans.

Plaatje's life spanned a period of extraordinary change in South African history. At the time of his birth, Southern Africa was made up of a cluster of mutually independent British colonies, African protectorates and kingdoms, and Afrikaner republics. During his lifetime, this landscape was transformed by the mining revolution in Kimberley and on the Witwatersrand, by the Anglo-Boer War and the unification of South African territories in 1910, by the incorporation of all Southern African economies into the global capitalist economy, and by the theft of African land by the settler state and the concomitant process of rapid urbanization. By the time of his death, a powerful central state protecting white privilege and serving the interests of both international and local capital was securely in place.[5]

Besides the homage to Shakespeare, Plaatje's publications included the first novel in English by a black South African, *Mhudi*, completed in 1917, but only published in 1930,[6] and *Boer War Diary*, his impressions of the Siege of Mafeking. He wrote *Native Life in South Africa* as a protest against the 1913 Land Act, which made it illegal for black South Africans to own land in the Union. He praises the Cape's nineteenth-century Empire-builders for their generosity and non-racialism, the same qualities he saw and admired in Shakespeare. He includes a whole chapter bemoaning the passing of the Cape Liberal tradition:

[t]he one Colony whose administration, under its wise statesmen of the Victorian era, created for it that tremendous prestige that was felt throughout the dark continent, and that rested largely upon the fact that among its citizens, before its incorporation with the northern states, it knew no distinction of colour, for all were free to qualify for the exercise of electoral rights. . . . the old Cape Colony whose peaceful methods of civilization acted as an incentive to the Bechuana tribes to draw the sword and resist every attempt at annexation by Europeans other than the British . . . [a]ll this done without any effort on the part of the British themselves, and done by the Natives out of regard for Cape Colony ideals. . . . What would these Empire builders say if they came back here and found that the hills and valleys of their old Cape Colony have ceased to be a home to many of their million brawny blacks, whose muscles helped the conqueror to secure his present hold of the country?[7]

Shakespeare's capacity, on Plaatje's reading, to demonstrate vividly that nobility and depravity are not the monopoly of any colour made him the literary exemplar of this noble but embattled English tradition at the Cape, which strove to govern without enforcing any distinction of colour. Plaatje's third publication of 1916 was *Sechuana Proverbs with Literal Translations and their European Equivalents*, a collection of 732 Tswana proverbs. His aim in this collection was to demonstrate the universal relevance of these proverbs, to preserve for posterity the inherited wisdom of an oral tradition under severe threat, and at the same time to assert the value of his own African culture and identity.

Finally, lest Plaatje's homage to Shakespeare be read as exceptional for a colonial subject at this time, attention is directed to the similar views of contemporaneous colonial writers, both in South Africa and in other parts of the Empire. In the *Educational Journal*, a publication addressing the political interests of coloured teachers in South Africa, 'In the Editor's Sanctum' describes the journal's position regarding the First World War thus:

For us, as British subjects, there can be but one opinion as to the justice of the war. For us, as intelligent and thinking men and women, there can, too, be but one opinion. The fact that these two opinions coincide, fortifies our loyalty and enables us to look forward with calm confidence to the triumph of British might and British right. We are prouder than ever of being subjects of the glorious British Empire.[8]

As regards the cultural inclinations of the journal, these can be discerned in the short piece 'A Luxury of Life', which consists of a long quotation from De Quincey's *Essays on Shakespeare*. The passage quoted, presumably with approval, since there is no commentary indicating the contrary, includes the following not untypical tribute to Shakespeare's genius:

[I]t may be affirmed of Shakespeare that he is among the modern luxuries of life; that life, in fact, is a new thing, and one more to be coveted, since Shakespeare has extended the domains of human consciousness and pushed its dark frontiers into regions not so much as dimly descried or even suspected before his time, far less illuminated (as now they are) by beauty and tropical luxuriance of life.[9]

Taken together, the insistent pride in being British subjects and the unreflecting repetition of the opinion that Shakspeare

has improved life in formerly dark regions reflect a commitment to the English way that goes beyond mere gesture. These
passages instance members of the 'coloured races' actively
reproducing the ideological categories of the imperialist power,
thus complicating any simple opposition of colonizer–colonized.

Colonial writers in Ireland and India were also at this time
reflecting on their relation to British culture, with editions of
Shakespeare's plays for the first time being produced locally
and for local consumption instead of being imported from
England. These editions reflect on the same issues as Plaatje,
namely the relation of the colonial subject to the British state
and to British culture, and, with certain important differences,
reproduce the same contradictions. Writing shortly before Irish
independence, the editor of the 1920 Dublin edition of *Hamlet*,
described as An Examiner under the Board of Intermediate
Education, provides a unique and in many ways exemplary
introduction to Elizabethan England, including routinely ignored details like the following:

To bend Ireland to her will, Elizabeth maintained throughout her
reign an enormous army, sometimes numbering 20,000 soldiers and
more, engaged in active service against our chieftains and ravaging
our country of its growing crops. The magnitude of this effort may
be judged by the fact that for many years the English Parliament
devoted no less than *three-fourths of the entire Government revenues of
England*, recorded as £340,000 out of £450,000, to the prosecution of
the Irish wars.[10]

Any illusions about liberal England firmly buried, the Examiner none the less retains a profound admiration for Shakespeare, arguing that he matters enormously to the human
race, but that '[t]o solve in any way the great secret of Shakespeare's mind we can only consider his artistic career and
mental development in connection with the progress of events
contemporaneous with his life' (p. xvi). What follows is a
detailed chronology of Shakespeare's life, Irish history, world
economic trends, and England's domestic political history, with
incongruous entries that encourage a rather different reading
of the period and of Shakespeare:

1579. Expedition to Ireland fitted out by Pope Gregory XIII for
Seamus Fitz Maurice. Seamus killed at Barrington's Bridge,

near Limerick, by Sir William Burke, who is made Baron of
Castleconnell, and dies of joy in consequence.

Shakespeare leaves Stratford Grammar School, aged 15.   (p.
xvi)

The apparent contradiction between hating England but ven-
erating Shakespeare is mediated by two arguments: that
Shakespeare is a universal genius, and that he in fact displays
in his plays a rather more Irish than English temper. The
latter is established by proving that Hamlet's name is in fact
Gaelic and not Danish in origin, and by interpreting the moral
lesson of *Hamlet* as being drawn from the teaching of *Sinn
Féin*: 'confidence in our own *ego*, and our own initiative, active
under God's providence, not torpid to God's dishonour under
an assumption of divinely decreed fatality' (64).

Much closer in spirit to Plaatje's homage was the 1928
Bangalore edition of *Othello* edited by Ram Gopal and P. R.
Singarachari. The edition was conceived as 'an humble offering to my fellow citizens, and as signalising (*sic*) my admiration of and homage to the world's Great Teacher, in the hope
that his teachings would reach a large number of my country-
men'.[11] Shakespeare's favourable reception in India is attributed to 'the intellectual fraternity of mankind' (p. i), and the
editors substantiate this claim with selective reference to well
over twenty English, American, and European critics. Their
central argument is that although in the past the differences
between Europe and Asia were taken for granted, in fact they
share a common humanity nowhere more apparent than in
Shakespeare's plays. The conclusion makes the point with great
force:

Surely, the master-mind of Shakespeare, this universal brain, this
cosmopolitan genius,—dealt with humanity in general, irrespective
of the narrow, artificial, unstable and fleeting accidents of a particular time, place, birth or situation. He dealt not with Italy, or Venice;
not with Turkey or Morocco (*sic*); not with the shifting geographical
frontiers or ethnological walls and boundaries of a particular race
or country; not with Christians or non-Christians; not with brown,
black, or white colour; but with elemental human emotions and
passions, longings and desires,—Love, Faith, Credulity, Hatred, Pride
of power or success, Revenge, Envy, Jealousy, Malice, Ambition,
Greed, etc., etc., with a view to their right direction, discipline and
education.   (p. cxii)

As in the case of Plaatje's homage, no misgivings about the political and economic dimensions of the British Empire are voiced, and instead Shakespeare's purported commitment to international fraternity is celebrated. But, and this is perhaps the most significant point about these texts, even where opposition to British rule is voiced, Shakespeare remains exempt from criticism.

. . . And Shakespeare

The William Shakespeare Sol Plaatje might have encountered in the Cape Colony in 1916 was a figure of contradictory qualities. At least three aspects of his identity emerge in descriptions of him current at the time: his status as quintessential English hero defending Albion from the Germans; his universal humanity transcending national boundaries; and his unique abilities as instructor of youth in ways of obedience and moral rectitude.

In England in 1916 great emphasis was placed on Shakespeare's Englishness. The tercentenary of his death was marked by a performance of *Julius Caesar* on 2 May 1916 at Drury Lane Theatre, and was attended by the King and Queen. The tercentenary committee was made up of Prime Minister Asquith (Honorary President), the Earl of Plymouth (Chairman of the Executive), the Lord Mayor of London (Honorary Treasurer), and Professor Israel Gollancz (Honorary Secretary). The sentiments of those present can be adduced from the foreword to the programme by W. L. Courtney, who pledges that '[t]o all artists the memory of the Great Englishman is as dear to those who recall with gratitude his patriotic love of his native land'.[12] Further, 'at a time like this, so unpropitious to the higher levels of imaginative creation', Shakespeare's plays provide inspiration and succour.

The perception of Shakespeare as typifying a certain kind of Englishness was also announced by the major English critics of the time. Some years before, King Edward VII Professor of English at Cambridge Sir Arthur Quiller-Couch had described Shakespeare's plays as celebrating 'the fierce joy to be an Englishman', and that they 'serve as a handbook to patriotism, should that sacred passion need one'.[13] In like spirit, Sir Walter Raleigh, Merton Professor at Oxford, argued in 1916 that Shakespeare stands as pre-eminent spokesman of the English race, implacably opposed to 'foreign cruelty, pedantry and intellectual dogmatism'.[14] The most urgent expression of this fervour for enlisting Shakespeare in the battle against the Hun is Francis Colmer's 1916 publication *Shakespeare in Time of War*. Colmer looks to the arts for sustenance in this hour of need:

[England] has denied and proscribed the arts, without which the martial spirit must faint, and just retribution falls on her. Where shall she look among those whom she has neglected for one clear rallying cry and cheering note? . . . There is only one poet who has identified himself deeply with the nationality of our race and who has made himself the mouthpiece to interpret it in every mood and aspiration, who is himself, indeed the typical Englishman. Our one and only *national* poet is William Shakespeare,—national, not merely in an insular, but, one might almost say, in an imperial sense.[15]

To revive the flagging martial spirit Colmer collects together a vast number of short passages from Shakespeare's works, arranging them with topical references. He finds quotations apposite for every aspect of the war, from the numerous battles to the statesmen and generals involved in running political and military affairs.

This is not to say that the notion of Shakespeare as the guiding light of *all* nations was entirely sacrificed in the atmosphere of heightened jingoism that characterized the war years. Emphasizing his Englishness coexisted in tension with a sense of his universal (and eternal) relevance to other peoples and contexts. This is summed up neatly in a poem by Israel Zangwill, published in the same collection as Plaatje's homage:

The Two Empires

If e'er I doubt of England I recall
   Gentle Will Shakespeare, her authentic son,
   Wombed in her soul and with her meadows one,
Whose tears and laughter hold the world in thrall,
Impartial bard of Briton, Roman, Gaul,
   Jew, Gentile, white or black. Greek poets shun
   Strange realms of song—his ventures overrun
The globe, his sovereign art embraces all.

> Such too is England's Empire—hers the art
>   To hold all faiths and races' neath her sway,
> An art wherein love plays the better part.
>   Thus comes it, all beside her fight and pray,
> While, like twin sons of that same mighty heart,
>   St. George and Shakespeare share one April day.[16]

The martial (St George) and the cultural (Shakespeare) function in concert to secure the future of the Empire, but, unlike Colmer, Zangwill stresses that the 'Impartial bard' is also for other races. And in the same way that Shakespeare 'embraces all', England's Empire includes other races within her bounty by a process 'wherein love plays the better part'.

In South Africa, the universal—as opposed to uniquely English—aspect of Shakespeare's art is stressed. The programme of the Johannesburg Shakespeare Tercentenary Celebration declares that '[t]here is, in fact, a strong and enduring conjunction between the nerve-centre of South Africa and the "master who spake through myriad mouths" ',[17] and further, that the 'cultured' white community of South Africa should be aware 'that for all his strange waywardness the Philistine has not managed to lock, bolt and bar the door against the higher revelations of art' (2). Having established the legitimacy of Shakespeare's position in Johannesburg, the Shakespeare Committee pledges itself to making 'the higher revelations of art' available to other 'Philistine' races. 'Philistine' could include both Afrikaans-speaking and black South Africans, and their resistance to official English culture reflects a reluctance to relinquish their own national identities. What is important here is the desire, however grudging, on the part of the colonial defenders of 'high culture' to leave a space within their ranks for those Philistines willing to open themselves to the benign music of Shakespeare.

The Cape Town Tercentenary Celebration was held on 24 April, and took the form of a concert which included an address by the last prime minister of the Cape Colony, John X. Merriman, music by the Cape Town Municipal Orchestra, recitations and songs from Shakespeare's works, and excerpts from his plays. The production was under the patronage and performed in the presence of the Governor-General and Lady Buxton, and the proceeds of the evening were to go to one of the war charities. According to the *Cape Times*, the Celebration 'was a notable occasion which attracted a large audience and abounded in glorifying England's great dramatist and poet'.[18] Introducing the evening's proceedings, Lord Buxton observed that enthusiasm for Shakespeare in the Cape was reflected in the fact that during the preceding few days more than 2,000 people had been to look at the Shakespeare manuscripts which were on display at the South African Public Library.

The prologue published in the programme of the Shakespeare Tercentenary Celebration was composed by W. R. Dudley and spoken by E. C. Dudley, and concludes as follows:

> Thou art the mightiest conqueror of the world,
> And holdest sway wherever men have raised
> Their minds above the sordid things of earth.
> Thou rulest even in the hearts of those
> Who hate thy England: and thy wizard voice
> Pierces the severing walls of race and speech.
> We too, whose land, in thy day dimly known
> As haunt of savage beast and man,
> Is now the home of ordered life and law,
> Join with the countless millions whom thy voice
> Has dowered with untold wealth of golden thought,
> And gladly lay our homage at thy feet.[19]

The universalizing themes are again to the fore: Shakespeare (not the British Navy and Army) subdued foreign nations; Shakespeare's truth transcends the boundaries of race and language; Africa (and particularly South Africa) has but recently emerged from a state of darkness and savagery; and, having emerged, its subjects have the capacity to appreciate Shakespeare's genius. In the stress on universal genius rather than national (English) hero, the potential is thus created for members of races massively 'inferior' to the English to appreciate Shakespeare in their terms.

Merriman's speech was recorded in detail in both the *Cape Times* and the *Cape Argus* on 25 April, with the former reproducing the full text. Merriman also emphasizes Shakespeare's quintessential Englishness, his status as a world genius, the fidelity to life of his plays and characters, and his particular relevance in time of war. In repeating these familiar themes, he tells an anecdote to reinforce Shakespeare's inspirational qualities, and particularly those of his historical plays:

A young friend of mine—a true South African, whose claim to that title would not be disputed by even the straitest of the sect of nationalistic pharisees—the very flower of our English public school and university culture—met his death in Flanders the other day. When he was picked up it was found that the bullet that had killed him had passed through a copy of 'Henry IV'. Fit companion for such a gallant soul.[20]

As if nervous to explore the implications of this death—would a thicker book have saved his life? Why exactly should 'a true South African' have to die in the mud 6,000 miles from home?—Merriman immediately quotes at length an exchange between Hotspur and Lady Percy, and moves on to pay tribute to the characterization of Falstaff and Master Robet Shallow. In the final paragraph, he quotes from Arnold's poem 'The Epilogue to Lessing's Laceoon' (sic), which includes the lines 'Beethoven, Raphael cannot reach / The charm that Homer, Shakespeare teach' (8). From this, he concludes that '[Shakespeare's] genius is the heritage of mankind, and his name lives enshrined in the hearts of the English-speaking folk. The greatest Englishman of us all' (8).

The story of Merriman's young friend dying in Flanders is a curious sequel to Arnold's story of the death of Arthur Mynors in Natal. Sharing a common identity forged on the playing-fields of English public schools, both young men are sacrificed for an ideal of Englishness that has Shakespeare as one of its defining coordinates. What is of course different about Merriman's deceased friend is that he is 'a true South African', although for Merriman this does not seem to disqualify him from also being English since in concluding he announces to his Cape Town audience that Shakespeare is 'the greatest Englishman of us all'. Quite where Englishness faded and South African identity emerged for Merriman is difficult to discern, and indeed his use of personal pronouns would seem to suggest that he saw the two as coterminous. Indeed, this uncertainty is confirmed in Sir James Rose Innes's description of Merriman as 'a great Englishman, a great South African, and without doubt the most brilliant intellect in the

political life in my time'.[21] What is clear, however, is the subordination of the colonial identity to that of the metropolis,
with the cultural markers of England (like Shakespeare) enjoying hegemony among the élite of the settler community.

Merriman's denial of a South African identity independent
of England is echoed in the writings of John Clark, the Arderne
Professor of English at Cape Town University from 1903 to
1928. Clark included in his literary output a long poem entitled 'An Ode on the Occasion of the Visit to South Africa of
the Prince of Wales'. Divided into seven parts, part 5 is headed
'Colonies are Nations in the Making, and, like Youth in Families, often Exhibit in Intenser form the Spirit and Polity of
their Parentage', and his short book *Aristotle's Poetics and
Shakespeare's Tragedies* confirms this observation.[22]

In following Bradley, in setting out to 'know definitely what
Shakespearean Tragedy means in substance',[23] Clark at the
same time elaborates the third aspect of Shakespeare's identity, namely his role as exemplary moral instructor of youth.
In addition to being national hero and universal genius, Shakespeare is also the Great Teacher. His principal lessons are
clarified in the course of the essay, with the first introduced
in the six-page second paragraph: 'The main part of tragedy,
the core of it, we might, then, from a new aspect declare to be
the deeds that are expressive of character, or the character
that manifests itself in action' (22). And '[t]he prevailing element, the causal factor in the tragic events of Shakespeare's
dramas is this or that deed, or series of deeds, of the hero'
(23). The tragic hero is *responsible* for his end: he 'procures his
own doom by deeds, or, from another point of view, by the
neglect of deeds' (24).

Connected to this is the question of the moral framework in
terms of which the hero's deeds are to be judged. Concepts
like 'fate', 'poetical justice', and 'divine law' do not quite capture the sense of moral order Clark detects underlying all the
tragedies. He argues that these rather mystifying terms can be
replaced by simpler ones: 'In a further statement of the position that the ultimate power in the world of Tragedy is vitally
concerned with Morality, let us stop using terms like justice
and merit and push our argument with simple terms like
"Good" and "Evil", which are primarily concerned with

morality, but may also connote what is admirable, or what is reprehensible, in a general way, in the conduct of human beings' (28). Evil, in Clark's definition, is 'that which leads to disaster, which is the cause of death and sorrow' (28), and 'that which causes convulsions in the order of the world' (29).

Clark's metaphysical pretensions are more modest than Bradley's—notions of Good and Evil are adequate for conveying his views on the morality of tragedy—but in describing the effect of the plays on 'us', he draws on the Aristotelian principles of fear and pity: 'Shakespeare has pity and terror in his tragedies, as is requisite, but commingled with the feelings they generate is an emotion of sorrow' (25). He argues that 'witnessing of the spectacle does not leave us hopeless in our thoughts or insurgent in our attitude' (30), and concludes that 'as we see this we agree with rightness of the catastrophe, although we do not sit or feel inclined to sit in the seat of the judge, and although we are far from losing the feeling of pity and fear' (30).

Clark does not quote any critics in exploring these themes, but his arguments are a very close paraphrase of Bradley. He repeats Bradley's emphasis on character and action, on the transcendent moral order of the tragedies, and on the capacity of the plays to purge the anti-social sentiments of the audience. Indeed, the final point is phrased in almost the same words as Bradley: for Clark, the spectacle does not leave us 'hopeless or insurgent', and for Bradley, it does not leave us 'rebellious or desperate'.[24]

For both Bradley and Clark then, Shakespeare teaches the need to cultivate a sense of personal responsibility and a respect for order. Their reading, in less displaced terms, was reproduced in the syllabuses and examination papers for the colleges and schools of the Colony.[25] Mary Penrith summarizes the syllabuses of the three main South African colleges at this time. They all had three consecutive courses in English: the first comprised essay, history of English literature, history of language, and special authors; the second included the close study of the literature of a specific period, Chaucer, Shakespeare, and special authors; and the third course contained a wider range of material, notably Middle and Old English, but again included Shakespeare and special authors. Before 1918 the English examinations were still set by the University of the Cape of Good Hope, and all the colleges were therefore obliged to work their way through the same syllabus. The most intensive dose of Shakespeare was in the Second Paper of the BA Pass examination, where for 1916 students were expected to 'know' *Love's Labour's Lost*, *Romeo and Juliet*, *Henry IV Part 2*, *Twelfth Night*, *King Lear*, and *A Winter's Tale*. This involved answering questions like:

5. Analyse the character of Lear with special reference to character development. Consider the *denouement* of *King Lear* from the standpoint of poetical justice.
6. How far is *Romeo and Juliet* a tragedy of character and how far a tragedy of circumstance? In what does the tragic fault lie?

or

Compare the character development of Romeo with that of Juliet.[26]

Two events of interest took place in the Cape schools in 1916. The first was the not altogether surprising mention of the Shakespeare Tercentenary, which was to be marked in the manner laid down in the *Education Gazette*:

The Tercentenary will naturally be celebrated in our schools, and our teachers will doubtless find more than one opportunity during the next few weeks of dealing appropriately with the man and his work. For such celebrations short addresses, recitation competitions, tableaux, etc., are appropriate, and in all schools, we feel sure some effort will be made to mark the occasion.[27]

The reasons for the celebration are elaborated, with a range of authorities summoned to support the cause:

In the case of the younger pupils readings from Shakespeare as have been suggested will prove suitable; but in the case of the older pupils what is wanted is that they should learn to appreciate the greatness of Shakespeare's genius, to know with Jonson that 'He was not of an age, but for all time.' It is the permanent and universal element in Shakespeare that the young student must learn to realise and learn to capture, so that he may ultimately recognise, in the words of Gladstone, that the works of Shakespeare stand 'entirely unrivalled in all literature for largeness and variety with depth'; and in time to come to appreciate that Shakespeare, as Carlyle insists, was 'the greatest intellect who, in our recorded world, has left record of himself in the way of Literature'.   (1022)

To assist teachers in cultivating love and respect for his universal genius, it is suggested that they read Carlyle's essay on Shakespeare in *On Heroes and Hero-Worship*, John Masefield's *Shakespeare*, Raleigh's *Shakespeare*, and Sir Sidney Lee's *A Life of William Shakespeare*.

Whether any teachers read these books is uncertain, but the injunction to expose their charges to Shakespeare was enforced in another way, namely through the introduction of the new English syllabus. Before 1916 the English literature syllabus amounted to no more than a stipulation as to the number of lines of poetry that had to be memorized in each standard. The rationale for this method of literature teaching in the Cape education system is set out by F. H. Sykes in terms that echo Arnold quite precisely. Sykes argues that '[n]o part of true education is of greater importance than the memorizing of passages from our best authors [since] [t]he influence of literature on the formation of character is a fact beyond dispute'.[28] But although this conviction continued to hold sway in the minds of education administrators, the means of ensuring the transfer of noble thoughts from the works of 'our best authors' to the minds of pupils were adjusted in the new syllabus. Instead of memorizing Shakespeare, the syllabus demanded that students answer questions about the plot, characters, and themes in a selected play. The syllabus itself has not survived, but an article in the *Educational News* of 1916 responds to anxieties regarding the requirements of the new syllabus by publishing a sample examination paper in which some sense of what students were expected to know can be discerned. The questions include:

4. What effects of the unusual life that Miranda had led are to be seen in her character? Give detailed reference to passages or incidents in the play.

And;

7. Who was Enobarbus? Describe the part that he takes in the events of the play. Why did he desert Antony?[29]

Forcing pupils by an examination system to know about Miranda's character and Enobarbus' desertion, however, did not entirely satisfy the Cape's educational administrators. The aim of the new syllabus is defined by H. Redfern Loades as to instil 'a definite liking for English Literature [and] a love for further reading'.[30] In the same article, he invites English teachers to respond to seven questions regarding the capacity of the syllabus to achieve this ideal. In a subsequent issue of the *Educational News* he discloses the results of his survey, concluding from the teachers' responses that 'the present syllabus is *not* such as to foster further reading',[31] and, further, that the general pattern as regards pupils' reading habits is for them to treat 'the books set "as lessons" but [turn] to lighter, more exciting and ephemeral matter for pleasure and relaxation' (195). There is an opposition set up here between Shakespeare, who is 'good for pupils', and lighter reading, which is perceived as potentially subversive.

Shakespeare's position as reliable instructor of youth is reinforced in the introductions and notes to the school editions of the period. This is evident in the first South African school edition of a Shakespeare play, the 1913 Juta edition of *The Tempest* edited by the English master at Sea Point Boys' High School, S. J. Newns. After a few introductory remarks on the features of the Elizabethan Age, Newns establishes why *The Tempest* is accepted as the last play Shakespeare wrote and then summarizes the plot. As in the late Victorian editions of the plays, much detail is then given to delineating and explaining the characters, and the triangle of Prospero–Caliban–Miranda is reproduced in the same terms as contemporaneous English editions: Prospero, seen as a kind of surrogate schoolmaster, is described as 'a man of great intellectual powers [whose] fine character makes us pass lenient judgment on him';[32] Miranda is 'the embodiment of simplicity, and beauty of character' (8), and her obedience to Ferdinand is singled out for special praise; and Caliban, [a]though he is a brutal and debased creature, yet he has moments . . . of rugged eloquence' (9). In the concluding paragraph, familiar themes recur: Shakespeare's universality is announced—'[t]he characters . . . are of a different realm; and yet the wonderful thing is, that in spite of this, they are singularly human, and appeal to everyone' (10)—and the Bard's veneration for order is emphasized in the unquestioning acceptance of Prospero's final dispensation: 'Thus while the guilty obtain pardon, the innocent gain something; Ferdinand —a beautiful wife, and Miranda—a good husband.... The whole play is a vindication of virtue, and brings out clearly the ultimate triumph of right, and the condemnation of wrong; and even there, judgment is tempered with mercy' (10). At all stages of the Cape's education system, Shakespeare therefore instructs young minds by insisting upon detailed knowledge of complicated plots, exhaustive speculation about character development and fatal flaws, and stern reminders of the need always to respect the prevailing moral order.

Some sense of the impact Shakespeare might have had upon pupils can be gained from Z. K. Matthews autobiography, *Freedom for my People*. Matthews was in the same class at high school in Kimberley as Plaatje's son, St Leger, and he recalls his English lessons in 1915 and 1916 with Thomas Leah affectionately: 'Mr Leah got across to us his love of language and its poetry. Here was an Englishman reading English poetry to a class of African children without the fact that we were Africans making any difference to him. It says something for Thomas Leah and for Shakespeare that somehow we did gather up a share of the spirit in which those great plays were written and of the feeling Mr Leah had for them.'[33] It would obviously be dangerous to generalize on the basis of this one testimony, but it shows that particular teachers working within the education system managed to instil an enthusiasm for Shakespeare and the cluster of values associated with his name. As for Plaatje, so too for Matthews, Shakespeare the universal genius transcended Shakespeare the English national genius, and his position of enforced authority within the schooling system did not dim his aura.

The Assimilated Phase

The first reading of the relation between the colonial subject and Shakespeare explored is the one produced in the years of decolonization by anti-imperialist writers from former European colonies. Several of these writers reflect in some detail on the contributions of Plaatje's generation to the struggle against all forms of Western domination.

Frantz Fanon, in *The Wretched of the Earth*, identifies three phases in the history of the native writer responding to the colonial experience. In the first phase, 'the native intellectual gives proof that he has assimilated the culture of the occupying power. His writings correspond point by point with those of his opposite numbers in the mother country. His inspiration is European and we can easily link up these works with definite trends in the literature of the mother country. This is the period of unqualified assimilation.'[34]

In the second phase, the native intellectual's memories of the pre-colonial past are rekindled, the fragile coherence of the assimilated identity is disrupted, and a reimmersion in the life and culture of the colonized takes place. In Fanon's phrase, 'We spew ourselves up' (179). The third and final phase, the one Fanon himself registers in his work, is the fighting phase, in which 'the native, after having tried to lose himself in the people and with the people, will on the contrary shake the people' (179). He becomes 'an awakener of the people', his writing becomes 'a fighting literature, a revolutionary literature, and a national literature' (179).

Fanon argues that the black middle class in developing countries should repudiate its own nature, which is to be the tool of Western capitalism, and 'make itself the willing slave of that revolutionary capital which is the people'; it should 'put at the people's disposal the intellectual and technical capital that it has snatched when going through the colonial universities' (120). Unfortunately, instead of following this 'heroic, positive, fruitful and just path' (120), the colonial bourgeoisie such as it exists betrays its destiny, functioning as a 'little greedy caste, avid and voracious . . . glad to accept the dividends that the former colonial power hands to it' (141). He concludes: 'It remembers what it has read in European textbooks and imperceptibly it becomes not even the replica of Europe, but its caricature' (141). Of the European textbooks that pervert the mind of the native intellectual, Fanon again refers to literature. Elaborating on the crises of national identity engendered during the assimilated stage, Fanon observes that such intellectuals occupy what they describe as a 'universal standpoint' (176). He explains:

This is because the native intellectual has thrown himself greedily upon Western culture. Like adopted children who only stop investigating the new family framework at the moment when a mini-mum nucleus of security crystallizes in their psyche, the native in-tellectual will try to make European culture his own. He will not be content to get to know Rabelais and Diderot, Shakespeare and Edgar Allan Poe; he will bind them to his intelligence as tightly as possible. (176)

In *Towards the African Revolution*, Fanon repeats this negative judgement of the early native intellectual:

Having witnessed the liquidation of its systems of reference, the collapse of its cultural patterns, the native can only recognize with the occupant that 'God is not on his side.' The oppressor, through the inclusive and frightening character of his authority, manages to impose on the native new ways of seeing, and in particular a pejor-ative judgement with respect to his original form of existing. . . . Guilt and inferiority are the usual consequences of this dialectic. The oppressed then tries to escape these, on the one hand by proclaim-ing his total and unconditional adoption of the new cultural models, and on the other, by pronouncing an irreversible condemnation of his own cultural style. . . . [T]he oppressed *flings himself* upon the imposed culture with the desperation of a drowning man.[35]

However, in *Black Skin, White Masks*, he explores in greater detail the psychological dimensions of colonial oppression, setting out to 'help the black man to free himself of the ar-senal of complexes that has been developed by the colonial environment'.[36] In rather more sympathetic terms, he again emphasizes the imposition of Western culture and its debil-itating effect:

Every colonized people—in other words, every people in whose soul an inferiority complex has been created by the death and burial of its local cultural originality—finds itself face to face with the lan-guage of the civilizing nation; that is, with the culture of the mother country. The colonized is elevated above the jungle status in propor-tion to his adoption of the mother country's cultural standards. (18)

Towards the end of the book, Fanon describes how European archetypes have in the colonies insinuated themselves into the unconscious of the colonized, and he notes the role of literature in this process:

The *anima* of the Antillian Negro is almost always a white woman. In the same way, the *animus* of the Antilleans is always a white man.

That is because in the works of Anatole France, Balzac, Bazin, or any of the rest of 'our' novelists, there is never a word about an ethereal yet ever present black woman or about a dark Apollo with sparkling eyes. . . . But I too am guilty, here I am talking about Apollo! There is no help for it: I am a white man. For unconsciously I distrust what is black in me, that is, the whole of my being.   (191)

In *The Wretched of the Earth* and *Towards the African Revolution*, Fanon dismisses the crises of conscience suffered by the emergent colonial bourgeoisie, identifying their assimilation of Western culture (including Shakespeare) as inextricably bound up with their betrayals of 'the people'. In these more polemical works, he emphasizes the systemic inequalities of the colonial situation and pursues strategies for overcoming them, perceiving the subtleties of the relationship of a privileged élite of collaborators to Western culture as a rather less urgent concern than the immense suffering and humiliation of the vast majority. In these works, he flattens out the contradictions determining the struggles of his forebears, constituting himself in the three-stage teleology as the heroic colonial thinker who has transcended the intellectual constraints of 'the assimilated stage'. In *Black Skin, White Masks*, however, he is more sympathetic to the likes of Plaatje, conceding that the psychological scars of cultural imperialism are complex and not easily transcended.[37]

Amilcar Cabral echoes the Fanon of *The Wretched of the Earth* when he dismisses the assimilated colonial intellectual as an isolated phenomenon:

[Western culture] only leaves its mark at the very top of the colonizer's social pyramid—which created colonialism itself—and particularly it influences what one may call the 'indigenous petit bourgeoisie' and a very small number of workers in urban areas. . . . They are prisoners of the cultural and social contradictions of their lives. They cannot escape from their role as a marginal class. . . . [Their conflicts are] played out according to their material circumstances and level of culture but always resolved on the individual level, never collectively.[38]

The honourable route Cabral prescribes for such intellectuals is for them to relinquish their privileged position and commit themselves to 'real involvement in the struggle for independence

... not only against the foreign culture but also the foreign domination' (162). What is needed is for Western culture to be recognized as 'no more than a more or less violent attempt to deny the culture of the people in question'.[39] Assimilated intellectuals subject to this onslaught must resist by undergoing 'a spiritual reconversion, [a] *re-Africanization* in our case' (145).

Albert Memmi's *The Colonizer and the Colonized*, on the other hand, is closer in spirit to *Black Skin, White Masks*, providing detailed psychological portraits of the colonizer and the colonized, and consciously leaving aside economic analyses and political strategies. However, in his description of the colonized, Memmi argues that the colonial relationship is ultimately determined by a common motive: 'the colonizer's economic and basic needs, which he substitutes for logic, and which shape and explain each of the traits he assigns to the colonized'.[40] These traits combine to function as a stereotype which the colonized comes to internalize: 'Wilfully created and spread by the colonizer, this mythical and degrading portrait ends up by being accepted and lived with to a certain extent by the colonized' (153). Central to this process for Memmi is the reduction of the colonized to the status of object, and the systematic denial of any significant pre-colonial past.

Faced with the formidable forces of the colonizer, the colonized has two choices: assimilation or petrifaction. Since the latter involves a total withdrawal from the colonial situation, something frequently impossible, Memmi deals at greater length on the processes of assimilation, in terms that echo Fanon's ideas on the first phase in the evolution of the native intellectual. Memmi explains the contradictory psychological pressures of attempts to assimilate in the following way:

> The first attempt of the colonized is to change his condition by changing his skin ... to become equal to that splendid model [the colonizer] and to resemble him to the point of disappearing in him. ... This fit of passion for the colonizer's values would not be so suspect, however, if it did not involve such a negative side. The colonized does not seek merely to enrich himself with the colonizer's virtues. In the name of what he hopes to become, he sets his mind on impoverishing himself, tearing himself away from his true self. (185–6)

Memmi argues that no amount of effort on the part of the colonized to assimilate can bring success, since it remains limited to being an individual solution, and '[i]n order for assimilation of the colonized to have a purpose and a meaning, it would have to affect an entire people; i.e. that the whole colonial condition be changed' (192).

Unlike Fanon, who sees appeals to a universal equality purely as pernicious bourgeois myths perpetrated to facilitate the recruitment of collaborators from the ranks of the oppressed, Memmi argues that the ideal must be retained:

As for the failure of assimilation, I do not derive any particular joy from it, especially since that solution carries a universalistic and socialistic flavour which makes it *a priori* respectable. . . . Moreover, and this is the essential thing, assimilation is also the opposite of colonization. It tends to eliminate the distinctions between the colonizers and the colonized, and thereby eliminates the colonial relationship. (215–16)

It would be easy to argue that Memmi in this passage falls for the same myth of bourgeois freedoms that had beguiled Plaatje forty-one years before, but his argument also brings out the complexities of writing—as Plaatje, Fanon, and Memmi do—from a weak defensive position outside the ramparts of Western Culture. The faint cries from within for universal brotherhood echo alternately as genuine messages of conciliation (for Plaatje and Memmi), and as cruel lures to trap the naïve and unwary (for Fanon and Cabral).

As regards the reading of Shakespeare in this tradition of anti-imperialist thought, loosely three positions can be identified. The first, a minority position, is perhaps best represented by C. L. R. James, who, in like manner to the Examiner of the Dublin 1920 *Hamlet*, vigorously opposes British imperialism while at the same time embracing Shakespeare. Defending Lenin from charges of vanguardism, James audaciously points out that '[n]ext year [1964] is the 400th anniversary of Shakespeare. It is also the 40th anniversary of the death of Lenin.'[41] He explains the connection between Shakespeare and Lenin thus:

Who should govern, what he should aim at, what philosophy of society he should adopt, what should be a political leader's personal philosophy in a time of revolution, who are the political types he is likely to meet, on all this and the exposition of it, Shakespeare stands second to none, neither to Aristotle, to Rousseau nor to Marx. He is surprisingly close to Lenin. (30)

A second position, more frequently expressed, is to treat European High Culture as fatally compromised by its foundations in imperialism. The most eloquent version of this argument is Aimé Césaire's *Discourse on Colonialism*, where Cesaire does not name Shakespeare, but insists on the congruence of Western racism and humanism:

Yes, it would be worthwhile to study clinically, in detail, the steps taken by Hitler and Hitlerism and to reveal to the very distinguished, very humanistic, very Christian bourgeois of the twentieth century that without his being aware of it, he has a Hitler inside him... Whether one likes it or not, at the end of every blind alley that is Europe... there is Hitler. At the end of capitalism which is eager to outlive its day, there is Hitler. At the end of formal humanism and philosophic renunciation, there is Hitler.[42]

The third position is to appropriate Shakespeare, and interpret the plays as anti-imperialist documents. The play lending itself most obviously to such rereadings has been *The Tempest*.[43] Roberto Fernandez Retamar's treatment of the play, for example, focuses on Ariel as the symptomatic colonial intellectual faced with a familiar choice:

The Ariel of Shakespeare's great myth, which we have been following in these notes, is, as has been said, the intellectual from the same island as Caliban. He can choose between serving Prospero—the case with intellectuals of the anti-American [the continent, not the USA] persuasion—at which he is apparently unusually adept, but for whom he is nothing more than a timorous slave, or allying himself with Caliban in his struggle for true freedom.[44]

To sum up: both Plaatje and Shakespeare are for the most part represented in negative terms by this first group of writers. As regards Plaatje, there are limited qualifications: Fanon, in *Black Skin, White Masks*, and Memmi demonstrate some sympathy for the colonial writer struggling within and against economic imperialism and Western culture. However, Fanon, in *Wretched of the Earth*, and Cabral equate the colonial subject's love of Western culture with political betrayal. As regards Shakespeare, although Memmi and James argue that the universal humanism in Western culture should be seized upon as a message of hope, the far more frequent view is that Shakespeare serves the interests of the imperialist powers.

An Agent of Foreign Capital

In Marx's writings, two different sets of texts might be cited as originating two versions of the relation between Europe and its colonies. The first set is his articles on India in the 1850s.[45] Marx argues here that Western capitalism is the principal agent of world history, and that the historical path of the West leads ultimately to socialism:

England, it is true, in causing a social revolution in Hindustan, was actuated by only the vilest interests, and was stupid in her manner of enforcing them. But that is not the question. The question is, can mankind fulfil its destiny without a fundamental revolution in the social state of Asia? If not, whatever may have been the crimes of England she was the unconscious tool of history in bringing about that revolution.[46]

He argues further that 'Indian society has no history at all, at least no known history';[47] and suggests that socialism in India is unlikely 'till in Great Britain itself the now ruling class shall have been supplanted by the industrial proletariat' (85). The world outside Europe thus awaits liberation from within Europe, specifically from the Western working classes.

The second group of texts is certain letters written in the 1880s, and reflecting on the history of Russia. In his brief letter to Vera Zasulich, he insists upon the historic specificity of different struggles. Regarding the genesis and expansion of capitalism, he asserts that '[t]he "historical inevitability" of this course is therefore *expressly* restricted to *the countries of Western Europe*'.[48] And in a letter to the Editorial Board of the *Otechestvenniye Zapiski*, he warns that one must not 'metamorphose my historical sketch of the genesis of capitalism in Western Europe into an historico-philosophic theory of the general path every people is fated to tread, whatever the historical circumstances in which it finds itself'.[49] The world outside Europe has its own history and dynamic of change, including the potential to achieve revolutionary liberation.

The 1850s Marx is developed by V. I. Lenin in *Imperialism, the Highest Stage of Capitalism*, where he argues that England's 'art' resides not in the liberal sentiments of its greatest writer, but rather in the capacity to secure and expand its material interests.[50] He links England's vast sphere of influence to its position as a major capitalist power, making the crucial connection between the transition from competitive to monopoly capitalism and the scramble for the colonies. In this relationship, the economic framework allowing Shakespeare to overrun the world was structured:

For Great Britain, the period of the enormous expansion of colonial conquests was that between 1860 and 1880, and it was also very considerable in the last twenty years of the nineteenth century. . . . We saw above that the development of pre-monopoly capitalism, of capitalism in which free competition was predominant, reached its limit in the 1860s and 1870s. We saw that it is *precisely after that period* that the tremendous 'boom' in colonial conquests begins, and that the struggle for the territorial division of the world becomes extraordinarily sharp. It is beyond doubt, therefore, that capitalism's transition to the stage of monopoly capitalism, to finance capital, *is connected* with the intensification of the struggle for the partitioning of the world.[51]

Lenin's short book analyses with economy and skill the extraordinary concentration of power and capital in the hands of the international capitalist class during this period, thus throwing into relief Sol Plaatje's presumptions regarding an equal place within the Pax Britannica for black South Africans. In focusing on the economic forces shaping the production and distribution of resources, Lenin demonstrates the hollowness of claims made from within English culture regarding the liberty and equality of humankind, claims upon which Plaatje and others had placed great store in their struggles against settler governments.

A striking absence in Lenin's argument is his lack of interest in cultural imperialism. Concerned with the flow of finance capital and the production and distribution of material resources, he does not discuss the related deployment of intellectual capital, or the cultural institutions and practices serving the colonial enterprise. As a result, he sheds little light on why Plaatje pays tribute to Shakespeare and not to the London Stock Exchange; or, for that matter, on the relation between Shakespeare and the London Stock Exchange. Plaatje's support for British interests did not take place in isolation: material interest was explained and legitimized by the stories generated by the dominant English culture—including stories about Shakespeare's universal wisdom and authority—and the hegemony of those stories was enforced by educational and cultural institutions both in Britain and in the colonies.

Contemporary Western Marxist theory continues to focus primarily on economic relations.[52] Michael Barratt Brown summarizes the method: 'Marxists will tend to collect facts about societies in different epochs according to the economic or property relations that are to be found, and not according to the ideas that men had about them.'[53] Furthermore, the terms of structural economic analysis do not permit of much speculation regarding the consciousness of the different actors living the colonial experience. Barratt Brown's contribution in this area consists of two quite valid, but obviously limited, observations: the first is that colonization 'led to an artificial world division of labour maintained by free trade, in which countries restricted to primary production became dependent upon those with diversified and mainly industrial output' (63); and the second is that the international division of labour made Third World development very difficult, since 'its national bourgeoisie, for instance, had become agents of foreign capital' (69).

For the most part Western Marxism therefore continues to script the working classes in the West as the revolutionary actors, with colonial subjects left in the wings. A. Sivanandan savagely parodies this tradition in his review of Bill Warren's *Imperialism: Pioneer of Capitalism*:

Imperialism, in other words, creates its own contradiction in creating Third World capitalism, and capitalism creates its own contradiction in creating the working class that is destined to overthrow it. The result: socialism. Without imperialism, then, there is no capitalism (for the Third World); without capitalism, no socialism. So if we want socialism, we had better embrace imperialism.[54]

A more philosophical variant of this argument is put forward in Perry Anderson's *Consideration on Western Marxism*. Arising in tension with the same social forces as Warren's Marxism, this tradition eschews the heroic fantasy and reflects at length on the failures of European revolutionary impulse. Anderson describes the context in the following way:

Thus, from 1924 to 1968, Marxism did not 'stop', as Sartre was later to claim; but it advanced via an unending detour from any revolutionary political practice. . . . The hidden hallmark of Western Marxism as a whole is thus that it is a product of *defeat*. . . . its major works were, without exception, produced in situations of political isolation and despair.[55]

The tradition described by Anderson also marginalizes those outside the West, but in a different way to Warren. Where Warren's message to Third World struggles is: wait for the great white working-class hope to deliver you unto socialism, the Anderson message is more gloomy: the great white working class has failed, so you might as well give up too in your struggles for socialism.[56]

The non-European Marxist tradition overlaps substantially with the writings of Fanon's generation. Cabral in particular acknowledges a debt to Marxism, although they disagree with Western Marxists in key areas, notably in their insistence on the revolutionary agency of the peasantry.[57] Kwame Nkrumah follows this trajectory. Observing the main contours of Lenin's economic analysis, Nkrumah none the less differs fundamentally from the Western Marxists in allocating the African oppressed the major role in socialist transformation. He stresses the role of indigenous élites in securing capitalist interests, describing them as 'a small, selfish, money minded, reactionary minority'.[58] Enforcing an education assiduously copied from English public schools, the colonial powers sought to 'train up a western-oriented political elite committed to the attitudes and ideologies of capitalism and bourgeois society' (36–7). Although the bulk of African intellectuals seek to benefit from the system rather than to change it, Nkrumah praises the minority, 'who reacted strongly against its brainwashing processes and who became genuine socialist and African nationalist revolutionaries' (39).

South African communist historians hold similar positions in this regard. Jack and Ray Simons's standard text *Class and Colour in South Africa 1850–1950*, sets out in cogent detail the break-up of the consensus forged in the nineteenth century between the Eastern Cape African peasantry and the English merchant class at the Cape, under the pressure of the mineral revolution in the north. But in referring to Plaatje's close allies

in the ANC who were in the early twentieth century still appealing to that consensus, their judgement is brief and harsh: 'The
conservatives [including Plaatje's political allies] and their
white liberal advisers never quite understood their society or
its power structure. They persisted in believing against all
the evidence that liberation would come to them through
reasoned argument, appeals to Christian ethics, and moderate,
constitutional protest.[59] Cast as victims of a false consciousness, the contradictions of their position are again flattened
out, and they are depicted as early travellers on the first stage
on the journey to a revolutionary socialist consciousness.[60]

How then is the relation between the colonial subject and
Shakespeare expressed in this extremely diverse tradition? Although there are very important differences between writers
calling themselves Marxists (Marx himself, of course, loved
Shakespeare), certain generalizations might be ventured. The
colonial intellectual of Plaatje's generation is for the most part
seen as an agent and apologist for capitalism, a traitor to the
African masses. Shakespeare, though rarely specifically cited,
is part of the ideological weaponry of Western capitalism, part
of capital's 'brainwashing processes', and love of Shakespeare
in colonial intellectuals is seen as synonymous with a politics
of capitulation.

A Gifted Old Chap

In the early 1970s a small number of academics at South
African universities turned their attentions to black South
African writers, and to Plaatje in particular.[61] Their research
is detailed, careful, and sensitive, and their reasons for studying Plaatje were several.

In the first place, they felt suffocated by the conservatism
of English departments at all the South African universities.
Tim Couzens explains by quoting at length from a news-letter
reporting on the main debates at the 1977 inaugural conference of South African English lecturers:

It revealed that South African university teachers of English are still
much concerned with the debate between text and context, i.e. the

study of the text as autonomous as against the belief that the text is part of wider cultural, historical and social structures which require equal attention. . . . Prof. Gillham offered a closely reasoned and dispassionate statement of the classical 'prac. crit.' approach, expressing his concern 'to reinstate criteria that are in danger of being attenuated.' He expressed his conviction that 'really great works of art have the habit of providing their own relevant knowledge; . . . the work will itself suggest the criteria by which it should be judged'.[62]

Although there were dissenting voices at the conference, Couzens reports that the sympathies of the 'silent majority' were firmly behind Gillham, a position Couzens regarded as anachronistic and inappropriate.

That Couzens's hostility to South African English department orthodoxy took him towards social history was due also to the fact social history as an academic discourse *was available*. The work of English radical historians like E. P. Thompson and Christopher Hill represented an escape route from the claustrophobia of English studies. Brian Willan, in the preface to his superb study *Sol Plaatje: A Biography*, echoes E. P. Thompson's professed objective in *The Making of the English Working Class* of 'seeking to rescue the poor stockinger, the Luddite cropper, the "obsolete" hand-loom weaver . . . from the enormous condescension of posterity',[63] when he writes that Plaatje's neglect is due to

South Africa's capacity to obscure and distort its own past, to neglect the lives of those whose ideals and aspirations have been in conflict with official orthodoxies, past and present. The South African historical memory, to put it another way, has been highly selective in its recall. I hope this book may contribute to challenging the dominance of this form of historical memory; and in showing that it is possible to write a book such as this, I hope I may encourage others to undertake biographical research into the lives of other men and women of Plaatje's background and generation.[64]

The methodological assumptions of this approach are determinedly empirical, as Couzens explains in his biography of Herbert Dhlomo, *The New African*: '[E]ven "facts" which follow in this book may have to be modified in the light of further information, [and] in time it will be replaced by more and more accurate studies.'[65]

The choice of social history as the most appropriate form of academic writing was presumably also due in some part to the fact its expressed intention intersected with Steve Biko's injunction to rewrite the past from the point of view of the black oppressed, since

with an unnerving totality the colonialists were not satisfied merely with holding a people in their grip and emptying the Native's brain of all form and content, they turned to the past of the oppressed people and distorted, disfigured and destroyed it. . . . No doubt, therefore, part of the approach envisaged in bringing about 'black consciousness' has to be directed to the past, to seek to rewrite the history of the black man and to produce in it the heroes who form the core of the African background.[66]

The division of labour within South Africa's culture of resistance, however, meant that Biko's appeal was answered not by black political activists but by professional white historians and critics.

The third reason for the interest in the 1970s in black literature and black literary history lies in the broader context of South Africa in the 1970s: the wave of strike action and rapid growth of trade unions, the escalation of the war in Angola, the crisis in black education that culminated in the Soweto Uprising of 1976, and the emergence of a defiant black consciousness political movement. It is more difficult to write about these connections, but it is possible at least to phrase the relation negatively: in the mid–1970s, the absurdity of enthusing about really great works of (Western) art at the same time as Soweto was exploding became too difficult to sustain, and a literary–critical–historical discourse that at least acknowledged the reality of that explosion was sought.

A final reason for the choice of Plaatje no doubt also rested upon the sympathy these historians felt for Plaatje's position: alienated from white South African culture and with no political or institutional base in radical black culture, their writing tries to mediate tensions not unlike the ones Plaatje tried to reconcile between liberal white patronage and an emergent militant black working class.[67] And in their commitment to human equality and democratic values, they share Plaatje's dreams of a more just South Africa. They seldom announce these convictions—the genre does not encourage it—but in using Plaatje to talk for them, their own concerns are expressed in displaced form. This is perhaps shown most clearly in the concluding paragraphs of an early Couzens article on *Mhudi*, where he argues that Plaatje's novel suggests implicitly that the revolutionary solution 'is only to be tried as a last resort', and, further, that Plaatje's belief that ' "[b]rotherhood is not only between man and man, but between nation and nation, and race and race" . . . is not a facile one [but] a solution won in the teeth of harrowing experiences'.[68] Writing at a time when relations between races continued to be far from fraternal in South Africa, Couzens's citation of Plaatje's dogged commitment to non-racialism stands as validation of Couzens's own commitment to the same ideal fifty-five years later.

As to what light the work of these writers sheds on the relation of Plaatje to Shakespeare, it is clear that they offer a wealth of biographical and anecdotal detail that provides a far more subtle and sympathetic portrait of Plaatje. Introducing a special centenary edition of *English in Africa* commemorating Plaatje's birth in 1976, Couzens and Willan conclude their introduction by quoting the opinion of an old friend of Plaatje's: 'Plaatje . . . was a gifted old chap. Very much gifted in that he could penetrate into what was going to come. And analysing what is taking place at the present time. And then also he had the background, you understand . . . what had been happening.'[69] In short, Plaatje was a reasonable black man trapped by impossible contradictions. And this sympathetic portrait of Plaatje is matched by a rather more generous impression of Shakespeare. Implicit in the work of these writers is the belief that English liberal culture of Plaatje's time represented a humane alternative to the more brutal racism of the Transvaal, and further, that Shakespeare offered a route for Plaatje to the world beyond South Africa. The encounter between colonial subject and Shakespeare was therefore more than simply the cultural equivalent of the economic transaction between De Beers Consolidated Mines and African mineworkers; it was a complicated exchange which *included* certain valued achievements of Western culture becoming available to colonial subjects for the first time.

The Other Plaatje

During the 1980s there was a massive increase in the amount of research carried out on 'colonial discourse' in Western universities. Although writers like Ngugi wa Thiong'o have continued to write in the spirit to Fanon's generation, the major 'colonial discourse theorists'—Edward Said, Gayatri Chakravorty Spivak, Abdul JanMohamed, and Homi K. Bhabha—have approached matters colonial and post-colonial in a quite distinct fashion.[70] In general, these recent writers concentrate less on the political struggles and strategies, social histories, and material conditions of the colonized, focusing rather on culture, identity, subjectivity, and consciousness.[71] Shakespeare studies have not been ignored in these developments, with *The Tempest* in particular being reread in the light of this new work.[72] To explain the emergence of these concerns is less easy, and it is tempting to accept David Simpson's cynical conclusion regarding the rediscovery of history in English studies in order to explain the study of colonial discourse, namely that 'the discontinuous, uncontingent autonomy of the academic subculture [is] responsive not to the larger movements of history (whose very existence might indeed be disputed) but to the mere demand for change'.[73] But the search for novelty still does not explain the timing or the selection of a particular area of critical interest (like colonial discourse), and therefore several further factors might be mentioned. These would include: the rise to positions of power within English and American universities of students from the Third World who studied in the West in the 1960s, the existence of a heterogeneous student body still interested in the legacy of imperialism, and the extraordinary media focus via Live Aid etc. on Third World poverty and devastation. Also, the reversals or containment of revolutionary victories won in the 1960s and 1970s in Mozambique, Angola, Algeria, Vietnam, Nicaragua, and Iran have made the threat to official Anglo-American culture posed by the study of anti-imperialist struggles in its universities far more slight. As Edward Said confesses, 'I feel outnumbered and outorganized by a prevailing consensus that has come to regard the Third World as an atrocious nuisance.'[74]

The critical project undertaken by this group is accordingly modest. Unlike Fanon, who saw his critique of colonialism as directly related to the violent overthrow of oppressive regimes, these writers seek by their work to change the syllabuses in English departments at élite Western universities. Henry Louis Gates Jr. acknowledges the limitations of theoretical interventions in the field:

Scores of people are killed every day in the name of differences ascribed only to race. This slaughter demands the gesture in which the contributors to this special of *Critical Inquiry* are collectively engaged: to deconstruct, if you will, the ideas of difference inscribed in the trope of race, to explicate discourse itself in order to reveal the hidden relations of power and knowledge inherent in popular and academic usages of race. But . . . when thousands of people willingly risk death to protest apartheid . . . the gesture that we make here seems local and tiny.[75]

Abdul JanMohamed and David Lloyd are similarly conscious of the scope of their intellectual labour. Seeking to challenge 'the systemic relegation of minority concerns to the periphery of academic work', they conceive their principal function as minority intellectuals as being to provide a 'critique and re-formulation of the traditional role of humanist intellectuals and of the disciplinary divisions which sanction that role'.[76] They concede that real acceptance of diversity and difference in Western society will involve 'radical transformations of the material structures of exploitation', but none the less argue that intellectual work should not therefore be relegated to 'perpetual adventism', since '[o]penings for intervention are various and multiple at any moment, and indeed . . . most of the terms of a minority discourse have been forged precisely in the practices of engaged minority groups' (15). In England, the emphasis has been similar, with careful intellectual endeavour directed to explicating the language of colonialism conceived as a viable form of political intervention: the 1984 Essex Conference on *Europe and its Others* described the objective of the conference as to provide 'a general archaeology of europocentric discourses'.[77]

Some idea of the critical method employed by these critics can be gained from their stated aims, but it is difficult to summarize their collective contribution, as their ideas and methods differ in important ways. Benita Parry identifies four critical strategies employed:

to expose how power secretly inheres in colonialism's system of 'natural' differentiations and to show that in the process of producing meaning, these dualisms are undermined and repositioned as interdependent, conjunct, intimate; to decentre the native as a fixed, unified object of colonialist knowledge through disclosing how colonialism's contradictory mode of address constitutes an ambivalently positioned subject; to dislodge the construct of a monolithic and deliberative colonial authority by demonstrating the dispersed space of power and a disseminated apparatus, wielded by diverse agents and effecting multiple situations and relations; and to dispel the representation of brute, institutional repression by making known the devious techniques of obligation and persuasion with which the native colludes but simultaneously resists.[78]

In order to provide some sense of what 'Plaatje' becomes when these strategies are applied to him, one aspect implicit in Parry's summary requires special emphasis, namely the rejection of empiricist modes of representation. Said describes the most important task facing him and other like-minded critics as 'to ask how one can study other cultures and peoples from a libertarian, or nonrepressive and nonmanipulative, perspective',[79] and for Bhabha, that perspective must radically subvert '[t]he historical and ideological determinants of Western narrative—bourgeois individualism, organicism, liberal humanism, autonomy, progression'.[80] Spivak takes this to involve

the charting of what in post-structuralist language would be called the subaltern subject-effect. A subject-effect can be briefly plotted as follows: that which seems to operate as a subject may be part of an immense discontinuous network ('text' in the general sense) of strands that may be termed politics, economics, history, sexuality, language and so on. . . . Different knottings and configurations of these strands, determined by heterogeneous determinations which are themselves dependent upon myriad circumstances, produce the effect of an operating subject.[81]

Bhabha similarly insists on the fragmentation of the colonial subject, and of the need for critics to focus on how it is

structured ideologically and discursively in relation to poly-
morphous processes of signification. He suggests that the point
of intervention 'should shift from the *identification* of images
as positive or negative, to an understanding of the *processes of
subjectification* made possible (and plausible) through stereo-
typical discourse'.[82]

This anti-humanist, anti-empiricist, deconstructive reading
strategy produces another Plaatje that can perhaps best be
represented as 'Plaatje', since the construction of his subjectivity both in his own times and since is seen as crucial. The
radical relativism of this position, with its emphasis on the
psychic constitution of the colonial subject, none the less still
produces a version of Plaatje that competes with those of
Fanon, Lenin, and Willan.

This can be adduced, for example, in Bhabha, whose critical
vocabulary includes terms like 'ambivalence', 'hybridity', 'po-
lyphony', 'lability', and 'liminality', all of which are utilized
to convey the psychic subtleties and complexities of colonial
subjectivity. Their deployment results in a quite distinct version of the colonized, as his suggestive discussion of mimicry
as a strategy employed by the colonized in contesting the
definitions of the colonial relationship demonstrates. He argues
that there is a third choice for the native intellectual in addition to those offered in Fanon's alternatives of to 'turn white
or disappear', namely 'the more ambivalent, third choice: camouflage, mimicry, black skins/white masks' (120). He quotes
Lacan's observation that mimicry should be seen as a process
of harmonizing not so much against a background as 'against
a mottled background of being mottled—exactly like the technique of camouflage practised in modern warfare' (121), and
argues by extension that mimicry on the part of the native
frequently marks 'those moments of civil disobedience within
the discipline of civility: signs of spectacular resistance' (121).

How then would the relation between Plaatje and Shakespeare be represented in terms of this critical discourse? In
the first place, the very act of juxtaposing the canonical and
the colonial writer would be enthusiastically embraced: Said,
in particular, insists that to understand the great Western writers, one cannot 'exclude their relationship with the protracted,

complex, and striated work of empire'.[83] Secondly, in reading
the colonial writer the emphasis would be placed upon 'the
immense discontinuous network' of different discourses functioning to produce his effect as 'a sovereign and determining
subject'. This would involve detailed consideration of the
discourses *constituting* both 'Plaatje' and 'Shakespeare'. In
Plaatje's case, this would include attending to the discourses
of mission education, Tswana culture, Christianity, Englishness, and Afrikaner settler culture, which would in turn provide a basis for showing both how 'colonialism's contradictory
mode of address constitutes an ambivalently positioned subject' and, further, how repression works not only by direct
brutality but by 'devious techniques of obligation and persuasion with which the native colludes but simultaneously resists'. Following these concerns, emphasis might be placed
firstly on the contradictions of English culture in the Cape—
Shakespeare for everyone against Shakespeare the ultimate
Englishman—and on the efforts of Plaatje to negotiate that
contradiction in the act of appropriating Shakespeare, and
secondly, on the patterns of collusion (in reading Shakespeare)
and resistance (in reading him as a champion of non-racialism)
in Plaatje's relation to the culture of colonialism. Finally, an
argument might be made, following Bhabha, to see Plaatje as
engaged in a strategy of mimicry in which 'the words of the
master become the site of hybridity—the warlike sign of the
native' (104): Shakespeare, the master's master, redefined by
Plaatje in an act of subversion and defiance.

As Plaatje came to resemble the social historian Couzens
writing in 1970s South Africa, so in colonial discourse theory
he is likely to resemble diaspora intellectuals working in
New York and London: an isolated, fragmented subject mediating discontinuous discourses. This tendency of selecting and
recasting figures from the past in the image of the present is
unremarkable: if Plaatje is to be taught at Yale, it is perhaps
inevitable that he should be read in ways that students in
such institutions might recognize. What is more worrying is
that given the cultural authority such institutions enjoy, these
readings are globalized (at least in the English-speaking world),
and the 'hybridized' Plaatje displaces all other versions.[84]

The Real Sol Plaatje

I have presented four Plaatjes: Fanon's obedient native reading European textbooks; Lenin's agent of British imperialism; Willan's reasonable black man shunned by white racists; and Spivak's fractured colonial subject produced by a discontinuous discursive network. Instead of offering the real Plaatje, I offer in conclusion an incident which took place four years after Shakespeare's tercentenary, and which dramatizes most acutely for me the resonances of the relation between the colonial subject and Shakespeare.

In 1920 De Beers Consolidated Mines, for whom Plaatje had recruited native labour during times of personal hardship, donated £30,000 to the University of Cape Town for the establishment of the De Beers Chair of English Language.

The De Beers Directors' Report of that year discloses that the Company's total annual wage bill for '2696 men, 324 lads and 13781 Natives' (28) amounted to £36,113, and that after-tax profits (and after the donation to the university) to be distributed among shareholders amounted to £5,153,695.

Thus the exchange: in order for the English teachers at the University of Cape Town to examine more colonial students about Shakespeare, extraordinary profits are extorted from the labour of the 17,000 De Beers mineworkers.

4

Minorities against English Studies:
The 1930s

Introduction

What is at stake for minorities studying Shakespeare? The question is expressed in different ways in different contexts. South African critic Njabulo Ndebele writes about black South Africans learning English in the following terms:

What may need to be emphasised is that if the recognition that English belongs to all who use it is more than academic, then in multi-cultural societies, English will have to be taught in such a way that the learners are made to recognise themselves through the learning context employed, not as second class learners of a foreign culture, or as units of labour that have to be tuned to work better, but as self-respecting citizens of the world. The idea of teaching English through the exposure of second language learners to English culture, should be abandoned. If English belongs to all, then it will naturally assume the cultural colour of its respective users.[1]

Crucial here is Ndebele's desire to destabilize the authority of the English language and culture in the South African education system. His challenge is posed on behalf of a constituency defined as marginal despite representing a numerical majority, and he seeks to inscribe a central defining stake for them in post-apartheid educational dispensations.

Writing about women students of English in Britain—another numerical majority without adequate representation in the discipline—Ann Thompson and Helen Wilcox observe:

Even in what is perceived as a 'feminine' subject like English, female students still find themselves in a curiously subordinate position: while they are in the majority as 'consumers' of tertiary education courses, most of their teachers are men and they spend most of their time studying texts by male authors and male critics. The potential power of their numbers is undercut by the lowliness of their status and by the limitations on their input into course planning and administrative control.[2]

The essays assembled in their collection *Teaching Women* offer a variety of strategies for trying to overcome this painful anomaly.

Also writing in Britain, Alan Sinfield describes how the personnel of English studies has been recruited from successive subcultural groups without the central assumptions and practices of the discipline being changed. Indeed, the energies of those select individuals from subcultural groups enlisted in the service of English literature have been crucial in sustaining the profession. For Sinfield, the challenge is to reverse this pattern:

In a collective ethos, a community would advance in wealth and dignity together, not clambering up on each other's shoulders, thrusting the others back down. My preferred alternative is that academics should reverse the move away from subcultures of class, gender and sexuality. We should seek ways to break out of the professional subculture and work intellectually (not just live personally) in dissident subcultures.[3]

Sinfield speaks for constituencies on the margins of English studies, encouraging them to challenge the centralizing authority of the discipline by exploiting the resources of the English studies industry, rather than by being co-opted on an individual basis into the profession.

US critic Abdul JanMohamed reflects on the fate of minority literatures in the Western academy in the following terms:

Western academic institutions, which ultimately mediate the production of minority literatures and criticism that are written in European languages, provide the context wherein the hegemonic process subconsciously attempts, usually successfully, to incorporate the Third World intellectuals and to ensure the elimination of any oppositional or alien attitudes and tendencies. This is done through the presentation of Western humanism . . . as a universal philosophy superior to the traditional world views of Third World cultures.[4]

Surveying recent attempts to incorporate black US literature into a liberal humanist critical project, JanMohamed argues with some urgency on behalf of those outside the US English studies consensus that minority criticism 'must articulate and help to bring to consciousness those elements of minority culture that oppose, subvert or negate the power of hegemonic culture' (298).

Ndebele, Thompson and Wilcox, Sinfield, and JanMohamed in different ways express a political opposition to the liberal humanist consensus underlying English studies, and they all articulate the hope that the discipline might be transformed by their critical interventions on behalf of those currently excluded from its procedures and privileges. What I explore in my survey of South African and English Shakespeare teaching and criticism in the 1930s is an important fragment of the long and complex history of marginal voices arguing on the discursive fringes of English studies. In particular, I show two things, namely that the figure of the Victorian gentleman critic casts a long shadow over English criticism in the twentieth century, and *all* critics writing after the First World War define themselves as in some way trying to occupy the centre vacated by Bradley and his generation. This applies to critics in England, but with particular force to critics in the Cape. In seeking the origins of this marginal voice, I emphasize the sense of inadequacy lurking in the prose of the professional critic, suggesting that the paradigmatic voice of the twentieth-century critic is that of the aggrieved mandarin, the extremely clever person haunted by a sense of being excluded from the (now absent) centre of the discipline.[5]

And second, I show that the accommodation of dissenting critical voices in the academy has no predictable effect in the practice of English literature teaching at school level. Shakespeare occupied a central place in the educational institutions of Britain and the Cape Colony towards the end of the nineteenth century, and, further, he was a confident, unified figure authorized by the great critics of the time, and studied by students memorizing the broad contours of his character. There was a consistency in how he was described from school to university, but this changed in the 1920s and 1930s as a significant variety of critics saw him quite differently from the way he was described in schools. This asymmetry between the high-school and university Shakespeare I take to be important in securing the relation of minorities to the teaching of English.

Very Small Minorities

The 1930s in England have been remembered as a time of upheaval, uncertainty, commitment, and extremism. Even the secluded pastures of literary studies were invaded by concerns traditionally excluded, and guardians of culture were under pressure to go beyond preferring Milton to Donne and to declare their political allegiances. In a radio broadcast in 1941 George Orwell summarizes the cultural ethos of the decade as follows:

The writers who have come up since 1930 have been living in a world in which not only one's life but one's whole scheme of values is constantly menaced. . . . In a world in which Fascism and Socialism were fighting one another, any thinking person had to take sides, and his feelings had to find their way not only into his writing but into his judgements on literature. Literature had to become political, because anything else would have entailed mental dishonesty.[6]

The nature and form of the politics that intruded into the world of literature was dictated by the complex of economic and social tensions dominating the period. The traditional Victorian economy based on cotton, coal, and heavy industry had contracted dramatically after the First World War, leading to economic depression, mass unemployment, and instances of bitter industrial dispute.[7] That this did not destabilize the state further than it did can be attributed to several factors: organized labour was incorporated into the parliamentary process with the complicity of the Labour Party leadership; the mass production of consumer durables, undertaken increasingly by monopolistic corporations, expanded and provided employment for a significant percentage of the surplus labour; the domestic market for these new products expanded rapidly; the state, although nowhere near on the scale of Nazism or the New Deal, sought in desultory fashion to address the most extreme inequalities confronting it; and wealth was generated on an even larger scale than before by Britain's 'invisible' sources of income, namely overseas investments and the financial services provided by the City of London. None the less, these factors that together preserved the form of the British state did not arrest the gradual decline of British industry with respect to its capitalist competitors, for both the traditional and the new consumer industries failed to sustain and increase their export markets, or to modernize their capital assets.

In addition to these economic struggles and shifts within Britain, there were political developments beyond its borders which contributed to the sense of crisis in English culture. The example of the Soviet Union, the first workers' state, with its spectacular material advances and language of equality, provided a proximate and attractive alternative to the cruel differentials of wealth and poverty in Britain. The rise of Fascism in Italy, Germany, and especially in Spain also occupied a central place in the English national consciousness, representing as it did another and altogether more brutal way out of the world-wide crisis of capitalism that had culminated in the Depression. These developments, in conjunction with the visible vulnerability of the British state, prompted a questioning about the natural superiority of the English way, and substantial sections of the intelligentsia defected to a range of anti-establishment positions.

Of the factors contributing to the containment of the crisis threatening the British state in the 1930s, one requires special emphasis, namely the role of the colonial Empire. Although it did not impinge on the English national consciousness to the same extent as European politics,[8] the British Empire reached its zenith during the inter-war years, consolidating its administrative, economic, and political hold in the colonies after the initial phases of rapid imperial expansion, and generating in the process more revenue for the central state than ever before. The colonies functioned primarily as producers of cheap raw materials for Britain and as markets for British manufactured products.

Shakespeare criticism, a central part of the English literary industry, was not immune from these tensions; indeed, all the criticism of the period is marked by a general sense of English culture having moved some distance from the relative harmony of both Elizabethan and late Victorian England. This sense of distance is expressed alternately as nostalgia or as liberation, but the common reading of English history implicit in the criticism is of a movement from settlement to crisis.

G. Wilson Knight in *The Imperial Theme* locates his study 'directly in the tradition of A. C. Bradley's *Shakespearean Tragedy*'.[9] He identifies certain transcendent key motifs, images, coherences, or atmospheres which are immanent in the plays and occur 'in loose dissociation from the story' (p. viii), a process he believes 'will lead us from multiplicity and chaos toward unity, simplicity, and coherence' (19). Shakespeare's great work is thus appreciated 'in its wholeness and its power [because] by concentrating on a part and forgetting the whole, [other critics] quite failed to do justice to the essential life and amplitude of the work concerned' (p. xi). Attention to character in isolation from the play as a whole is the most common version of their flawed method. But this totalizing vision does *not* extend beyond the text to the social and intellectual context of the plays, 'since what is most important in his work is best compared, not with his contemporaries, but with his great peers across the centuries' (p. xiii). The plays are themselves the sole authentic source of meaning.

Of all the images that occur in Shakespeare, the most important for Wilson Knight are those of 'music' and 'tempests':

Their interplay is the axis of the Shakespearean world. Style of verse, types of play, imaginative themes, 'character', veins of imagery—all pass in turn, alternating, changing, blending, as the great planet swings over: but all revolve on the 'tempest'–'music' opposition. These two correspond to the most fundamental of ideas necessary to natural, human, or divine realities: conflict and concord; evil and love; death and life. (29)

A particularly prominent version of this opposition is that of order (music) versus chaos (tempests), the former normally invested with positive value and the latter with negative. Honour, kingship, and war are values that cluster around the idea of order, and they all have a continuing application today: ' "honour" ... suggests a quality which extends further and may be applied in any age or place, in war or peace. The equivalent to-day might well be a form of business competition'

(5–6). In plays like *Hamlet, Measure for Measure,* and *King Lear,* order, honour, etc. are grouped together with love and set against a series of negations that oppose them, whereas in *Julius Caesar, Coriolanus,* and *Antony and Cleopatra,* love and honour are in opposition. But this apparent inconsistency does not deter Wilson Knight, since ultimately '[t]here is re-grouping and re-arrangement, but essentials persist' (19), and the imaginative response of the sensitive critic will always disclose those essentials.

For Philip Henderson, Shakespeare's essential qualities are to be divined in a different fashion. Consciously refusing the intellectual legacy of Bradley, Henderson, in *Literature and a Changing Civilisation,* provides in his chapter on the Renaissance a lengthy introduction to the Elizabethan age, emphasizing the avarice of English explorers, the cruel suppression of the Irish, and the terrible poverty of the English peasantry.[10] He characterizes the period as one in which '[t]he despotism of the Church is exchanged for the despotism of money—soon to grow to nightmare proportions in Big Business and High Finance',[11] and argues that these factors must be appreciated in coming to terms with Shakespeare's genius, since he 'reflected many of the national ideals and aspirations of his time' (53).

Where Wilson Knight reads in Shakespeare an anxiety about the disorder of his age and a sympathy for the 'positive values' of order and kingship, Henderson perceives in the plays evidence only of a 'disgust with the social system of his day' (50). To support this contention, Henderson imputes speeches from characters in *Timon of Athens* and *King Lear* to Shakespeare, arguing that their damning social critique is the product of 'the individual mind of man broken loose from the moorings of religious and social order' (51). In spite of this imploding disorder and chaos, Henderson concludes that 'everything [Shakespeare] touched he transfigured with the grandeur and nobility of his mind' (53).

Where Wilson Knight's critical persona might be described as aspirant heir to Bradley, and Henderson's as angry young Marxist challenging Bradley, L. C. Knights defines his relationship to Bradley in a more ambivalent way. Part of the new generation of professional literary critics employed in the universities in the 1920s to teach English literature, Knights wrote as a member of an intellectual vanguard defining itself not only against the philistine mass, but also against the genteel amateurism of the Victorian gentleman scholar. The *Scrutiny* group's self-definition as an embattled minority is spelt out by F. R. Leavis: 'In any period it is upon a very small minority that the discerning appreciation of art and literature depends. . . . Upon this minority depends our power of profiting by the finest human experience of the past; they keep alive the subtlest and most perishable parts of tradition.'[12] And in the decades to follow, despite considerable institutional success, this identity was never relinquished. For example, Raymond Williams recalls that '[o]ne must remember that by this time [the 1960s], although [Leavis] still thought of himself as an outsider in his last years, he had completely won'.[13]

Combining a version of Wilson Knight's textual analysis and Henderson's insistence on context, L. C. Knights, in *Drama and Society in the Age of Jonson*, undertakes to provide 'a study of economic conditions and the drama, *in conjunction*, in order to throw light on one of the more important problems of our own time: the relation between economic activities and general culture'.[14] Reviewing Marxist attempts to perform this task, he observes: 'Methods of production and cultural superstructure may be related in the realm of abstract dialectic, but no one (anthropologists dealing with primitive peoples apart) has yet established the relation in terms of fact and experience' (16). A sense of Knights's method is best conveyed by describing the organization of the book: after an introduction on Shakespeare and profit inflations, there are four chapters on the economic, social, and political background to Elizabethan and Jacobean drama, followed by six on the dramatists, and concluding with two appendices on Elizabethan prose and seventeenth-century melancholy.

This structure, with 'background' and 'dramatists' dealt with in separate sections, reflects Knights's difficulty in showing the connections between economic activities and culture, and it is in the short appendix on melancholy that he provides his most sustained attempt to correlate the two spheres of activity. Surveying the most common explanations for the increased prevalence of melancholy in the early seventeenth century—

that there was a collective emotional recoil after the excessive exuberance of the Renaissance; that writers had exaggerated the extent of melancholy for various reasons; and that there was a greater preoccupation with death—Knights suggests that although these arguments have some substance, what has been insufficiently stressed has been the influence of the economic and social life of the time. Quoting extensively from sermons, pamphlets, letters, and plays, Knights demonstrates the presence of an upwardly mobile class thwarted in their ambitions by the constraints imposed by their society. He concludes:

In the economic and social organization of the state the early seventeenth century was a period of transition. The relatively stable medieval society had decayed, and the new economy was not yet understood. Throughout the sixteenth century the Tudors had followed a policy of encouraging the middle classes, but by 1600 neither the new aristocracy nor the new commercial classes had altogether adjusted themselves to the changed conditions.... [C]ommerce and industry were not yet sufficiently developed . . . to provide attractive careers. (273)

And it was this state of affairs that constituted the most important key to understanding the atmosphere of disillusionment and melancholy.

This passage also encapsulates Knights's understanding of Shakespeare's age as one of transition and uncertainty. Sensitive to the enormous inequalities of wealth and opportunity occasioned by the shift from feudalism to capitalism, Knights none the less sees Elizabethan society as uniquely homogeneous, citing with approval Yeats's image of the period as one when 'the art of the people was as closely mingled with the art of the coteries as was the speech of the people . . . with the unchanging speech of the poets' (20). Reproducing F. R. Leavis's arguments in *For Continuity* about the organic community that forged Shakespeare's English as a vital medium, Knights concludes gloomily about the disappearance of that community:

To-day, unless he is exceptionally lucky, the ordinary man has to make a deliberate effort to penetrate a hazy medium which smothers his essential human nature, which interposes between him and things as they are; a medium formed by the lowest common denominator of feelings, perceptions and ideas acceptable to the devitalized products of a machine economy. The luck of the Elizabethan in *not* having to pierce, in being able to obtain whatever satisfactions were possible at first hand, was of course due to 'the prevailing methods of production and exchange', to the fact that mass-production, standardization, and division of labour, although not unknown, were still exceptional and undeveloped.   (21)

Although Wilson Knight, Knights, and Henderson might share the same problematic, their differences are substantial. In their attitudes to literature, to social order, to political change, and to the place of history in literary criticism, they occupy positions that range from the aesthetically detached to the politically engaged. To elaborate on just one of these areas, they display extremely divergent feelings for the social order: for Wilson Knight, nostalgia for the threatened values of order and authority, for Henderson, anger at 'the system' and desire for its destruction, and for Knights, bitterness at the passing of a culture and way of life based on values of community.

However, there are also important similarities in their arguments. In the first place, they all distance themselves in different ways from the inherited tradition of Shakespeare criticism: Wilson Knight seeks simply to refine or improve upon the threatened pattern of coherence and overarching order celebrated in the plays by Bradley's generation; Henderson attacks what he perceives as establishment misreadings of the plays, promising to disclose their true meaning; and Knights through scholarship offers a professional account of Shakespeare's relation to the Renaissance. Where the Victorian scholar pronounced confidently upon the plays on the basis of his class, birth, and breeding, these critics of the 1930s justify their views on the basis of their trained intelligence, scholarship, or political commitments. Their relation to the practices and discourses of English criticism is accordingly one of critical insecurity, determined by their status as recent recruits to a profession under pressure to prove their credentials: am I clever enough to belong to the club?

Further similarities relate to what they have to write about Shakespeare. First, they all take as given Shakespeare's transcendent genius, which they locate not in the subsequent critical and dramatic reproduction of him, but in the innate excellence of his plays.[15] This essentialist humanism enables them, notwithstanding their different critical methods, to treat the plays as repositories of infinite wisdom and beauty, as uncontroversial touchstones for a variety of arguments. Second, and closely related to the first point, they accept the empiricist separation of 'literature' and 'society', and the mediation of these categories by the more or less transparent medium of language. Their work is premissed at all times on the existence of a reality or truth which the various Elizabethan playwrights represent with a greater (Shakespeare) or lesser (Dekker) degree of verisimilitude. Finally, they all focus on the same general themes, reading in the plays of Elizabethan England their anxieties about English society in the 1930s.

Keeping his Eye on the Ball

South African critics in the 1930s continued for the most part to gaze with unwavering respect at the English masters of Bradley's generation. Their attitude to African intellectual resources was extremely patronizing,[16] and the influence of more contemporary metropolitan critics like Leavis, Richards, and the English Marxists was only registered in their writing towards the end of the decade.[17]

A piece that exemplifies this intellectual dependency is the Hon. Patrick Duncan's essay on *Hamlet* published in the first edition of the *Critic*. The aim of the journal as set out in the prologue was to fill the absence in South Africa of any English critical periodical. H. A. Reyburn explains its attitude to politics carefully:

One of the conditions of the development and maintenance of a sound literary and critical tradition is a spirit of intellectual freedom, and a journal of this kind can assist to provide the right atmosphere. Freedom, of course, is often misinterpreted and identified with a spirit of revolt, just as, for some people, criticism means adverse criticism. That is not the view taken here. The purpose of the journal is not to seek out alleged abuses of those in authority, and it has no pet scheme to advocate for the regeneration of an oppressed world.[18]

As the first article in the journal, Duncan's *Hamlet* essay must presumably have combined for the editor in particularly skilful fashion the dual demands of exercising the right of intellectual freedom without at the same time challenging authority in an impolite way. And indeed in its unqualified endorsement of Bradley on Hamlet's character, it remains true to the spirit of respect for authority and in no way stretches the boundaries of intellectual freedom. Conceding at the outset that he is not 'able to say anything new',[19] Duncan provides a summary of the plot, and then turns to his main interest, namely Hamlet's character. He identifies two schools of thought, that of critics seeing Hamlet's character as inexplicable, as 'an imperfectly co-ordinated patchwork', and second, that of a more distinguished critical tradition which sees Hamlet as 'a human soul' (13). Duncan identifies himself with this latter view, and in particular with its latest representative, A. C. Bradley, whose 'conception of the character . . . is to my mind at once the most profound in understanding, and the most in consonance with the text of the play' (14). Quoting extensively from 'Bradley in the remarkable study I have already mentioned', Duncan reproduces a reading of *Hamlet* which concentrates almost exclusively on seeing the character of the main protagonist as fatally flawed by his 'brooding melancholy' (16). His conclusion regarding the total effect on the audience of this tragic spectacle is also very close to Bradley: '[I]t should leave us with heightened perceptions, and purified emotions, and with a deeper comprehension of the world in which we live' (19).

Quite how watching *Hamlet* might have provided a deeper comprehension of South Africa in the 1930s—the world in which Duncan and his readers presumably lived—is left unclear, but the assumption that Shakespeare constituted a vital resource also underlies the teaching and criticism of Duncan's contemporaries. For example, Shakespeare's language was the central concern of the first De Beers Professor of English Language, W. S. Mackie, who held the chair from 1921 to 1951 and included in his publications a history of the Mowbray

Golf Club.[20] Mackie had a paper published in the *Modern Language Review* on 'Shakespeare's Language: And How Far it can be Investigated with the Help of the *New English Dictionary*', and also inspired a couple of his students to undertake similar studies. According to A. M. Lewin Robinson,[21] the only two MA theses completed in the University of Cape Town English Department in the 1930s on Shakespeare were C. M. J. Morris's 'Shakespeare's Vocabulary in *Love's Labours Lost*: The Effect of the Elizabethan Age and the Renascence on the Creation, Use and Interpretation of Words', and D. N. Vaughan's 'Satire upon Language in the Plays of Shakespeare and Ben Jonson'. As to Mackie's preferred method of study, he sets this out some years later, where he expresses reservations about the grand aims of the Cambridge English mission, but goes on to endorse its insistence on disciplined reading in terms that unite his interests in literature and golf:

[T]here can be no doubt that [practical criticism's] technique and its possibilities have been developed by Dr. Leavis and the Cambridge School with quite amazing success. Whether it will do all that its more enthusiastic disciples claim for it, whether it will go on producing bright-souled missionaries to spread the light of a new culture in our schools and colleges . . . the older among us may be inclined to doubt. . . . [But by] no means the least [of its merits] is the training that it gives in intelligent attention; as in another sphere of activity, the learner must keep his eye on the ball.[22]

In addition to Mackie's focus on Shakespeare's language and Duncan's interest in character, a third strand of criticism rather more concerned with Shakespearean society and the politics of theatre can be discerned in the work of two other critics who wrote at different ends of the decade. The first is W. A. Sewell, Senior Lecturer in the UCT English Department from 1929 to 1934. In his extension lectures on 'Shakespeare', Sewell warns against the excesses of bardolatry, arguing that '[i]f criticism, textual or circumstantial, has an object, that must surely be to make Shakespeare more certain for us'.[23] This demands a robust intellectual approach, a 'strenuous clearing of the mind for action' (9), since, as he quotes W. J. Lawrence, '[t]here is heavy need for Shakespeare scholarship to go out into the open and do some missionary work' (11). Dismissive of critics like Coleridge and Bradley who treat Shakespeare's plays as literary texts rather than *as plays*, Sewell prefers either those critics like W. J. Lawrence who provide historical detail about the theatre in Elizabethan England, or those like Harvey Granville Barker who stress the dramatic nature of the plays. In this spirit, Sewell sets out first to describe the conditions under which Shakespeare produced his plays, concentrating largely on the pressures exerted by the audience. Insisting that the Elizabethan age was not one of chaos and licentious- ness, he none the less describes the audiences of the time variously as 'a motley crew', 'superstitious', 'imaginative', as liking above all else a good story, but as ultimately not 'cul- tured' (12–13). In the final lecture, Sewell goes on to explore his second concern, how a better understanding of the theat- rical conventions of Shakespeare's day might inform contem- porary productions. For him, '[t]he ideal is, then, to miss none of the essentials in the play and, so far as modern technique can help us, to focus the play down as far as possible to those essentials' (15). This involves, among other things, dispensing with elaborate sets and costumes, and paying particular at- tention to the language of the play.

Sewell left Cape Town at the end of 1934, and the next South African Shakespeare critic to pay attention to Eliza- bethan society in any detail was A. J. Friedgut in his 1939 article for the *Critic* entitled 'The Rise of the Caliban Drama'. The 'politically neutral' stance of the *Critic* had changed by this stage, with articles on Fascism by John Strachey from the *New Statesman and Nation* and a defence of Marxism by George Sacks appearing in its pages. Friedgut's appraisal of English drama too displays a marked shift from Duncan's piece on *Hamlet*, reflected not least in his citing of the generation of English critics that succeeded Bradley, with I. A. Richards and T. S. Eliot particularly prominent.[24]

Friedgut declares in his opening sentence that 'it is essential for the critic to be familiar with the *Zeitgeist* of the dramatist under consideration, with the literary and social conventions of his age, and the nature and tastes of his audience',[25] and in his penultimate paragraph quotes I. A. Richards's view that 'the arts are our storehouse of recorded values' (12). Between the materialist sentiments of his beginning and the idealist

notions of the conclusion, Friedgut tries to show how Elizabethan, nineteenth-century, and contemporary drama were
structured by their age. But instead of drawing his understanding of these different periods from historians, he looks
to the likes of literary critics such as Eliot and Raleigh. For
example, in characterizing the Elizabethan age as one of emotion and imagination as opposed to subsequent periods of
scientism and reason, Friedgut gives prominence to Eliot's
observation that 'the general attitude to life of the Elizabethans,
is one of anarchism, of dissolution, of decay' (4). With insights
like this guiding him, Friedgut's conclusions about the drama
produced in such a society remain somewhat superficial:
'Knowledge stirred the emotions of the Elizabethan dramatists, paradoxical though this may seem. . . . This accounts
largely for Elizabethan drama, notably tragedy, being written
mainly in verse and modern drama mainly in prose' (4).
However, Friedgut's interest in some form of materialist
social critique is never entirely submerged by his reliance on
conservative English critics as he still writes favourably of the
dramatic techniques employed by both Shaw and Auden in
trying to bring social evils to the attention of a wide audience.

   The final South African critic of the 1930s of interest was
arguably the most energetic, since he was the only one to
have his thoughts on Shakespeare published as a book, and
he was also the only one to deviate substantially from the
pattern of following English Shakespeare critics. F. C. Kolbe
opens *Shakespeare's Way: A Psychological Study* with the confident declaration: 'My justification for writing a new book on
Shakespeare's Art is that I really have something new to say.'[26]
That this was indeed so is acknowledged by G. Wilson Knight,
who describes Kolbe's work as sharing with his own and that
of Caroline Spurgeon a quite original thesis: 'that Shakespeare's
plays showed significant coherences that could be, pro-
visionally, discussed in their own right in loose dissociation
from the story; they had, as it were, key-*motifs*. With Caroline
Spurgeon these were necessarily "images"; with Kolbe, they
might be images, ideas, or just things, as with the moon in
Midsummer Night's Dream.'[27] Wilson Knight thought he was
cleverer than the other two—Kolbe's study 'was, as far as it
went, sound, though with a value varying greatly according

to his insight into different plays' (p. viii)—but none the less he never challenged the novelty of Kolbe's contribution.

In his preface, Kolbe pledges to pursue a scientific course of study, one aimed at producing 'something new, something solid, something important', and which is the 'product of analytic induction, not fanciful sentiment'.[28] Dismissing the relevance of theory in this process, Kolbe explains his method:

What I have done is to select and marshal a great array of facts, which have never been shown in this light before, in order to prove that Shakespeare consistently adopted for the unifying of his plays a device familiar in the sister arts of music and painting. It may be called dramatic colouring. (p. ix)

And in his chapter on *Macbeth*, he elaborates:

My thesis is that Shakespeare secures the unity of each of his greater plays, not only by the plot, by linkage of characters, by the sweep of Nemesis, by the use of irony, and by appropriateness of style, but by deliberate repetition throughout the play of at least one set of words or ideas in harmony with the plot. (2)

In the next twenty-nine chapters, Kolbe demonstrates this method, uncovering in close readings of each play a key motif or motifs: in *Macbeth*, they are blood, sleep, darkness, and confusion; in *Hamlet*, it is the concept of mental and moral analysis; in *The Tempest*, it is enchantment and Divine Providence; and in *Othello*, desecration of love is harped upon 250 times.

The psychology referred to in the title is meant to connote a scientific impulse, but Kolbe reassures the reader that it is the 'psychology of daily life as understood by the average man' (p. vii). But his flirtation with psychology goes further because he also sets out in two paragraphs that are only loosely connected to his earlier arguments an understanding of a collective unconscious that is presumably meant to shed light on Shakespeare's creativity. There is a subconsciousness that functions as 'the artist's cornucopia' (p. xi), and knowledge of it is not something new: 'From the first moment of our organic existence, which we start of course with a racial inheritance, every experience of our organism registers itself and becomes part of our treasure-house of possible knowledge. . . .

This treasure-house, i.e. the sum total of our organic experience, the early thinkers called Memoria' (p. xi). This subconsciousness is the wellspring of creativity, and it is this quality that makes it 'the Paradise of Poets' (p. xii).

These themes—the search for unifying imagery in the plays, and the belief in a subconscious treasure-house sustaining the race—occur *simultaneously* in English culture in the work of Wilson Knight and I. A. Richards. Indeed, it could even be argued that Kolbe preceded these metropolitan writers as he had been working on his book for the previous thirty years. But what is perhaps more interesting is that the ideas in Kolbe's book had no immediate impact on English teaching in South Africa. Only at the end of the decade—and 'brought back' from Cambridge—did the kind of close reading performed by Kolbe gain any institutional base in South Africa, and only in the late 1940s did it become hegemonic.[29]

A Possibility of Escape

Arguments in South African criticism in the 1930s about the women characters in Shakespeare also looked to the late Victorian scholars for guidance.[30] In A. Milligan's essay on Lady Macbeth, for example, the main concern is to understand Lady Macbeth's character, and the views of Dowden, Swinburne, Hallam, and Mrs Jameson are followed before the conclusion is reached:

> By the strength of her will she cuts herself off from her better nature, and by sustained nervous energy she suppresses her womanly feelings in order that she may bring greatness and power to her husband more than to herself. The strain proves too much for her delicate frame, and she is killed by the revolt of her womanhood against the unnatural restraint she endeavoured to impose upon it.[31]

While Lady Macbeth suffered for denying her essential womanhood, other female characters were rewarded for being true to their nature. This is explained in an essay by American actress Margaret Anglin published in the *Cape Times* for the Tercentenary Celebrations of Shakespeare's death:

Miranda, to me, expresses the miracle of latent woman; Portia measures equally the proportion of womanly grace and intellect; Katharine has in the mere pronouncement of her name the incisive rhythm of quick temper; Viola reflects the mauve quality of a violet, and conjures up the sadness of romantic love. Rosalind is the full-blown rose.[32]

Writing to assist the actress in preparing for her role, Anglin recommends the reading of literary criticism, and in particular the work of Mrs Jameson, which she describes as 'saturated with the most penetrating analyses of womanly characteristics' (9). Her insights—like the fact that Portia is chaste and dignified in love—leave us 'mentally stimulated, and our conceptions are enriched by a wider range of understanding' (9).

In this short article, Anglin reads dominant stereotypes of womanhood into Shakespeare's plays. She argues that Shakespeare has unique insight into the female soul, holding up domesticated versions of his women characters as proof of this. The woman critic she cites, Mrs Jameson, registers in her title her subordination to male authority, and in metaphors that announce with great force the internalization of the patriarchal Bard, Anglin credits her ideas with the capacity first to 'penetrate' and then to 'stimulate' the mind of the female reader. Although written originally for the *New York Times*, Anglin's argument reinforces equally the allocation of women in the Cape to narrowly designated social roles. The exchange —male patronage and protection in return for a generation of good wives and mothers—underwrites this translation of Shakespeare's female characters into obedient role models for twentieth-century women.

Unlike Mrs Jameson, most women writing criticism at this time did not pay special attention to female characters or to women's issues raised in the plays. Instead, they focused on the same themes as their male colleagues. An instance of this pattern is G. Newman's 'The Fairy Lore in *A Midsummer Night's Dream*', published in the South African university women's journal the *Bluestocking*.[33] Written without any references or footnotes, the essay combines three strands: a concern with the imagery and unifying motifs of the play, of which the moon and dreams are seen as primary; an interest in the social context of the play, with insights regarding Elizabethan court politics and popular notions of fairies drawn upon to explain aspects of the play; and thirdly, a desire to affirm by quotation the beauty of Shakespeare's language. The article ends with a homily about the power of the imagination and Prospero's lines 'We are such stuff as dreams are made on.'[34]

The subordination of women to the patriarchal Shakespeare was also enforced in the high schools. This is nowhere more evident than in the arguments surrounding the uncertain passage of the subject English literature in the 1930s. Besides being taught in the compulsory subject of English, literature was also taught at South African high schools in the optional subject of English literature. It was conceived of as a subject primarily for girls: according to M. E. Wright, 'it has afforded a possibility of escape from some other subject, e.g., Mathematics, which girls often find difficult after the Junior Certificate stage.'[35] During the course of the decade, the syllabus underwent several changes. When first introduced in 1929, candidates were required 'to study a prescribed period or department of literature and to show special knowledge of *six* prescribed works representative of the period or department'.[36] Questions on the prescribed texts dealt with their subject-matter and the lives of their authors, and the examination paper comprised two sections: in section A, there were three compulsory 60-mark questions of a general nature, like 'Select one of the following authors and write an essay on his (or her) life and work:—Pope; Jane Austen; Dr. Johnson; Goldsmith' (1930 examination paper); and in section B, candidates had to do two of six 40-mark questions on their set books, which included Pope's *Essay on Man*, *Gulliver's Travels*, Sheridan's *The Rivals*, *Emma*, a poetry collection, and a prose anthology. There was no Shakespeare.

In 1933 the second, more demanding syllabus came into effect. It sought to remove the stigma attached to English literature of being a 'soft option', setting out its requirements as follows:

A brief account of the following periods of literature; (*a*) Elizabethan, (*b*) Classical, (*c*) Romantic, and (*d*) Victorian, illustrated by the study of specified works by a few outstanding authors from the first three periods, and a larger number from the fourth. The specified works (not more than twelve in all) will represent the following departments of literature:—(i) Drama, (ii) Poetry other than drama, (iii) The novel, (iv) Prose other than novel. These works should be studied from a literary standpoint and with reference to their significance in the department in which they belong.[37]

According to M. M. Miller, T. Tyfield, and M. M. Krige, the Principal and teachers of the subject at Good Hope Seminary, this syllabus provided an extremely popular course of study for those who followed it. They insist on the excellence of the syllabus from both an enjoyment and a 'cultural point of view',[38] and argue that if it were a qualifying course for university, far more pupils would study it.

The third syllabus came into effect in 1939, retaining substantially the same structure as its predecessor, but with the crucial difference that the choice of books set for study was curtailed, and included those set for the compulsory English course. The change was strongly criticized in the same article by Good Hope Seminary's guardians of literature, who argue that in effect 'the present innovation . . . reduces the course to the level at which it originally stood' (266), i.e. as a 'soft option' for those not wanting to go to university. A further aspect of the 1939 syllabus they criticize is the absence of Shakespeare from the choice of Elizabethan texts to study: 'Moreover, it cannot be affirmed too strongly that no literary work arouses such intense enjoyment, or proves as intellectually and emotionally stimulating to pupils, as a good play; and of all plays, those of Shakespeare create the profoundest impression upon the minds of children. To do away with the detailed study of a play will prove a very great cultural loss' (265). The scale of the great cultural loss occasioned by the removal of Shakespeare from the English literature syllabus was perhaps softened slightly by the small number of pupils who had chosen to do the subject—eighty-nine in the Cape in 1939, according to the Superintendent-General of Education's Report—and by the fact that virtually all of them (96 per cent) passed the final examination.

As regards what happened in English lessons for South African girls, there are two reports that suggest the experience was less than inspiring. Mrs Max Drennan (as she signed herself, the wife of the Professor of English at the University of the Witwatersrand) notes with alarm the gulf between South African schoolgirls and Shakespeare. She discovered that pupils claiming to have ' "done Shakespeare" . . . could tell me nothing of the play', and her overall impression was that although the *idea* behind the teaching of literature was excellent, 'in actual practice it is the letter and not the spirit of the curriculum that is followed'.[39] Instead of living up to their noble calling, English teachers 'are boring a fresh generation with even more disastrous results' (3), and consequently South African children never come to appreciate 'the vastness of the worlds to which a knowledge of English furnishes a key' (4). Writing of her years in Thelma Tyfield's English classes at Good Hope Seminary in the 1950s, Lyndall Gordon is similarly unenthusiastic:

[S]he was alive to literature and we sat up to her judgements. But they were her judgements. . . . It was Miss Tyfield's custom to dictate notes designed as fodder for matriculation examiners. Needless to say, these notes ignored class discussion; they aimed at compromise between her own acuteness and the plodding detail, the laborious learnt quotations, of a system which rewards feats of memory. . . . At the same time, she was teaching our future role of obedient passivity—that we had nothing to offer, and had best attend to the judgers and doers. So we learnt to defer to opinion, and most of us remained silent for years to come.[40]

Together these few pieces of criticism and commentary convey a sense of the relation of South African women to the discipline of English literature. In the first place, there is an identification of English literature as not 'useful', and that only as a component of the subject English—taught as one of the official languages and in conjunction with composition and grammar—will it receive serious consideration. Both the embattled progress of English literature and Mrs Drennan's perceptions of anomie in the English class would seem to bear out this conclusion. Closely tied to this is the perception of it as peculiarly suited to women. While men and boys got on with useful subjects like mathematics, women teachers prepared girls for English literature examinations which were set by men (the 1939 paper, for example, was set by Professor P. Haworth and moderated by Mr S. B. Hobson and Mr H. Z.

van der Merwe). Also, the ultimate authority for syllabus planning and indeed the very existence of the subject lay with male administrators in the Cape Department of Public Education. And thirdly, women's access to Shakespeare was mediated and controlled in a number of ways. For instance, Shakespeare was absent in the 'soft' first and third versions of the English literature syllabus, suggesting that his presence automatically connoted standards demanding some greater degree of (masculine) intellectual rigour. Further, although the lack of references makes it difficult to establish the point, it is arguable that Newman's 'Fairy Lore' essay also resides in the shadow of male authority in that it reproduces faithfully the concerns of metropolitan male critics (Wilson Knight's search for motifs, the *Scrutiny* and Marxist interest in Elizabethan society, and everybody's enthusiasm for Shakespeare's verse).

Native to our Genius

In the 1930s, as access to the cultural riches of South Africa (like Shakespeare) were conceded to women, so too certain political privileges also advanced. But there was an important trade-off in this exchange, as E. Schreiner explains:

We, as women, have long laboured under the unjust theory that any human being, born a woman, is *ipso facto* and for the rest of her life, unfit for the duties of citizenship. Now the price the country is to pay for the removal of one ancient wrong is the endorsement of two other principles, equally untenable:

(a) That any man with a white skin . . . is competent to exercise the rights of citizenship.
(b) That any man with a black skin . . . is unfit ever to become a citizen of the country of his birth.

In other words, women's rights have been granted in order to secure the extension of manhood franchise to the Cape, and in order to swamp the Cape native vote, already in imminent danger of extinction.[41]

Although it was by no means a view shared by all who contributed to the journal,[42] Schreiner concludes by arguing that women should use their newly acquired voting power to oppose the disfranchisement of black people:

> only a few months ago we stood side by side with the black man as unrecognised members of the State, with no rights except to contribute to the public revenue. It seems inconceivable that we should follow the course our generous liberators so confidently predict and use our new power to shut the doors of hope and opportunity in the face of the native peoples. (5)

These hopes that liberal white women would protect the interests of 'the native peoples' came to nought, but none the less certain black intellectuals during this period did at least manage to gain access to white South Africa's cultural domain. Under the often uneasy patronage of white English liberals,[43] a small black élite read and claimed to enjoy Shakespeare. This took place both at colleges like Lovedale and at reading circles set up by white intellectuals and aimed at increasing racial contact and understanding. The most well-known figure emerging from this context was Herbert Dhlomo, who, in his essay 'African Drama and Poetry', reviewed B. W. Vilakazi's arguments regarding the rhyme schemes of Zulu poetry.[44]

Rejecting Vilakazi's proposed rhyme scheme as too rigid and inflexible for dramatic purposes, Dhlomo invokes Sir Arthur Quiller-Couch's *On the Art of Writing* and argues that the passions and furies of drama 'burst through the stagnant, dam-like banks of rhyme, and can only be contained in the wider and less defined sea-basin of blank and parallel verse'.[45] As to what poetic forms might be suitable models for Bantu dramatic work, Dhlomo has two suggestions. The first is that of the ancient Hebrew writers, 'for it is natural to African genius and to our Native speech' (89). He quotes in detail the views of Laurence Binyon on Hebrew poetry and of Professor Lestrade on Bantu poetry in order to demonstrate what he sees as their common disavowal of rhyme and their reliance on rhythm to structure poetry. The second model for Bantu poetry that Dhlomo suggests is Shakespeare, whose poetic form 'comes naturally and without effort to the African writer. It is native to our genius' (90). Quoting again from Quiller-Couch, Dhlomo establishes that Shakespeare depended 'less on line structure, on any orderly and regular sequence of sound within the line, and more . . . on the balance of sentences and on emphasis' (90), a method of writing entirely at one with African poetry. Dhlomo refers to the work of *Gestalt* psychologists to support his contention that the Bantu poet's mind is structured by tribal society in a way that produces a love of rhythm: 'The tribal African was under the rigid rule of pattern. . . . This love of pattern certainly had grave disadvantages, but it gave birth to a marked sense and love of rhythm' (90). And since 'there is a kind of rhythmic law underlying all great literature' (90), the African writer can draw upon the forms and techniques used by the unquestionably great Shakespeare.

Dhlomo's piece drew an angry response from Vilakazi, which was published as a letter to the editor in the July 1939 edition of the *South African Outlook*. Essentially, he argues that Dhlomo does not know what he is talking about and that his extended quotations from Quiller-Couch and other white scholars are merely smoke-screens obscuring the extent of his ignorance. Although he sneers at Dhlomo's reverence for 'his White Masters of poetry',[46] and declares his own 'unshaken belief in Bantu languages and their literature' (167), Vilakazi uses two rhetorical devices that illustrate deeper congruences in his and Dhlomo's positions. The first is his deployment of Latin phrases to clinch particular points: of Dhlomo's knowledge of Hebrew literature, he declares 'Nescio, quidem ipse nescit', and of his pride in black culture, he writes 'Ego sum quod sum' (166–7). And the second is his citing of another 'white master' to refute Dhlomo's Quiller-Couch:

I have sat before a number of Professors of English lecturing on Shakespearean forms; but all my learned masters could never agree and I have always left the lecture theatres very ignorant. Prof. J. Y. T. Greig speaking on Shakespeare to the non-European Reading Circle of the Wits University in 1937, described his works as 'a bundle of contradictions inextricable.' I walked out satisfied. And to-day my friend tells us of *Shakespeare's easy-steps*. La, my dear Dhlomo! (167)

The hostility of this exchange might be attributed to several factors intrinsic to the arguments, like Dhlomo's greater respect for European models and Vilakazi's anthropological rather than literary interest in Zulu poetry. However, at least as important would have been their common desire to establish their credentials as worthy literary critics, as competent new participants in the discourses of culture defined by the likes of Quiller-Couch and J. Y. T. Greig, English professor at the University of the Witwatersrands in the 1930s. The pressure on the recently recruited critic was compounded by the pressure on them to defend their reputations as 'experts on black culture'. Writing for a constituency made up of an emergent black urban intelligentsia and a white liberal bloc, Dhlomo and Vilakazi introduced new material for discussion, but were still constrained in their exchanges by the conventions of literary debate in England. That they squabbled with each other under the watchful eye of white patrons, but did not collectively dislodge certain central assumptions of dominant English settler culture, might be read as confirming the continued hegemony of that culture. However, notwithstanding their shared respect for official European culture, they both express with rather more confidence than those of Plaatje's generation a desire to affirm and contribute to African culture, and in Vilakazi's article particularly, the seeds of a defiant black nationalist identity are evident.

The Batting of a Supreme Cricketer

The second part of my argument in this chapter is that the developments in literary criticism in the 1930s had very little impact on the teaching of literature in schools. For the most part, the pedagogical and discursive practices established in the late nineteenth century continued unchanged, though there were certain differences between England and South Africa.

In England, the major initiative in the control of English teaching after the First World War was *The Teaching of English in England*, the Newbolt Report of 1921.[47] The committee under Sir Henry Newbolt's chairmanship was made up of members of the English Association, and it sought to promote a sense of national pride by emphasizing the value of the English language and its literature, and also to give expression to a general desire for improved educational opportunity. Underlying these concerns was a commitment to using the teaching of English as a means of social control, and in particular as a means of containing the anti-capitalist sentiments of young workers. Section 233 records '[e]vidence as to the hostility among thoughtful working-men to literature',[48] and section 236 records that the middle classes too display 'an indifference . . . to the claims of literature' (256). Good English teachers, identified as missionaries of a kind (259), are made responsible for remedying this unhappy state of affairs.

The Newbolt Report was an important attempt to reconstitute English national unity after the war through education, though what I want to emphasize is that it offered nothing new in terms of cultural analysis or pedagogical innovation. The fears of class war, and of teaching English literature to try and forestall it, were familiar themes in the nineteenth century. Further, in terms of the teaching of Shakespeare in high-school class-rooms, there too there was little change as a result of the Report. For example, in J. H. Fowler's *The Art of Teaching English*, the author approves the eclipse of 'the old method of burying of Shakespeare under mountains of archaeological, philological and textual notes',[49] and sets out the correct order in which to study the 'infinity of things that may be studied in a play of Shakespeare' (95). First, the students must grasp the plot; then, they must clearly 'individualize the characters' (95); third, the language of the play, the 'magic of the words' (96), must be imbibed (this would include reading aloud and learning by heart great passages from the plays); and finally, metre must be appreciated. Fowler's scheme of study was already inscribed in certain Shakespeare texts in the 1880s and 1890s (recall, for example, Lewis Maxy's 1892 edition of *Hamlet*), and by the 1930s the plot–character–theme focus had become the norm.

John Hampden's 1930 edition of *Hamlet* is part of a series that sets out to 'make the reading of Shakespeare's plays as easy and straightforward as possible',[50] and insists on Shakespeare's continuing and permanent relevance:

There is no political situation to be explained or historical setting to be described. Hamlet belongs to all time. We can picture him if we choose at the court of eleventh-century Denmark, living in a half-savage world; but that the barbarities of the play do not merely make it a thing of the past the history of the years 1914–1918 bears terrible witness. Recently, the whole drama has been successfully staged in modern dress, with only some minor points of action . . . that seemed incongruous with a Hamlet in plus fours and Ophelia in a Parisian gown. Shakespeare's company always acted the play in modern dress. (9–10)

After the text of the play, the editor concedes that notes are a necessary evil, and then provides scene-by-scene notes; aids to further study (background on Shakespeare's life, sources of the play, etc); fifty-nine questions 'On Thinking it Over', which would presumably be used as examination preparation, and which include a large percentage of questions on character-ization and plot (Bradley's thoughts on Hamlet's melancholy nature are prominent); a number of simpler exercises; and a list of further reading.

Guy Boas's 1934 edition of *Othello* also emphasizes Shake-speare's universality, concentrating extensively on the charac-ters, and displaying an intellectual dependence on Shakespeare critics of Bradley's generation. In his introduction, he quotes with approval Bradley's view that the audience leaves *Othello* elevated and comforted, and after the text of the play, he structures his commentary in the same way as Fowler sug-gests, with a modest supplement of notes, an appendix on Shakespeare's life, the order of the plays and the Elizabethan theatre, longer essay questions, and finally detailed questions on the play. The essay questions concentrate on character and action:

3. Contrast Othello with Macbeth and Brutus as tragic figure, or Desdemona with Ophelia and Cordelia.
5. Consider the importance of the part played in the plot by a mere handkerchief.
7. To what extent is the character of the easy-going popular Cassio typical of a certain type of young Englishman?[51]

A more original commentary is provided in Edward Thompson's 1934 edition of *The Tempest*, which makes some attempt to relate the play to its context:

The Empire was being founded; and there was a nation's will be-hind it. . . . Shakespeare was too sensitive to the life of his day to be untouched by what was the common steady topic of several years;

and all the ferment of the beginnings of colonisation stirs in his play.[52]

Also notable is Thompson's criticisms of Prospero—we must, he argues, recognize 'how overbearing Prospero is and how maliciously he enjoys the infliction of petty suffering' (p. xxii)— and his efforts to ask questions that encourage reflection on issues other than character–theme–plot. For example, in addition to asking students to '[c]ontrast the characters of Caliban and Ariel', he asks:

'There are many things in life that must take precedence of literature.' Discuss this statement, and indicate any things which seem to you more important. How far do you think Shakespeare would have agreed with you, judging by 'The Tempest'? (135)

But notwithstanding these ideas, which suggest a rather less conventional construction of Shakespeare and *The Tempest*, many familiar assumptions and arguments are repeated. Shakespeare's universal genius is celebrated in terms that recall the team-sports machismo of the 1870 Rugby edition of *Hamlet*:

The play's style is often casual, but so successful that no-one would criticise it; it is casual as the batting of a supreme cricketer is casual, when he is wearied with a long innings but his skill is too entirely at home for its seemingly careless slashes to miss their aim. (p. xiii)

Further, Thompson's commentary includes for the students' benefit the normal wealth of 'safe knowledge' they needed to pass examinations, namely, detail about the sources of the play, explanatory notes on the text, and questions on the play's characters and plot, and his judgement of Miranda is entirely in the spirit of Mrs Jameson: 'an elemental woman, unspoiled in thought and deed' (p. xxiii). The result is a reading of *The Tempest* that reproduces the concerns of more traditional editions, with the thoughts on colonization, Prospero's malice, and the possibility of there being things in life more important than literature, functioning as little more than provocative asides.

Compared to the situation in the late nineteenth century, when the readings of Shakespeare's plays that were deployed in the schools cohered substantially with the criticism of Bradley and his peers, in the 1930s that symmetry was to some extent fragmented. The rupture was by no means decisive—Wilson Knight's arguments, for example, do not significantly challenge the values inscribed in any of the school editions discussed—but none the less there does seem to have been some kind of time-lag, with the 1880 Shakespeare model continuing to be used in the schools, while at the same time new models were introduced at universities. Indeed, although traces of a dissenting interpretation of Shakespeare are evident in certain editions, no institutional endorsement of these ideas is apparent, with schools oblivious of even the existence of these new and in some cases anti-establishment models.

Setting the Big Things

Whereas Britain in the 1930s was dominated by conflict and tension, South Africa enjoyed a period of relative affluence.[53] The enormous wealth from the gold-mines was boosted further at the end of 1932, when South Africa abandoned the Gold Standard and the world price of gold in the following year increased by 45 per cent. The result was that between 1933 and 1937 South Africa was remarkable among industrial states in displaying budget surpluses. Besides cushioning the effects of the Depression far more effectively than the combination of measures undertaken in Britain, the massive increases in revenue from gold enabled the Hertzog government to carry out its rather more modest version of the New Deal, with state intervention in the economy directed to *inter alia* the improved provision of certain social services for its (white) citizens.[54]

The relative stability of South Africa compared to Britain no doubt contributed to the fact that there was no initiative in social engineering through education equivalent to the Newbolt Report. None the less, the political function of English literature was spelt out by South African English teachers in broadly similar terms. In a 1933 editorial of the *Educational News*, a diagnosis of the crisis facing education in South Africa is provided:

The tragic breakdown of the economic system of Western Civilisation, with the infinite miseries it has carried in its train, has dealt

severely with education throughout the world. . . . The situation
in the Cape is bad enough, though South Africa has escaped the
worst evils of the world depression. Here too poverty and under-
nourishment are rife; here too classes of 60 children are to be found
and here too, we see confusion in grappling with the problems of
State economy.[55]

Attributing the mismanagement of the economy to the absence of 'impartial discussion of public questions [and] of a
developed critical faculty in the voter', the editor confesses
that '[o]ur system of education cannot escape some measure
of responsibility for this lack of critical faculty in the masses'
(3). The solution? To adopt a holistic attitude to education as
outlined by Professor Haarhof. This means cultivating an attitude of mind which unifies the 'various portions of education that are incomplete or sterile until they are combined
into a significant unity' (5). And 'the appreciation of literary
beauty and significant values'—in both the Classics and English literature—is central to this. Haarhof suggests: 'I believe
in setting the big things, on occasion, before quite young children—a play of Shakespeare, for example. They will fail to
understand much of it, but contacts are made, echoes are made
in the mind that bear fruit later; they get a glimpse of something worth striving for' (5). The rapid shift from world
economic crises to brave new world is thus to be mediated by
the application of English literature to young minds.

That this places some burden on English teachers is something that was recognized by Louis Herman three years earlier in a two-part article in the same journal.[56] Although he
too does not make English teachers directly responsible for
world peace, Herman none the less constructs them as exceptional beings, endowed with the unique qualities necessary to
reconcile the interests of culture and the examination system.
However, the pressures of preparing for examinations can
lead teachers and pupils alike to forget that literature is to be
enjoyed. The analogy with sport is invoked:

Novels and poems are to be enjoyed, their assimilation being merely
the consequence of the pupils' interest in them, just as a good place
on the log of the schools' league is the probable consequence
of games played with gusto. The fact that school games are play,

recreation, amusement, is almost forgotten in the insane insistence on competition in sport. Just so are we inclined to forget that literature is to be read with pleasure, the examination only being a means of testing whether the prescribed reading has been done.[57]

The range of talents the English teacher must possess in order to ensure such instructive enjoyment of literature is considerable: a literary sensibility, which means 'being widely read outside the confines of academic syllabuses' (324); an extensive knowledge of the language and a broad general knowledge, since 'he will be called upon to explain a greater range of matter than any other member of the school staff' (324); enthusiasm for the subject and a heightened emotional intelligence, because 'emotion, however it is intellectualised, is the very stuff of art, and literature is primarily art' (324); an ability to read well, to quote and 'even sing a snatch of a song when the occasion demands' (325); and finally, the ability not only to distinguish good art from bad, but also the courage 'to appraise, to criticise, and to attack, if necessary, even works of acknowledged worth' (325).

In the second part of the article, Herman elaborates on what kind of books the English teacher may use in pursuing this heroic mission. Dividing reading done in leisure hours and reading done in the classroom, he argues that in the case of the former, the pupil should be free to explore whatever interests 'him', since a process of natural selection will operate, and '[h]e will get over the penny dreadful stage as he gets through the measles' (383). However, this 'purely laissez-faire policy' should be moderated in subtle ways by the teacher: 'Advise unobtrusively but do not tell. . . . Do not give the good and bad equal chances, but weight the scales in favour of the good where the opportunity occurs' (383). As regards the literature set in schools, the teacher must demonstrate that 'there is something worthy of esteem in the work' (383) by analysing it carefully, and not by simply gushing about the book's excellence. This process of careful reading is crucial, as '[u]nsympathetic reading, even of the best work, will arouse dislike instead of admiration' (384). As an unambiguous instance of such inept reading, Herman cites the letter of a Cape Town teacher to the newspaper complaining that studying

Shakespeare at school made boys and girls so dislike him that they never wished to read his works again. Such a response by the class is entirely the teacher's fault, since '[a]ny good teacher of literature will attest that no class about the age of Standard VII or VIII reads 'Julius Caesar' or 'The Merchant of Venice' or 'Richard the Second' or any one of the suitable plays without wishing to start on another play immediately' (385). There were other pieces produced in this decade which repeated similar cultural diagnoses and proposed similar solutions: J. Y. T. Greig[58] relies on Allen Tate and John Crowe Ransom in voicing his fears about the demise of culture and the triumph of the machine, and R. W. Watson bemoans 'the sacrifice of beauty for utility',[59] but sees salvation in the familiar form of dedicated English teachers instructing pupils in 'the best that has been thought and felt' (10). The arguments first put forward in nineteenth-century England about lost rural innocence, an embattled high culture, and redemption through literature, are therefore repeated here without adjustment. That none of these writers effects any alteration to Arnold's arguments in order to account for the different time and place of their own projects is some indication of the hegemony exerted by this strand of dominant metropolitan English culture in the Cape.

Many aspects of life at the Cape in the 1930s could be noted in order to emphasize the real differences between it and Arnold's England, but perhaps one will suffice to make the point. The Industrial Revolution had assuredly made deep impressions on the lives of English people by 1850, and Arnold's preoccupation with the ravages of industrialization is not eccentric, but there was in the 1930s a conspicuous absence of 'dark Satanic mills' in Cape Town, at least in so far as they affected the lives of white South Africans. For example, no mention is made of burgeoning industry in a 1933 article advertising Cape Town to English colonials: 'The Cape Peninsula is a land of out-of-doors, of oak and pine woods, and a profusion of wild flowers set in a green and pleasant countryside. It has long been a centre to which people of leisure and fixed income retire to lead a life full of interest.'[60] Less saturated in the literature and criticism of nineteenth-century England than their English-teaching cousins, the veterans of colonial service therefore perceived the Cape more as rural idyll than as a temperate variation of Birmingham.

As was the case in England, the developments in university production of Shakespeare were contained within their own sphere and the plot–character focus first established in the previous century continued uninterrupted at high schools. There were, however, some liberalizing trends in the school examination papers of the 1930s. For example, C. T. Loram's 1930 English Higher Senior Certificate paper reflects a slight shift from papers of previous years in that in addition to testing how many facts about the plays pupils remember, it encourages them to demonstrate some personal appreciation. The Examiner's Report in the *Education Gazette* of 1930 sets out that '[t]he questions were set to test the knowledge of the candidates of the books prescribed and also, generally in the alternate questions, to give opportunities for expression of criticism or appreciation'.[61] Loram's two questions on *Hamlet* in the 1930 English Higher examination satisfy this dual demand:

1. Choose *four* well-known quotations from this play (not more than one from any one speech) and in connection with each give (*a*) the name of the speaker, (*b*) the occasion on which it was spoken, and (*c*) its full meaning.

   or

   In about ten lines for each say what the following persons might think of this play:—

   (*a*) the moralist who looks for lessons on life and human nature from the drama;
   (*b*) the dramatic critic who is chiefly concerned with the way in which the play is constructed;
   (*c*) the ordinary school boy or school girl.[62]

The English Lower paper of the same year (for predominantly Afrikaans-speaking students) was set by A. R. Hewitt, and includes rather less scope for 'personal appreciation',[63] with standard questions about Hamlet's 'tragic failure' and a comparison of the characters of Laertes and Hamlet.

For the rest of the decade, the English syllabus remained unchanged, with instructions to study the six set texts 'from a literary aspect'.[64] Besides the Shakespeare play, pupils doing

English Higher for the Senior Certificate were questioned on a modern drama, epic or lyric poetry, a novel, a biography or travel book, and a collection of essays. English Lower required study of four of the six texts, with the Shakespeare play compulsory, and for the Junior Certificate, a novel and a collection of poetry were set for detailed study and two further prescribed texts had to be read. All the editions of the set texts recommended for pupils were ones published in England—for the Shakespeare plays, the Blackie editions at 6*d*. a copy were preferred.

For the 1939 English Higher Senior Certificate examination, the examiner was Professor P. Haworth of Rhodes University, and the set Shakespeare play was *The Tempest*. Again his questions test primarily the ability of pupils to remember plot details:

1. (*a*) Describe briefly with appropriate quotations the first meeting of Ferdinand and Miranda. What dangers and difficulties impede the course of their love, and how are these overcome?

   or,

   (*b*) Discuss the justice of the charges brought by Caliban against Prospero. Outline the action taken by Caliban to avenge his wrongs, and state the consequences.

   or,

   (*c*) Compare Prospero's treatment of Antonio and Caliban in frustrating their plans and punishing them. Criticise the scheme of poetic justice in this play.[65]

In an unusual departure, the Superintendent-General of Education's Report for 1939 includes the results of the different subjects written in the Senior Certificate examinations. There were 1,847 candidates who puzzled over Haworth's paper; 95 per cent passed; the average mark was 52 per cent; and the symbol breakdown was as follows: 0 As (80–100 per cent); 4 Bs (70–80 per cent); 19 Cs (60–70 per cent); and 34 Ds. The vast majority of students received between 50 and 60 per cent, suggesting that passing English literature was not too difficult, but being 'good at English' was another matter. The fact that there were no A aggregates suggests that no one writing Senior Certificate examinations in the whole of the Cape Province in 1939 had proved their excellence.

Before drawing conclusions regarding the regulatory function of English literature examinations in this context, a further set of statistics from the Report should be mentioned. In 1939 a very small percentage of school pupils in the Cape actually got to study literature, with the educational pyramid especially steep in the case of coloured and black pupils: of a total of 158,975 white pupils, 3,969 wrote the Senior Certificate examinations; of 122,029 Coloured pupils, 115 wrote; and of 202, 763 black pupils, 76 sat for the final exams. The need for rigorous and demanding examinations about English literature in the spirit of W. G. Dasent of the Indian Civil Service Examination Board is therefore rendered superfluous, since the selection process separating out an élite of professionals, administrators, and officials will have been completed long before pupils reach the higher standards and encounter Shakespeare.

This means that although a knowledge of English literature continued to function as a prerequisite for upward mobility, the high pass-rate suggests that the cultural and ideological baggage pupils internalized in the process of studying it was perhaps more significant. In summary, what this amounted to was a combination of, on the one hand, the Arnoldian narrative of cultural redemption, with its animosity towards industrialism (*not* capitalism) and enthusiasm for a narrowly defined and conservatively interpreted canon with Shakespeare at its apex, and, on the other hand, a practice of teaching literature by focusing on plot minutiae, character analysis, and themes of moral harmony.

Conclusion

Extremely important changes took place in English studies both in England and South Africa during the period discussed in this chapter: the gentleman scholar was replaced by the state-employed professional critic recruited from a subordinate group; the number of pupils studying English literature increased enormously, with previously excluded social classes given increased access. At the same time, certain things stayed the same: the pessimistic cultural analysis justifying the teaching of literature continued to hold sway; the vast majority of pupils studying English in Britain and South Africa experienced the same version of Shakespeare as their parents' generation had done; and the educational hierarchies continued to admit only a small minority to positions of institutional power.

What these ruptures and continuities point to is a need for circumspection in assessing the impact of minority groups and their critical discourses on the subject of English studies. The presence of minority voices within the English common-room has no necessary connection with the collective improvement of their constituencies. English studies has over a long period been remarkably adept at recruiting talented thinkers from marginal groups and directing their energies to the service of the central (conservative) educational and cultural ends of the discipline.

5
Shakespeare and Apartheid: The 1950s

Introduction

In an interesting digression in the *Grundrisse*, Marx attempts to explain how the mediating term between two opposed extremes accrues to itself the greatest power. He is principally concerned with identifying how bourgeois wealth effects this by standing as 'the mediation between the extremes of exchange value and use value',[1] but then extends the pattern to further examples: 'Thus, in the religious sphere, Christ, the mediator between God and humanity—a mere instrument of circulation between the two—becomes their unity, God-man, and, as such, becomes more important than God; the saints more important than Christ; the popes more important than the saints' (332). In this chapter, I extend this dialectical mode of thinking to the opposition of apartheid and Shakespeare in 1950s South Africa, arguing that here too those mediating the relation between these opposed extremes—South African English teachers—confer upon themselves a centralizing power.

The mediation is effected differently in different areas, and I focus on the following three: the criticism of Geoffrey Durrant, D. R. C. Marsh, and Christina van Heyningen, the three most prolific Shakespeare critics from the white English-speaking universities; the syllabuses, school editions, and study aids produced for Shakespeare study at South African high schools; and the book reviews and literary criticism in the anti-apartheid political journals of the period. In each case, I try and point to what is announced and what is excluded in constructing and defending this limiting binary.

This chapter therefore continues the reflection in Chapter 3 of the relation between liberal humanism and colonial racism. However, whereas in the nineteenth century racism and humanism were compatible elements of a coherent world-view for the likes of Matthew Arnold and Langham Dale, in the 1950s English critics like Durrant and Marsh claimed to speak for a humanist faith and externalized racist thought by identifying it with Afrikaner Nationalists. My interest here is accordingly less on demonstrating the connections between humanism and racism than on exploring the rhetorical strategies used in reworking a once-unified world-view into a binary opposition. This focus deflects the discussion towards a more detailed consideration of the cultural mission of English studies in contemporary South Africa: in particular, it questions the basis of Shakespeare's credentials as a resource in the struggle against racism.

Between the Two Extremes

During the Second World War a significant number of British writers produced investigations and manifestos that looked forward to how the poverty of the Depression and war years might be avoided in a new and better Britain.[2] Drawn largely from the narrow dissident fraction of the English ruling class, these writers—referred to collectively by military historian Corelli Barnett as seekers for 'a New Jerusalem'[3]—produced various plans for social reconciliation via state intervention. The most famous set of proposals was Sir William Beveridge's Report of 1942, which elaborated a minimum programme for a more just post-war dispensation, but there were also a number of more explicitly socialist projections, like Harold Laski's *Where do we Go from Here?*, George Orwell's *The Lion and the Unicorn*, and John Strachey's *A Faith to Fight For*. Disillusioned with Western capitalism and Soviet communism alike, these works shared a common desire to see Nazism vanquished and some form of democratic socialism established in Britain. Like Arnold a century earlier, they saw the state as benevolent mediator between the different social classes. Their proposals accordingly related to how the state might mediate those opposed interests by *inter alia* eliminating absolute poverty, guaranteeing equality of opportunity in education and employment, and expanding meaningful participation in political decision-making processes. That they captured the mood of the moment is evident from their impressive sales figures: Beveridge's Report sold 635,000 copies (including in summary form), and Laski's pamphlet over 80,000.

The scale of similar such interventions in South Africa at this time was more modest, but there was at least one pamphlet infused with a like spirit. Geoffrey Durrant, educated at Cambridge in the 1930s and serving in the Army Education Unit during the war, wrote *Propaganda and Public Opinion* as an attempt to direct public and government opinion in South Africa towards a more democratic post-war settlement. Durrant's pamphlet is of interest for several reasons: it is the only text by a member of the new wave of Leavisite critics and teachers who were to dominate South African university English departments after the war which connects their cultural mission in any detail to their understanding of the state and of political struggle; and secondly, set against the colonial context it seeks to transform, the *Scrutiny* project (in Durrant's modified form) itself stands out in clearer relief, with silences and omissions occluded in England's pluralist culture, but less easy to overlook in South Africa.

Concerned with how 'thought can be made free, not only from government tyranny, but also from the more subtle and pervasive tyrannies of a commercial society',[4] Durrant first identifies the crippling apathy of modern industrial societies, then analyses the role of the mass media in South Africa in producing this state of affairs, and finally puts forward his own 'positive programme for democracy' (1). His basic premiss is that together the various institutions of the mass media have induced in 'the common man' a cynicism and intellectual torpor inimical to 'a reasoned attitude to national affairs' (3), and that the organization of each major media form therefore needs to be transformed. Starting with the press, Durrant bemoans the fact that in South Africa 'there is now not one editor or journalist with a national reputation for fearless and impartial comment . . . no Low, and no *Manchester Guardian*' (7). Instead, there is an English press, 'reverential in its attitude to the gold mines and to the economic policy that they favour' (6), and an Afrikaans press dedicated to furthering the ends of the National Party. Only in periodicals and journals like

Trek and *Forum* does Durrant see any examples of reasoned news commentary. In broadcasting, initial hopes of bringing 'light to the darkest minds in the remotest places' (13) have been disappointed, at least in so far as the South African Broadcasting Corporation (SABC) is concerned, and Durrant attributes this to an absence of both political debate on official airwaves and of any democratic participation by listeners in the running of the SABC. As regards film, Durrant notes the overwhelming presence of American movies in South Africa, a presence he insists is not neutral: '[T]he films give us a definite outlook on the world and have definite political influence. . . . [I]t is Hollywood culture and Hollywood politics that we unconsciously absorb' (19). Finally, he considers the refinement of advertising techniques, and registers his concern that advertisers manipulate 'group prejudice [and] basic human passions' (21) in ways that might easily be extended to the political field: 'If an advertiser may sell a quack remedy by playing on our fear of vitamin deficiency or halitosis, why should a politician not sell his policy by appealing to our fear of the Native?' (23)

In similar fashion to Arnold, Durrant looks to a revised education system to mend these ills: the 'channels of knowledge and discussion' (4) must be opened, and the principal means of doing so is by education. The educational initiatives Durrant suggests include: analyzing newspapers as part of the language training of schoolchildren; teaching the criticism of film at schools, since '[a] study of the humanities which merely purveys established opinions about the classics is of no use in helping us to understand and master the modern environment' (20); setting up a national system of adult education in which employees in offices and factories might regularly attend classes discussing 'questions that really affect the man in the street and his family' (24); and revitalizing educational radio broadcasts so that they might extend to all, not only to 'children and natives, [as] neither of these groups are citizens' (29). Durrant recognizes that his commitment to providing a framework for open discussion would be opposed because the refusal to raise contentious issues 'favours those groups which would like to prevent all discussion and keep everything as it is. In other words, it takes the side of the rich

and the powerful' (26). The only available agency for counter-
ing this resistance is the government: 'But in these days of
great capital accumulations, of monopolies, and of mass movements, the isolated individual is almost helpless. It is therefore
the duty of the government, not merely to act according to
democratic principles, but to act so that these principles will
live and be strengthened' (26–7). He therefore concludes that
'the need to-day is for positive government action to create a
free opinion' (31).

The first point to note about Durrant's argument is that it
is a distinctly left version of the *Scrutiny* analysis. Although it
reproduces *Scrutiny*'s main themes—the hostility to advertising,
the horror of commercial society, and the need for interventions in education—in its attack on the South African English
press, its antipathy to the Hollywood equation of success and
'getting a lot of money' (18), and its desire to stimulate discussion that would disrupt the hegemony of 'the rich and the
powerful', Durrant's pamphlet provides the basis for a radical critique of South African culture. Indeed, in these areas,
and also in his suggestions regarding increased participation
in broadcasting and in film production, he anticipates the
analysis of cultural struggle undertaken by Raymond Williams
in the final section of *The Long Revolution*.[5]

Notwithstanding these radical elements in his discussion,
Durrant's implicit understanding of the state ('the government' in his terms) and of the colonial relationship, reveal his
continuing commitment to a liberal paradigm. His benign view
of government as an agency that would 'guarantee the conditions for full and free consultation'[6] derives from a long
tradition of liberal political thought in which the neutral state
is seen to mediate between capital and labour, balancing the
interests of both and thus ensuring social equilibrium.
Durrant's ability to imagine a government committed to democratic reforms contrary to the interests of capital rests less on
an analysis of contemporaneous South African political history
than on his borrowing of projections plausible in England:
Beveridge and his ilk conceived a benevolent state for post-
war Britain, and Durrant simply took over their ideal and
imposed it on (the very different) South African social polity.
For both Durrant and his heroes in England, the bourgeois

state did indeed act as a sovereign representing the interests of all subjects, allocating material and cultural resources in the society on the basis of the collective good.

As regards the relation of England to South Africa, Durrant follows a well-worn path in attributing positive qualities to the metropolitan and negative to the colonial. For example, impartiality and objectivity reside in England: the *Manchester Guardian* tells the truth in a way no South African newspaper does, and teachers in America, Australia, and England have been successfully trained to be impartial (he cites Thompson and Leavis in a footnote to support this claim). Durrant's self-appointed task is presumably to carry these impartial voices from England to 'the darkest minds in the remotest places', and then also to inoculate the white settler folk against cynical propaganda which might exploit 'our fear of the Native'. But perhaps the most telling phrase in this respect is Durrant's observation that radio broadcasts for natives and children are of less significance because 'neither of these groups are citizens'. Durrant's exclusion of black people from the citizenry of South Africa reflects not only on how he as settler critic perceives native subjects as an absence of white adult citizens, but also on the inscribed limits of the left liberal discourse he reproduces: democratic participation for everybody does not actually mean *everybody*.

The fate of Durrant's ideals of post-war social reconstruction can perhaps best be measured in an article he wrote on *The Tempest*. Published in 1955 in Natal University's literary journal, *Theoria*, 'Prospero's Wisdom' reveals no glimmer of the democratic fervour that characterized *Propaganda and Public Opinion*, setting out instead a tepid defence of Prospero's actions on the island. Establishing that Prospero is not Shakespeare but simply a character in Shakespeare's final work, Durrant argues by paraphrasing certain passages of the play that *The Tempest* demonstrates the need for a rational moral order (enforced by Prospero) in an imperfect world:

Yet the play as it stands offers no final reconciliation of heart and mind, of innocence and experience. Prospero's justice is necessary in a world where men are given to evil; and his moral reason is needed to keep in check the Calibans of our animal nature. . . . The artistic unity and harmony of *The Tempest* is of the surface only, for the play conveys the agonized sense of the disparity between man's heart and reason.[7]

There are continuities between Durrant's earlier pamphleteering and this piece of literary criticism. He sustains his commitment to reason (the desirability of nurturing on a large scale 'a reasoned attitude to national affairs', and approval of Prospero's corrective application of reason to 'the Calibans of our animal nature'). Second, he denies the voice of the colonial subject (native subjects perceived as either 'the darkest minds in the remotest places' or as non-citizens, and Caliban characterized as 'unregenerate animal nature' requiring the stern hand of the 'good humanist [schoolmaster]' (53), Prospero). And finally, Prospero's benign but firm interventionist state on the island echoes Durrant's own projections for how the South African state in 1944 should act. What is most striking in comparing the two texts, however, is the dramatic narrowing of Durrant's political ambitions, from optimistic pamphleteer in 1944 seeking to reach a wide audience and influence national educational policy, to literary critic in 1955 arguing about Shakespeare's humanist ethic in a small circulation academic journal.

In the years between the two texts, Durrant directed his energies primarily to arguing for the introduction of practical criticism into South African English departments, a campaign that was largely successful.[8] No doubt anticipating that 'the government' would not aid in unclogging the channels of communication in South African society, Durrant in his inaugural lecture as Professor of English at the University of Natal, Pietermaritzburg, entitled *English Studies and the Community* pins his hopes instead on English teachers: '[My] claim is that [English studies] will make possible, if rightly followed, a more intelligent political activity, a clearer sense of ultimate values and a generally higher standard of human life.'[9] Among other things, this would demand keeping 'the lines that connect us with England and America in good working order' (18), and more specifically, '[t]he maintenance of the highest standards of criticism, the cultivation of free and ordered expression in poetry and in the common speech, the study of living popular forms of dramatic and literary art, and the clarifying of language' (18). Durrant concludes the lecture with quotations from Arnold, Dante, and Milton, challenging his audience to intervene on the side of humane culture in their own hostile community: 'if we fail to influence the community in which we live, the very standards by which humane studies have lived may be swept away' (20).

The shift in Durrant's writing over this eleven-year period then might be summarized as instancing a gradual withdrawal from politics to literature, with the connections between the two being increasingly suppressed: from confronting directly the interests of the 'rich and the powerful' in 1944, to promoting 'a more intelligent political life' in 1945, to defending Prospero's moral justice in 1955. The shift is of course not unconnected to the rapidly changing possibilities available to the white English liberal in South Africa during this period. The election of the National Party in 1948 dramatically ended the period of English liberal influence over state policy. Former Natal Senator and prominent liberal educationalist Edgar Brookes summed up the loss of power in a 1950 public lecture: 'We may . . . never, never, never hold public office in South Africa, never speak of our beloved country in the outside world, never be reckoned as one of the family in our own country. As far as may be our freedom must be curtailed, our voices stilled, our pens struck from our hands.'[10] This change in fortunes can perhaps best be expressed by recalling the record of another prominent liberal of the pre-war years, C. T. Loram: besides setting the 1930 matriculation paper on *Hamlet*, Loram was at the same time able to influence significantly the government's native policy as a member of the Native Affairs Commission and the Native Churches Commission. In the 1950s Loram's descendants in this liberal tradition could still set English literature examination papers, but their control over native policy (or any state policy for that matter) had passed into the hands of apartheid bureaucrats.

Whereas in 1944 Durrant's argument for a benevolent state mediating between opposed social classes was plausible, by 1955 the brutal intentions of the apartheid state were clear enough to discredit its claims to act as mediator. That Durrant no longer saw the South African state as a potential mediator between the rich and powerful and the poor is implicit in his decision to stop writing about politics directly, and to pursue instead a much narrower cultural project. In this process, the old opposition between rich and poor, with the state as mediator, is replaced by a new one between the Afrikaner state and black South Africans, with English-speaking South Africa as mediator. In this revised schema, Shakespeare becomes the third term that resolves the contradiction between the state and its disaffected subjects. Prospero's wisdom is greater than that of the apartheid state, and he effects a reconciliation beyond the means of South Africa's political rulers.

As a result of conceding control of the state to Afrikaner Nationalism, South African literary critics of the 1950s made only very rare direct reference to politics,[11] with their opposition to apartheid implicit in their criticism. This is most vividly borne out in the work of D. R. C. Marsh, English lecturer at Natal University and a senior official of the South African Liberal Party, who was imprisoned in 1960 for anti-apartheid activities. Marsh completed his major work on Shakespeare's final plays, *The Recurring Miracle*, while in Pietermaritzburg prison, a fact referred to in the acknowledgements and the flyleaf (written by Durrant) of the text. Marsh himself wryly thanks the Minister of Justice of the Union of South Africa, 'whose insistent hospitality gave me time for which I had been vainly seeking',[12] and Durrant sets out the circumstances in which the book was written in only slightly more detail:

Mr. Marsh wrote the greater part of the book whilst imprisoned, without charge or trial, in the Pietermaritzburg jail during the troubles of 1960. It says much for the liberality of the South African government that he was allowed access, during the months of his imprisonment, to the unexpurgated text of Shakespeare's *Plays*. The result is something more than a work of criticism; it is also a work of rare humanity.

In his discussion of the plays, Marsh makes no explicit connection between his opposition to apartheid and his devotion to Shakespeare, confining himself instead to a detailed defence of the final plays and of *Cymbeline* in particular. He argues that 'the relevance of these plays to life is as direct as anything that Shakespeare ever wrote' (4), and that:

In the scene-by-scene account of the play that forms the main part of this study, I shall endeavour to show that this central theme in *Cymbeline* is the theme common to all the plays of this group, the necessity of recognising the value of life. The tragic circumstances which are depicted in these plays call for the virtues of love, acceptance, understanding and detachment from selfish aims, before harmony can be restored. Piety, love and self-knowledge are shown as the central virtues, and the characters are good or bad insofar as they are able, through these virtues, to free themselves from the demands of self. (12)

The critics he draws upon most frequently in establishing this argument are G. Wilson Knight and Derek Traversi, although their influence is reflected more in terms of method than in terms of their views on the plays. That Marsh relied on these critics, with their exhaustive close readings and search for unifying themes, rather than on more sociological critics (or the English Marxists for that matter), might be attributed to several factors: by 1960 the left Leavisite tendency represented in Durrant's early work, which connected English studies and the fight against totalitarianism, had disappeared from South African English department language (not that it had ever been more than a marginal presence), and it had been replaced by a more self-enclosed and conservative version of *Scrutiny* discourse, with the result that writing about Shakespeare and politics in the same argument had become literally unthinkable; connected to this, drawing on the arguments of, for example, the English Marxists, was almost impossible because of the unavailability of the books in South Africa;[13] and thirdly, the political culture of the time allocated little space to exploring the relations between immediate political struggles and the literary canon. Notwithstanding these qualifications, Marsh clearly found in the ostensibly less 'politically engaged' methods of the conservative Scrutineers an adequate means of giving expression to his own commitments, of preserving his own identity in conditions of some duress.

The tensions between Shakespeare and South African politics come closest to surfacing in Marsh's chapter on *The Tempest*, where he concedes that the play is for him Shakespeare's 'most puzzling' (163), particularly with regard to Prospero's treatment of Caliban. Marsh awkwardly relates Caliban to anti-imperialist struggles in Africa:

Caliban, meanwhile, is rightly attributing to Prospero the punishments that plague him. In something of the state of the African in many colonial countries at the present time, he is sternly disciplined 'for his own good' and yet denied any possibility of improvement, so that he is ripe to be deceived by any other offers of advancement. . . . (To say this is not to try to impose a modern political interpretation on this part of the play, but rather to use a modern illustration to illuminate Caliban's state of mind.) (197)

This is as far as Marsh goes in introducing the theme of imperialism, and he focuses instead in detail on the dramatic unfolding of character and plot, locating the ultimate meaning of the play in 'universal' themes that cohere closely with his own liberal values.

Marsh argues firstly that 'always in Shakespeare, the right attitude seems to lie between the two extremes' (180), and he isolates several oppositions that direct the audience to a middle path: the spiritual (Ariel) against the physical (Caliban); innocence (Miranda) against knowledge (Prospero); chastity against abundance; and control against exuberance. Prospero's journey in the play is to achieve the right balance both in his own life, which was initially dominated by an austere Apollonian ethic, and in the social regime of the island. This preoccupation with balance is consistent with the pervasive myth among English-speaking South Africans at this time that they were mediators between African and Afrikaner nationalisms, humane interlocutors containing fiercely opposed extremes.[14] Like Durrant, Marsh therefore sees *The Tempest* as confirming Shakespeare's faith in a state form capable of mediating between opposed extremes.

Connected to this first theme is Marsh's concern with the need to transcend self-interest: 'the poison of self-interest has, in this and in the other plays, brought about all the suffering' (175). Prospero's search for knowledge has not been entirely disinterested because he has studied partly in order to exact revenge, and hence he needs to temper his learning with compassion. The qualities endorsed most clearly in *The Tempest* then are ones that correspond 'to the teachings of the Christian religion' (197), although direct reference to Christianity is absent. Marsh expresses the ultimate value taught by the play in the following terms: 'One must care about something, more than one cares about oneself, for whatever the sufferings or responsibilities involved in such a caring, to do so gives a value and a purpose to life, and redeems it from the sterility of self-interest' (197).

A third emphasis is on the need for the individual characters to find themselves: 'To find oneself, to know oneself truly, is the great quest of life, and in it lies the only freedom that matters, freedom from the self' (189). Only once they have overcome their own personal failings do the characters have any hope of dealing with the wider problems of their island society. Marsh makes a similar point in an unpublished lecture on *Hamlet* in 1960:

One can interpret Hamlet as a sort of Christ-figure who takes on the sins of his society and has to die for his sins. Yet he seems agnostic in that he is unaware of what will happen after death. It seems that the play is based on a Christian framework, yet Hamlet does not regard duty as religious—he acts out of a sense of justice, related more to an ethical creed than religious creed. This was typical of Shakespeare's time, when people didn't know what to believe in. One finally believes in oneself or a sense of justice.[15]

Faced with a corrupt society, Hamlet in Denmark—like Prospero on the island, or Marsh in South Africa—was obliged to look to his sense of self, his personal code of justice, in order to know how to act. The absence of a viable religious framework and the vast sinfulness of the society excluded the possibility of a social solution, and the integrity of the individual was therefore the only remaining resource.

This dilemma and the liberal response to it is given perhaps its definitive treatment in the novel *Cry, the Beloved Country*, written by Marsh's leader in the South African Liberal Party, Alan Paton. The exemplary liberal figure in the novel, Arthur Jarvis, is a man with Shakespeare on his bookshelves,[16] and is 'well known for his interest in social problems, and for his efforts for the welfare of the non-European sections of the community' (66). Already dead when the action of novel commences, Jarvis remains a central presence through articles and letters his father discovers and reads. In one essay, entitled 'Private Essay on the Evolution of a South African', he sets out his personal ethic:

I shall devote myself, my time, my energy, my talents, to the service of South Africa. I shall no longer ask myself if this or that is expedient, but only if it is right. . . . I shall do this, not because I am a Negrophile and a hater of my own, but because I cannot find it in me to do anything else. I am lost when I balance this against that, I am lost when I ask if this is safe, I am lost when I ask if men, white men or black men, Englishmen or Afrikaners, Gentiles, will approve. Therefore I shall try to do what is right, and to speak what is true. (151)

In his desire to serve, to make sense of a bewildering and hostile society, to seek the right balance, and to do what is right, Jarvis therefore resembles not only (Marsh's) Hamlet, but also Jesus Christ, William Shakespeare, and South African English teachers. Marsh's application of the close reading techniques associated with practical criticism to the plays thus enables the production of a Shakespeare closely resembling the 1950s South African liberal living out the virtues of selflessness, moderation, and service.

Accepting the opposition thus conceived between English–liberal–Shakespeare and Afrikaans–racist–apartheid was less straightforward for one of Marsh's colleagues, Christina van Heyningen.[17] The daughter of an Afrikaner civil servant who fought the English in the Anglo-Boer War, and an Anglican mother descended from the 1820 settlers, van Heyningen was born in one of the notorious English concentration camps. She attended Stellenbosch University at the same time as Verwoerd and Donges, but then went on to Somerville College, Oxford, where she completed a degree in English in 1926. In her two textbooks, *English: Intelligent Reading and Good Writing* and *On the Printed Page*, as well as in her criticism, she carries forth her version of the *Scrutiny* cultural mission with great zeal: the first footnote of *On the Printed Page* refers the reader to the work of the Leavises, Denys Thompson, and Stephen Potter, and the introduction concludes with rousing quotations from Arnold, Coleridge, and Lawrence, exhorting critics to 'be emotionally alive in every fibre, intellectually capable and skilful in essential logic, and then morally very honest'.[18] Like her colleagues, she was deeply committed to the methods of practical criticism, to teaching students to read 'with intellect, emotions, senses, all moving and working at the same time'

(1), and paying only secondary attention to historical and biographical detail. Implicit in this commitment is the belief that teaching good reading habits will ultimately contribute to good political practices, an assumption which generally translated as: practical criticism leads to English liberal politics.

For van Heyningen, however, the unspoken exclusion of Afrikaans and the Afrikaner people in this argument needed addressing. She argued that apartheid and Afrikaner were not the same thing, and attempted to challenge the construction of Afrikaner as the negative term in the opposition between apartheid and Shakespeare. In an essay on 'Christian National Education', she argues that what started out as a legitimate attempt to oppose Lord Milner's anglicizing policy in state education had been transformed with the National Party's coming to power in 1948 into a programme aimed at indoctrinating all South Africans in Nationalist ideology. Detailing the injustices wrought by the new education measures, she none the less remains convinced that the majority of Afrikaners, 'with their spontaneous warmth and naturalness',[19] reject them, and in fact only support the National Party grudgingly: 'Loyally—though with secret black misgivings—they vote for the party, no matter what the evidence against it' (55).

In an article on 'Afrikaans Translations of Shakespeare', Van Heyningen makes similar appeals to a nobler Afrikaner soul, one that has the capacity to transcend the limits of petty nationalism and to commune with High Art. She dismisses in the first place the need for Afrikaners to read translations of Shakespeare, as they should understand enough English to appreciate the original: 'Ersatz Shakespeare is all very well for those who can't get the real thing, but to provide it for people who can is, at the best, far worse than feeding them on powdered egg when fresh ones are as cheap'.[20] After reviewing a number of the nuances missed by L. I. Coertze, in his translation of Hamlet, she argues that where difficulties arise, greater use should be made of Dutch: 'Surely the only way to translate pre-Afrikaans literature into Afrikaans is to draw freely from Dutch and use the more formal and more ramified constructions of the days before our speech was cut small for us, like meat for children, by the influence of the comic strip, the bioscope, and the tabloid newspaper?' (21). This argument serves two separate convictions: the endorsement of the pessimistic *Scrutiny* diagnosis of contemporary mass culture; and the faith in a pre-Nationalist Afrikaner, worthier in spirit than the racists of the 1950s. Translating Shakespeare into a more Dutch version of Afrikaans would rescue him (and Afrikaans-speaking readers of the translations) not only from the taint of apartheid Afrikaans, but also from contemporary machine age Afrikaans. In concluding, van Heyningen equates the grandeur of metropolitan culture and colonial landscape in reaffirming the advantage to be gained by putting Afrikaners in contact with the original Shakespeare: translations are 'an imitation of the real thing almost as little like it as a snapshot of Table Mountain is like the great mountain itself' (25). Afrikaners should be equally free to ascend either summit.

The Moral Order that is so Strong

It would be dangerous to assume that behind their practical criticism of English literary texts all English literature lecturers at South African universities in the 1950s felt any deep opposition to apartheid, that they were prepared to risk imprisonment as Marsh did, or to argue publicly for a more democratic culture as Durrant did, or to concern themselves with the imposition of Christian National education as van Heyningen did. Indeed, while the general liberal sentiments of these three might have been more widely shared, most of their peers were clearly content to avert their gaze from the political transformations sweeping the country and concentrate instead on teaching Shakespeare to the small white student élite passing through their classrooms. Inaugural addresses[21] by English department heads and articles in the literary journals[22] of the period reveal very limited interest in either popular educational and cultural issues or wider political struggles, and the overwhelming weight of intellectual labour was directed towards keeping abreast with metropolitan critical concerns. For the English lecturer in South Africa, apartheid politics carried on in a sphere entirely separate from

Shakespeare, and it was only with the latter that he (more typically) concerned himself. Therefore, while occasionally the confinement to matters literary concealed a sincere opposition to apartheid, more frequently it facilitated a complacent acceptance of the sweet life white South Africans enjoyed during the 1950s.

For those teachers and bureaucrats concerned with the teaching of Shakespeare at schools, the same degree of detachment was impossible, and the relationship between Shakespeare and the apartheid state had to be negotiated in a different way. The schooling system was a central agency in the plan of grand apartheid, and as state employees of one kind or another directly implicated in carrying out this plan, the writers of English syllabuses, school Shakespeare editions, and study aids could not present themselves, as university critics did, as mediating between the racist state and its oppressed subjects. Indeed, the manner in which the (supposedly) inherently liberal, anti-apartheid English studies project fitted in with the neo-Nazi forms of social engineering undertaken by the Nationalists during this period complicates the simple oppositions assumed by Shakespeare teachers in more protected enclaves.

Between 1930 and 1950 the South African economy underwent a rapid transformation, from a small-scale capitalist economy with monopolies in mining to one dominated in *all* areas by monopoly capital. The boom in gold-mining initiated by South Africa's departure in 1933 from the international Gold Standard had generated a surplus which provided the basis for secondary industrialization, a process accelerated further by policies of import substitution and by the munitions industry's contribution to the Allied war effort. Besides creating new labour needs, these changes occasioned other tensions: rapid urbanization produced housing and crime problems; the underdevelopment of the rural reserves accentuated existing patterns of dependency; and organized opposition to these conditions in the form of trade unions and national political campaigns challenged the state's hegemony.

Although the post-war period saw changes in South Africa's white universities, most notably in the rapid growth in student numbers,[23] far more dramatic changes took place in the schooling system, as the state attempted to meet the sometimes contradictory demands of its own white constituency and the rapidly expanding economy. Attempts to contain political tensions via the education system were made in the next twenty years as a series of legislative fiats enforced racially segregated schooling: the Bantu Education Act of 1953, the Extension of University Education Act of 1959, the Coloured Persons Education Act of 1963, the Indian Education Act of 1965, and the National Education Act of 1967.

The official logic of these policies is well known, namely separate schools for different race and language groups under white (Afrikaner) guardianship. Afrikaner identity, threatened by Milner's post-Boer War education policies, would be protected in a differentiated schooling system where, as J. C. Coetzee explained in 1948, '[w]e as Calvinist Afrikaners will have our CNE schools: Anglicans, Lutherans, Roman Catholics, Jews, liberalists and atheists will have their own schools'.[24] But that separate in this sense did not also mean equal was made quite clear in policy statements regarding black education. In now notorious speeches to Parliament in the 1950s, the Minister of Education, H. F. Verwoerd, elaborated:

A Bantu pupil must obtain knowledge, skills and attitudes which will be useful and advantageous to him and at the same time beneficial to his community. . . . There is no place for him in the European community above the level of certain forms of labour. . . . For that reason it is of no avail for him to receive a training which has as its aim absorption in the European community. [A Western education would frustrate him] by showing him the green pastures of European society in which he is not allowed to graze.[25]

These notions accord most obviously with the racial policies of the Afrikaner ruling bloc: segregated schools with mother-tongue instruction effectively insulated Afrikaner cultural identity from harmful outside influence. But apartheid education was *also* congruent with the needs of both overseas and South African capital, which during this period required a supply of cheap, reliable semi-skilled labour to service the new manufacturing industries.[26] The inclination of liberal commentators in both South Africa and England to characterize apartheid as uniquely evil and deviant often serves to shift attention from the racist and élitist patterns in other capitalist societies.[27] David Yudelman explains:

South Africa represents in almost caricatured form the ugly side of most developing industrial states: the concentration of a disproportionate amount of growing wealth in the hands of a minority, the decline of civil and human rights, the centralization of power, and the systematic exploitation of the powerless. It is far more comfortable to relegate such a creature to a lunatic asylum than to conceive of living with it as a blood relative.[28]

Western capitalist states—led by Britain and the USA—were deeply implicated in the apartheid project via heavy investment in both mining and manufacturing sectors of the South African economy during the 1950s; returns on direct investment of around 20 per cent overcame any moral objections to doing business under the umbrella of a racist state.[29]

The programme of mass schooling initiated by the South African state in black education resulted in massive increases in student numbers: the number of black school pupils rose dramatically from 800,000 in 1953 to 1,800,000 in 1963.[30] The vast majority of black students received only four years of schooling, which involved a rudimentary training in the three Rs and the two official languages, a level of knowledge regarded as sufficient for semi-skilled work; secondary education was deliberately neglected because white labour was still able to meet the need for clerical, skilled, and administrative workers. Therefore, although the total number of black school pupils increased after the war, the percentage of secondary pupils of the total dropped from 1 in 11 in 1945 to 1 in 22 in 1961, with the decrease especially dramatic after the introduction of Bantu education.

Besides providing the appropriate schooling, Bantu education also served the interests of capital by deflecting the expense of creating an urban work-force in two ways. In the first place, when the burden of financing black schooling was transferred from the missions to the state in 1953, the state's contribution was fixed at £6.5 million, with the balance made up from the African general tax. As a result, annual per capita expenditure on black education decreased from R17,08 in 1953 to R12,46 in 1960, while expenditure on white students over the same period increased from R127,84 to R144,57 (for the Cape). A second, less direct, way in which the costs of producing and maintaining a literate work-force were kept down was by the migrant labour system. Bantu education, in conjunction with the pass laws, the labour bureau system, and housing regulations ensured that the costs of urbanization were borne not by capital or the state, but by the workers themselves. These measures contributed to the creation of an urban proletariat that was to a substantial extent still officially rural, and therefore in a weak position to demand social services like education.

How then did Shakespeare adjust to this schooling system? The teaching of English literature at South African schools in the 1950s continued along very similar lines to those followed in Britain at the same time and in pre-apartheid South Africa. For example, the 1951 'Proposed Syllabus in English as First Language' for the Cape repeats well-worn themes and phrases from the Arnold–Leavis cultural vocabulary:

The importance to the pupil of sound instruction in the mother-tongue cannot be over-estimated. It is his main means of communication with his fellow-men, and without it community life and civilisation would be impossible. It is the key to literature, the treasure-house of the wisdom, beauty and humour accumulated through the centuries by his race. It is the instrument by which men must carry on the activities of a democratic people, which demand intelligent participation in the social, the economic and every other sphere of public life.[31]

The sixth aim of teaching English was described as '[t]o introduce them, systematically, to the work and thoughts of great writers, with the aim, as they grow older, of training the imagination, developing taste and generally enriching their lives' (759), and to this end, students had to study four prescribed books in their final year of school, including a Shakespeare play. In describing literature as 'the treasure-house of . . . his race', and language as the facilitator of political participation, the syllabus slides together the teachers of Shakespeare (protectors of literature), and the architects of the state (guardians of 'intelligent participation in . . . public life').

Shakespeare is part of the state's ideological project, not in opposition to it, and the incorporation of the student mass into the apartheid social polity is to be effected in part by the study of English literature.

The spirit of the syllabus was followed in the schools, with Shakespeare's plays studied not as a critique of any state form, but as a body of facts to be memorized and as a lesson in the ultimate authority of the prevailing moral order. Examination questions continued to test students along the lines first established in Britain in the second half of the nineteenth century. The 1952 examination on *Antony and Cleopatra*, set by K. M. Hillhouse and moderated by Durrant, for example, is exemplary in its focus on the familiar areas of character–plot–theme:

1. (*a*) State clearly the causes of the quarrel between Antony and Cleopatra.
   (*b*) Give a character sketch of Antony.
2. Trace the part played by Octavius Caesar.
3. In the play, we witness Antony in conflict with Caesar, with his own baser nature, and with Cleopatra. Show this, pointing out the consequences in each case.[32]

At the end of the 1950s somewhat different types of question were set, with longer passages from the play cited and a more careful close reading of the text demanded from the candidates. The 1958 Cape Senior Certificate examination, for example, set out two passages from the play, and asked students the following:

19. Select one of the passages below, and use it to answer the following questions and requirements.
    (*a*) Name the speaker and describe the occasion on which the speech occurs.
    (*b*) What does the speech reveal about the speaker's character and of his state of mind at the time of speaking.
    (*c*) Discuss *three* different effective uses of imagery in the passage quoted, and explain why they are effective.
    (*d*) Explain in as few words as possible each of the *three* italicised phrases or short passages so as to show that you know its meaning in the context.[33]

Not surprisingly, study aids and the introductions and notes to school editions of the plays published in South Africa during this period seek to provide the pupil and teacher with the information needed to ease them through the examinations. They all provide some historical background on Elizabethan society and theatre, but here too the emphasis is on order rather than on dissent. J. L. du Plooy and V. H. Vaughan in their edition of *Macbeth* explain:

It was a period of development and prosperity, of adventure and discovery. England became the leading sea power in the world. Her fleets sailed the seven seas. The first English colony was established in the New World. England's wealth increased rapidly. The upper classes lived in luxury. The conditions of the common people were greatly improved. It was the golden age of poetry and drama in which Shakespeare played the supreme role.[34]

And P. de Munnik in her edition of *A Midsummer Night's Dream*, while conceding that there was some social turmoil, none the less insists that although 'Elizabeth's reign was by no means peaceful . . . it was orderly'.[35] Occasional insights into specific aspects of Elizabethan life were offered by other editors, with comparisons to the contemporary suggested. H. J. Oldendorf and H. Arguile, for example, in their edition of *The Tempest*, explain the Elizabethan fascination with witchcraft thus: 'Witchcraft and magic were probably as real to them as they are to most Africans to-day. Nations in their childhood tend to attribute all natural phenomena to the power of beings greater than men and to people the woods, the sea, the streams, with their mysterious beings.'[36]

The overwhelming weight of detail, however, is concerned with plot summary and character sketches. After setting out these superficial introductions to the Elizabethan age and establishing Shakespeare's pre-eminent genius, these editions furnish the reader with exhaustive plot summaries and character sketches. The character descriptions follow the long-established pattern of locating all responsibility for the action of the play exclusively with the characters themselves, and familiar prejudices are reproduced in the according of sympathy or disapprobation: in de Munnik's introduction to *The Tempest*, for example, Caliban is described as 'a brutish savage' and 'possessed of a certain low cunning', and Miranda as 'the incarnation of the Ideal Woman, gentle, obedient, yet with a will of her own'.[37]

Without exception, the combination of character and plot is read as moral fable, in which the triumph of order over chaos is celebrated. The most interesting version of this conclusion is that of I. S. Middleton and V. H. Vaughan's edition of *The Tempest*, who first quote at length from Gurrey's *Education and the Training of Teachers*:

In forming a concept of the characters, particularly in dramatic performance, the student stimulates his imagination and disciplines his attitudes towards the deeper meaning of the play; he begins to see the 'inevitableness of destiny' and the moral order that is so strong a part of life. . . . There can be no doubt that the reading and acting of these greater plays and many of the others provide the finest and most delectable education that can be prescribed.[38]

They then move on to explain what for them always threatens every moral order, and is therefore punished both in life and in Shakespeare's plays: it is a 'simple fact about human nature [that] it is by the heart and emotions that human beings are bound to one another . . . while the intellect is often the cause of their separation' (p. xxiv). Emotion can transcend intellectual differences, so 'a brilliant husband can get along amiably and lovingly with a wife much his intellectual inferior', and so too in *The Tempest*, the stories 'centred in the "warm family circle", [displaying] human heart and emotion' (p. xxiv) have a greater impact than more intellectual themes. Accordingly 'the emotional impact of a story lessens as the field selected moves further away from the focal point of the home' (p. xxiv). Against the emotionally vital regime of family, the amoral intellect. And more generally, against any form of centralizing authority (the state, the family, capital), the dissident impulse is to be policed and punished.

The extent and nature of the impact made by the plays on students is open to question. The school editions suggest some resistance. De Munnik, in the preface to her edition of *The Tempest*, acknowledges general antipathy to Shakespeare—'The very name Shakespeare seems to strike terror into the heart of the average reader'[39]—as do Du Plooy and Vaughan in their edition of *Macbeth*: 'Even amongst teachers there is a feeling that the time devoted to Shakespeare is . . . out of proportion to its real value to the student.'[40] The strategy for dealing with such opposition is uniform, namely to promise moral improvement as reward for studying Shakespeare, and again Middleton and Vaughan's justification provides the best example:

Count yourself fortunate . . . that you are about to have the opportunity of becoming acquainted with the work of one of the world's supreme geniuses, perhaps the greatest who ever lived. . . . The human mind absorbs impressions like blotting paper. That is why we should come in contact, in our literary studies, with what is fine and desirable. If you study Shakespeare eagerly and diligently, and with the object of enjoying him, almost certainly some of his magnificence and insight will brush off on you.[41]

What of course ensured that Shakespeare remained a part of the South African student's reading was less the general love of his work than the fact that examinations about him had to be passed, a fact certain educationalists took to be an obstacle to enjoying him. I. J. Kriel, for example, asks 'whether the school English course is meant to awaken the student's interest in and love of English literature, or whether it is meant to be nothing more than an exercise in memory training'.[42] Further harm is done to nurturing a sincere love of literature in South African students by the selection of prescribed texts, which in general 'have hardly changed since grandpa was a boy' (26), and as a result are hugely out of date. These constraints place an even bigger onus on the teacher, who Kriel believes should still be able to 'fan the sparks of the student's imagination to a steady flame that will illumine the path of his early cultural development' (27). Similar doubts about the success of the cultural mission of English literature are expressed by J. B. Gardener, where he notes that given a free choice the vast majority of students prefer to read sports books, with reading-lists indicating that 'the widest read South African author in English is [cricketer] Graeme Pollock!'[43]

The pattern in white schools of seeing Shakespeare's message as broadly consistent with the wider educational project in South Africa was repeated in black schools. In the 1950s black students completing a secondary education wrote the same examinations as their white counterparts, though with only 0.07 per cent (938 out of 1,338,424) of the total enrolment of black students in 1958 in the final year, the number reading Shakespeare was negligible. In 1959 the first black students started writing examinations set by the Department of Bantu Education, and the new syllabuses showed a dilution of the 'standards' established for white schools. English teaching made adjustments to suit the demands of the different racially constituted education departments, with state notions of black urbanization at times filtering into examination questions: in the same year that white students under Durrant's ultimate authority were writing about *Antony and Cleopatra*, the Native Standard VI English paper invited students to answer the following:

> 2(1) A neighbour's goats are constantly breaking into your garden. You have told him about this, but he does nothing. Write a letter of complaint to the headman of your location.[44]

The newspaper of the Non-European Unity Movement, *Ikhwesi Lomso*, records the removal of Shakespeare from the list of prescribed texts for the Junior Certificate syllabus, and observes with despair that '[t]he clouds of darkness and ignorance are rapidly engulfing our children as one by one the lights of learning are snuffed out'.[45]

Fears that Shakespeare would disappear completely from Bantu education syllabuses ultimately did not materialize, and ten years later the official publication of the Department, the *Bantu Education Journal*, provided guides for teachers to assist them in teaching the plays. These guides, as with the more detailed study aids designed for white students, do little to announce Shakespeare's opposition to racism. The author of the guides, D. N. Young, sets out the aim of studying Shakespeare as 'to enrich the pupil's knowledge of English, by exposing him to the rich beauty, vivid imagery and great sense of the superlative poetry of the texts',[46] and then summarizes what the pupils should know about the plays: the action and plot; the meanings of words; the background; and the dramatic dimension. Young concedes that 'Bantu pupils find great difficulty in seeing London society as it was [since] their own experience of life is far removed from all this' (32), but none the less believes that the enthusiastic teacher can overcome this and still convey to students that '[n]o work, except the Bible, has so universal [an] appeal' (32).

In a second article, Young reiterates the central importance of the content, but continues: 'What is of more permanent value is understanding, interpreting and appreciating the beauty, meaning and reality of the style, technique and expressions of ideas, facts and emotions of the characters who go to make up the content.'[47] The skill to develop in order to appreciate this more permanent truth is paraphrasing, and the rest of the article demonstrates how to translate Julius Caesar into modern English. Above a photograph of black students doing a gymnastics display entitled 'Mens sana in corpore sano', Young concludes by summarizing the procedure for dealing with the main speeches in the plays: explain the context of the passage; get the class to rewrite the original in their own words; read answers aloud and discuss them; provide a correct version on the blackboard; and finally, get them to correct each other's work from the teacher's answer on the board. Not as long-winded as experts writing for the white schools, Young's two short articles reflect the differences in how Shakespeare was packaged for black students: less freedom to speculate about character and theme, less need to demonstrate close-reading techniques, and a strong emphasis on being able to summarize the details of the plot. And the teaching methods recommended also reflect the enormous pressures on teachers at black schools, with Young's notes as much a survivor's guide to the examinations as a truncated version of the Shakespeare mission.[48]

A final development of importance in the teaching of Shakespeare in the 1950s was the beginning of annual Shakespeare productions at Maynardville in Cape Town. Started by Cape Town actresses René Ahrenson and Cecilia Sonnenberg, and with the help of London producer Leslie French, the first show, *The Taming of the Shrew*, opened in January 1956. It soon became the pattern for special performances to be reserved for schoolchildren, and in the choice of play, wherever possible preference was given to the school set work of the particular year. The *Maynardville Tenth Anniversary Programme* notes that the schoolchildren's 'appreciation has been unbounded',[49] and La Rochelle headmistress Miss D. C. le Roux agrees: 'It is impossible to try to sketch in a few words what these performances have meant and still mean to schoolchildren all over the Western Cape.'[50] Anecdotal testimony, both from actors who have survived performances for schools, and from schoolchildren themselves, suggests rather more mixed audience responses over the years.

Money for Maynardville Shakespeare productions came from various company sponsors, and from the Cape Town municipality. In an intriguing instance of Shakespeare in the service of capital, the advertisements in the *Tenth Anniversary Programme* link the company advertisements and a Shakespeare quote, so Koo Fruit juices are accompanied by 'Feed him with apricocks and dawberries, With purple grapes, green figs and mulberries' (24); Peter Stuyvesant cigarettes by 'All the world's a stage' (22); and Monatic Alba men's clothing by 'Apparel oft proclaims the man' (21). The connection between Shakespeare and municipal funding, however, was rather more difficult to sustain, as in the 1960s apartheid legislation laid down that the plays be performed before racially separate audiences. In debating the issue in council, Mr Gulzar Khan argued that 'if Shakespeare had been alive, he would have banned his actors from playing under the conditions of a segregated audience'.[51] Mr Khan's motion to oppose any application for a permit to have racially segregated audiences at Maynardville was defeated by thirty votes to eight (there were seven Coloured councillors). In effect, the white majority in council decided that Shakespeare could live with racially segregated audiences in much the same way that educational policy-makers decided that Shakespeare could survive, even thrive, within a racially segregated education system.

For those responsible for the teaching of Shakespeare at South African high schools, the relation then between apartheid and Shakespeare was therefore given little direct consideration. Shakespeare was for the most part a taken-for-granted component of the English syllabus which the philistine mass of students had to learn in order to pass examinations. The opposition between a humane English literary culture and a racist state constructed by Durrant *et al.* did not filter down to the high schools. Instead, the opposition in South African high-school English class-rooms was between Shakespeare, defender of social order and supporter of the state, and the resisting student population. Again English teachers play a mediating function, but in this case they are acting for the state and against the excluded masses. And Shakespeare is no longer a spiritual resource in the fight against apartheid; rather he is an important cultural weapon of a state education system dedicated to the production of a respectful and obedient workforce.

Through Shakespeare's Africa

I have used Shakespeare here as an emblem of English culture, symbolizing a contradictory cluster of values that, on the one hand, purport to be entirely opposed to apartheid, and, on the other, fit quite comfortably within the apartheid education system. To these two versions of the relation between apartheid and Shakespeare might be added a third, one which sees rather more complicated connections between English liberalism and Afrikaner racism than the opposition construed at the universities or the coherence assumed at the schools. Produced in radical political journals of the 1950s and 1960s, this third version attempts to understand the relation between the English cultural mission and the South African social polity.

The arguments about the relation between Shakespeare and apartheid can be organized in two loose groups. The first builds on the tradition of Plaatje and Dhlomo, insisting on a Shakespeare opposed to racism. In many respects, the arguments of this group repeat those of the liberal critics, deflecting them only very slightly to the left. The second group, much smaller in number, refuses the opposition, and argues that the relation between Afrikaner racism and English humanism should be rethought, with the uncritical exoneration of the latter in particular to be interrogated.

There are a number of variations on the way in which Shakespeare is constructed as the positive pole opposed to Afrikaner nationalism. The first versions are to be found in the work of the writers associated with the popular magazine, *Drum*.[52] Producing principally journalism and short stories, certain of these writers also wrote pieces of literary criticism. Most notable was Ezekiel Mphahlele, whose book *The African Image* examined literary representations of Africa and Africans. Predominantly educated at English mission schools, a schooling which involved immersion in liberal, assimilationist ideals and solid doses of Shakespeare, they strove in the 1950s to narrate their urban milieu and the shocking betrayals enacted by the apartheid state. They used Shakespeare variously, as opponent of apartheid, as witness to their sense of outrage, and as universal genius with prescient insights into the turbulent world of black South Africa.

Peter Abrahams in his autobiography, *Tell Freedom*, describes his first encounter with Shakespeare as an illiterate 11-year-old working in a Johannesburg bookshop. In the first act of kindness a white person had ever shown him in his life, 'the short-sighted Jewish girl'[53] who worked with him read to him from *Lamb's Tales from Shakespeare*. The effect on Abrahams was profound:

The story of Othello jumped at me and invaded my heart and mind as the young woman read. I was transported to the land where the brave Moor lived and loved and destroyed his love. (149)

The brief incident inspired Abrahams to go to school, and within a short time Shakespeare's world became for him a spiritually sustaining alternative to the deprivation and hardship of black South Africa:

With Shakespeare and poetry, a new world was born. New dreams, new desires, a new self-consciousness, was born. I desired to know myself in terms of the new standards set by these books. I lived in two worlds, the world of Vrededorp and the world of these books. And, somehow, both were equally real. Each was a potent force in my life, compelling. My heart and mind were in turmoil. Only the victory of the one or the other could bring me peace. (161)

The opposition Abrahams establishes here between a white settler culture that dominates and impoverishes black people (Vrededorp), and one that provides the route to an enlarged self-consciousness (these books), is not new : both Plaatje and Dhlomo had wrestled with forms of this contradiction. For Abrahams, no synthesis of apartheid and Shakespeare is possible; only the triumph of one or the other can produce psychic coherence.

In his article 'Through Shakespeare's Africa', Can Themba shares Abrahams's sense of Shakespeare's universal humanism, but differs in emphasizing the strong similarities between Sophiatown and Elizabethan London: 'Shakespeare would have understood without the interpolations of the scholars, and in this wise the world of Shakespeare reaches out a fraternal hand to the throbbing heart of Africa.'[54] The characters and situations dramatized in Shakespeare's plays are closely echoed in South Africa: 'In the Johannesburg of the 1950's there was the King of Jive, huge but electric Dumizulu. In the London of the 1580's, there was jolly old Falstaff, the merriest ruffian in literature' (151); and contemporary versions of the conversation between King Henry, Michael Williams, and John Bates in *King Henry V*, iv. i are repeated in shebeens in Soweto. But it is in the fate of Othello that Themba discerns the strongest parallels. He advises his readers to note the example of Othello closely:

Cultivate yourself into a superior being; grapple with something in their world and succeed: become a scientist, a literatus, talk as if the highbrow things come naturally to you: a theory, a poem, grand passion. . . . It is just this that Othello went and done. Worse still, he made himself indispensable to the state. It is this, also, that the urban African is continually doing. (153)

What affronted Venetian society most, however, was that Othello wooed a *beautiful* white woman, something Themba sees reflected in attitudes in his own milieu. He observes (uncritically) that 'the boys in Johannesburg would say: "Nay, man, Boeta Can, you got yourself a Jewess that's got background and bodice . . . [n]ot one of those weatherbeaten crows from Fordsburgville"'(154). Themba does not see Shakespeare as an anti-racist in the way Abrahams does, for in his conclusion, he expresses some regret that Shakespeare does not extend his sympathies to Shylock, choosing instead to join 'the carping, hounding, hate-fearing, anti-semitic rabble to make sport of the Jew' (154).

Bloke Modisane's autobiography, *Blame me on History*, takes Themba's comparisons one step further by using the words of

Shakespeare's characters in order to explain his own psychological processes, and especially in order to justify his often angry responses to the injustices he sees around him. For example, he quotes Laertes' graveside speech to convey his outrage at police violence against black protesters on a peaceful march;[55] his own feelings of exclusion from the riches of white South African society he likens to Othello's ambivalent acceptance in Venetian society (168); and Brutus' dilemma over whether he as a man of peace should use violence to defeat tyranny resonates strongly for Modisane because '[l]ike Brutus I am haunted by the immediacy, the direct presence of blood between freedom and oppression' (231). Modisane recognizes that his interest in Shakespeare and Western culture generally enabled friendships with certain white individuals (253), but he remained deeply conscious of the contradictions such interests produced:

[I]t shall be considered an impertinence for me to arrogate to myself a pretension for Western musical forms, art and drama. I am not ready for them; an early plunge might leave me bewildered. But I am a freak, I do presume an appreciation of Western music, art, drama and philosophy; I can rationalise as well as they, and using their own set of assumptions, I presume myself civilised. . . . [I]f I am a freak it should not be interpreted as a failure of their education for a Caliban, but a miscalculation of history.   (178–9)

Though Modisane therefore saw Shakespeare as a possession of the West, he appropriated him in order to explain the violent world of Sophiatown to his readers.[56]

A second tradition seeking to connect radical politics and literature found expression in journals of the Western Cape-based Non-European Unity Movement. The principal focus was on South African writers like Harold Bloom (see below), Sarah Gertrude Millin,[57] and on socialists like Bertolt Brecht.[58] But again, there were efforts to grapple with the dominant European tradition, the most extended one being Carter Ebrahim's 1952 essay 'The Drama and Society' in the Forum Club journal, *Discussion*.[59]

Not lacking in ambition, Ebrahim undertakes no less than a history of Western drama, relying on a loose interpretation of Maxim Gorky's *Aesthetics and Cultural History* in order to establish two criteria for judging drama. The first is the extent to which the drama is connected to its community:

Where its struggle was open and intense, the drama took on heroic proportions. And where again, its vision was blurred by false loyalties to power groups, its creativity pined and died. [Great dramatists] firmly planted their feet in the life-giving soil of the people's soul, found strength to wage a mightier battle, and they are the ones that stand out among the rest.[60]

And the second criterion, less clearly elaborated than the first, is a commitment to 'critical realism', to 'showing the age its "particular form and pressure"' (31). Shakespeare satisfies these two criteria to a greater extent than any other writer because the '"classless environment" of his, this world of the theatre . . . enabled Shakespeare to view his "external ambient" from an unprejudiced vantage point' (24). He concludes:

In presenting the truth that true heroism lies in warring against all forces inimical to humanity as a whole, he created a truly heroic drama. While . . . distilling out the essential qualities of an epoch, pointing out the flaws in its social structure and consequently the degree of poverty of its culture, Shakespeare also held the 'mirror up to nature,' reflected i.e. those eternal qualities of life . . . which would carry humanity forward to its highest approximation. (25)

With very few exceptions (pre-Stalinist Russian playwrights and Irish writers attached to the Irish National Theatre), the record since Shakespeare is dismal, with most dramatists no more than 'panderers to the whims of power groups' (26). Turning to South Africa in his conclusion, Ebrahim asserts that in the absence of any indigenous drama, 'anything that attains to an acceptable standard in technique, at least, has to be imported', and that this absence continues because the 'socio-economic structure deprives the masses of the oppressed people from even the rudiments of the forms of cultural expression' (30–1). The most urgent need in this context therefore is for an 'anti-Herrenvolk theatre [using] plays as a propaganda medium . . . to contribute in no small measure to the emancipation of the people' (31). Shakespeare for Ebrahim is therefore a champion of all oppressed groups, and until South Africa produces a similar figure, he remains the most important ally in challenging 'the Herrenvolk'.

The second group of essays is much smaller. Indeed, there are just two very short reviews that I would like to refer to, both of which suggest a different relation between Shakespeare and apartheid, a relation complicated by unacknowledged complicities and particularly an ignorance of class dynamics. The first is a review of Harold Bloom's novel *Episode*, written by 'Impressed' for the Non-European Unity Movement journal the *Torch*. Bloom's novel is written in the spirit of Paton, and as such is ideally suited for inclusion in the tradition of Shakespeare-loving, apartheid-hating English liberal culture. The reviewer, however, resists this path, and concludes in critical terms:

For Bloom the *Herrenvolk* are Kruger, Potgieter, Strydom and Verwoerd and not equally at least, Rhodes, Smuts and Strauss. He does not see the role of Britain at all. . . . Bloom shares this weakness with Paton and his friend Huddleston, who is one of the people to whom the book is dedicated. . . . Bloom's political myopia—he is a Liberal of the English school, if one may call it that—is coupled with a complete lack of understanding of the basic economic pattern of South Africa.[61]

In identifying the convergence of English and Afrikaner interests in the context of this short piece, the reviewer interrupts deeply embedded assumptions in South African political thought and literary culture, and directs the reader to an alternative binary, namely that between capital and labour. Since both Shakespeare and Verwoerd are included in the former term, this new opposition undermines the dominant ones between English and Afrikaans, black and white.

The second piece is from a writer in the Congress tradition. In the 1950s the ANC and its affiliates had a number of journals which protested against the establishment of the apartheid state, and all of them carried occasional articles on literary criticism and culture. A variety of subjects were covered, including Olive Schreiner,[62] Robert Tressell,[63] Nadine Gordimer,[64] Langston Hughes,[65] and Alan Paton.[66] However, articles were not confined to figures loosely in sympathy with the anti-apartheid struggle, and Sam Kahn, in an edition of *Advance*, wrote a carefully argued critique of one of the heroes of the established literary canon, T. S. Eliot.

Having found himself sharing the same passenger ship from Southampton to Cape Town, Kahn decided to write an open letter to Eliot, attacking the famous poet for 'his reactionary, anti-semitic, people-hating verse and prose'.[67] Quoting examples of anti-Semitism from Eliot's own poetry, Kahn then attacks Eliot's high regard for Ezra Pound, asking: 'By what right does anyone classify amongst the great poets the author of the views that this elite Fascist embodies in his work?' (4). Disgusted by Eliot's 'mysticism and misanthropy', Kahn then contrasts Eliot's élitist views on education with those of Milton, whose voice for him is 'more authentic of England' (4). His concluding judgement could not be more damning: 'T. S. Eliot's views are those adopted and being applied by Dr. Verwoerd and Dr. Eiselen' (4).

While Kahn leaves a space for reinventing the Shakespeare–apartheid opposition in the form of a Milton–Verwoerd split, he none the less articulates the seldom expressed complicity of at least a strand of official English literary culture in the ideology of apartheid, a complicity university English teachers at the time ignored in pursuing poetic allusions in 'Prufrock'. In a similar spirit to the Bloom review, Kahn challenges certain received truisms, introducing into literary criticism difficult questions as to how the socio-political and the cultural connect.

An African Dialectic?

Writing about the Negritude movement in *Myth, Literature and the African World*, Wole Soyinka notes the central place of dialectical method in the Western philosophical tradition, and questions its deployment in Africa:

Its reference points took far too much colouring from European ideas even while its Messiahs pronounced themselves fanatically African. In attempting to refute the evaluation to which black reality had been subjected, Negritude adopted the Manichean tradition of European thought and inflicted it on a culture which is most radically anti-Manichean. It not only accepted the dialectical structure of European ideological confrontations but borrowed from the very components of its racist syllogism.[68]

For Soyinka, to reverse the binaries between European virtue and African degeneracy so that Africa occupies the positive term is to remain trapped within a limiting Western problematic.

In South Africa, the dialectical habit of thought deviates along a different route, with the opposition Soyinka describes between Europe and Africa complicated by the existence of two distinct colonizing forces. The extremes are defined as being between Afrikaner racist and English humanist, with Africa for the most part written out of the encounter. For some, the English humanist intervenes on behalf of the dispossessed Africans, and for others Afrikaner racist and English humanist combine to ensure their continued subordination. Only when the terms of this opposition are refused—as in the criticism of Bloom's novel and of Kahn—do (very small) cracks emerge in the critical discourses of the 1950s. Even then, the new binaries (like capital and labour) introduced to challenge the old ones also derive from the West, and in themselves therefore cannot satisfy Soyinka's fantasy of voices emerging outside the hegemony of Western power.

6

Travelling Theory: To the Present

Introduction

In earlier chapters, some attempt to be comprehensive in describing the principal texts and actors in the history of South African English studies was made. There is no such attempt in this chapter, although some sense of the sheer volume of recent critical endeavour is indicated in the endnotes. Besides Shakespeare criticism, which is again a central concern, the criticism I am interested in here is that which is designated, and which designates itself, as radical critical theory. I am particularly concerned to explore how this radical theory has travelled to South Africa in the last twenty-five years. This focus is *not* based on any illusion that radical forms of criticism are dominant or likely to become so in English studies in either Britain and the US or in South Africa. What it is based on is the conviction that this criticism represents an interesting departure from previous formulations of English literature's social function.

Interest in how theory travels has grown in recent years, both in the US and in South Africa. Two key essays from US-based academics have been particularly influential. The first is Edward Said's 'Traveling Theory', which reflects on the transfer of revolutionary ideas from contexts of violent revolt to ones of more polite disagreement. Said details how the concept totality changes in meaning as it moves from Georg Lukács's usage in revolutionary Budapest in 1919, to Lucien Goldmann's modified sense in Paris after the Second World War, and to Raymond Williams's redefinition in Cambridge in 1970. He concludes that 'theory has to be grasped in the place and the time out of which it emerges as a part of that time, working in and for it, responding to it';[1] failure to recognize this can result in theoretical breakthroughs being contained, as they congeal into new orthodoxies no longer in tension with the context that produced them.[2]

The second essay is Adrienne Rich's 'Notes toward a Politics of Location'. Looking back at a time when she would have 'quoted without second thought Virginia Woolf's statement in *Three Guineas* that "... [a]s a woman my country is the whole world"',[3] Rich turns to a more materialist frame in insisting that the first question in *every* instance should be: 'When, where, and under what conditions has the statement been true?' (214). Travels to Cuba and Nicaragua led Rich to understand what it means to write from within the borders of an imperialist superpower; she started to grasp 'the meaning of North America as a location which had also shaped my ways of seeing and my ideas of who and what was important, a location for which I was responsible' (219–20). Noting how the struggles of women in the developing world, including South Africa, Lebanon, and Peru, had been 'unrecognised as theory in action by white Western feminist thought' (229), Rich's conclusion regarding radical Western theory's status as privileged export is scathing:

In my white North American world they have tried to tell me that this [Third World black] woman—politicised by intersecting forces—doesn't think and reflect on her life ... [t]hat only certain kinds of people can make theory; that the white educated mind is capable of formulating everything; that white middle-class feminism can know 'all women'; that only when a white mind formulates is the formulation to be taken seriously.   (230)

Conscious then that her 'feelings are not *the* center of feminism' (230), Rich opens the way for an expanded sense of 'theory' in which those outside Western academies might theorize in their own terms, rather than waiting for the arrival of metropolitan travellers and their theories.[4]

Writing from powerful centres traditionally associated with the production and export of theory, Said and Rich in different ways question what it means for theory to travel, with Rich in particular doubtful about theory journeying from the North to the South. In recent years, certain South African critics, writing from a specific periphery traditionally associated with the consumption and import of theory, have also assumed a more critical stance with regard to this transaction. This has been framed with particular urgency in the context of women's studies. Cecily Lockett, in the key paper for a special issue of the journal *Current Writing*, 'Feminism and Writing in South Africa', asks:

The question that needs to be considered by feminist critics in South Africa is whether these [Western] discourses can be imported into the South African context, or whether our special circumstances require a different kind of feminist project.[5]

Lockett distinguishes different strands of Western feminist thought, preferring what she takes to be the more politically engaged Anglo-American tradition to the (for her) more élitist and middle-class French tradition. Respondents to the paper for the most part accept the alternatives suggested by Lockett, with some offering a spirited defence of French feminism (Pamela Ryan) and others suggesting a more accommodating attitude to post-structuralism (Jenny de Reuck and David Schalkwyk). Sisi Maqagi, however, in terms that confirm Rich's desire for non-Western voices to announce themselves, refuses Lockett's initiatives and asks instead:

If the works of Ellen Kuzwayo, Boitumelo Mofokeng, Nise Malange, Gcina Mhlope are 'part of a coherent critical paradigm' why should Lockett seem to be excluding them from the process of theorising about their own work? It seems to me that the prerogative to theorise about black women's work should not be snatched out of their hands, even if they seem rather tardy about it.[6]

Resistant to the idea of accepting intellectual gifts from the (potentially treacherous) traveller, Maqagi chooses rather indigenous resources gathered together as part of 'the collective effort [that] has to emerge from within the ranks of those whose life is theorised' (24).

Recent debates in South African Shakespeare studies have also differed over what theories from the metropolis should be cultivated. Martin Orkin, in *Shakespeare against Apartheid*, has no hesitation in encouraging a generous reception for the British cultural materialists and the US new historicists:

It seems to me that in the work of these critics and others like them, the future of Shakespeare studies in South Africa should especially lie. It is my hope that the present book ... will encourage students more quickly to take up these critical works and to choose from those theoretical paths which they suggest. In so doing we may read the Shakespeare text in ways that no longer subtly encourage a passive acceptance of the apartheid system but rather in ways that promote more active awareness of the possibility of alternatives to it.[7]

If the correct theory is admitted to South African Shakespeare studies, the teaching of Shakespeare might form part of a pedagogical critique of the apartheid state. Orkin's fierce critic Lawrence Wright argues that cultural materialists and new historicists offer nothing particularly novel; they belong to a continuous tradition, 'which derives from the revisionary metaphysic of Matthew Arnold and passes through Bradley, Richards, Eliot, Leavis, Williams, Eagleton and Belsey'.[8] What unites this tradition is their shared assumption that 'the importance of literature resides in its relevance to their own vital concerns, their deepest 'religious impulse', and, against this tradition, Wright proposes 'a tradition of historical scholarship' (73–4) exemplified by Helen Gardner. Functioning as intellectual customs officials, South African critics thus seek to control the entry of foreign theory into the country. For Lockett, the decision is over how much Anglo-American and how much French theory should be admitted, with the latter obliged to pay for expensive visas. For Orkin, cultural materialists and new historicists are welcomed warmly, whereas for Wright older guests like Gardner are the more cherished.

Within this nexus of production and consumption, emission and reception of critical theory, I am concerned with two moves: with how theory has travelled within the West before being taken up in the English departments of Anglo-American universities, and with how that reformulated body of theory has then been imported into institutions in South Africa. In tracing these moves, I offer a critical commentary of the tendency in South Africa to privilege the analytical categories of the West, with writers summarizing the most recent European or US intellectual fashion, and then applying the summarized set of terms to a South African setting. The possibility should at least be entertained that the radical theorizing about Western revolutions might, if privileged uncritically at a different time and place, in fact function in a containing and reactionary fashion. The challenge then is to resist the reflex of installing the products of Western cultural projects— including the 'radical Shakespeare'—as *automatically* having the same political meaning and resonance in neo-colonial contexts.

My analysis is organized around the travels of one particular 'theory', noting its origins in France, and reflecting on how its meaning changes in travelling to Britain, to the US, and finally, to South Africa. The 'theory' I have in mind is associated with Roland Barthes's famous essay 'The Death of the Author'. Barthes defines the text as 'a multi-dimensional space in which a variety of writings, none of them original, blend and clash';[9] the multiplicity of writings in the text are focused not in the author, but in the reader: 'a text's unity lies not in its origin but in its destination' (148). For Barthes, seeing writing in this way represents a challenge not only to literary orthodoxies, but to all authority: 'In precisely this way literature (it would be better from now on to say *writing*), by refusing to assign a "secret", an ultimate meaning, to the text (and to the world as text), liberates what may be called an anti-theological activity that is truly revolutionary since to refuse to fix meaning is, in the end, to refuse God and his hypostases—reason, science, law' (147). This 'theory', i.e. that there is no transcendental signified, has become in some respects a commonplace assumption for many Anglo-American literary critics in the two decades since it was written; whether the revolutionary associations Barthes conferred upon the notion of semantic indeterminacy have travelled too is the question pursued.[10]

In the Introduction, I distinguished between the colonial Shakespeare taught in South Africa, and the radical 'Shakespeare' taught in Anglo-American universities. Much of the credit for adding scare quotes to the name 'Shakespeare' can be given to Barthes's essay, with Shakespeare, the most authorized of all authors, placed under fresh critical scrutiny in the light of Barthes's attempted (theoretical) murder. Extending the metaphor of international assassination plots, the question then is: has French theory killed off the English Hero, exposing him as the invention of a 300-year imperialist public relations exercise? Or has the addition of theory and history to Shakespeare studies instead revitalized the ageing icon?

From France to Britain

The direct contribution of European thought to British institutional academic culture before 1970 was largely conservative. Perry Anderson identifies a number of *émigré* intellectuals —Ludwig Wittgenstein, Karl Popper, Isaiah Berlin, Lewis Namier, and others—who took up residence in Britain and bolstered the conservative formations of their respective disciplines. What they all failed to do, according to Anderson, was to provide a theory of the social totality to fill the 'absent centre'[11] around which the various disciplines clustered in unconnected intellectual endeavour.

English studies, while not entirely without aid from the Continent (George Steiner fits the pattern outlined by Anderson), managed quite well on its own home-grown blend of empiricism and liberal humanism. Foreign theoretical thought was not welcomed, as F. R. Leavis demonstrated in his exchange with René Wellek in *Scrutiny* (March and June, 1937), and radical theory was positively opposed.[12] Although *Scrutiny* had ceased to publish in 1953, its imperatives continued to hold sway through organs like *The Use of English*, the seven-volume *Pelican Guide to English Literature*, and C. B. Cox and A. E. Dyson's *Critical Quarterly*. It would, however, be inaccurate to exaggerate the role of the Cambridge English School to the exclusion of other actors, since journals like F. W. Bateson's *Essays in Criticism* also played their part. Indeed, Bateson's arguments about how the teaching of the national literature might create democratic individuals exemplify the liberal ambitions of English teachers during this period: he anticipated that, if correctly pursued, English studies was 'destined in time to become the educational centre in English-speaking democracies'.[13]

Shakespeare too owed little at this stage to theories from abroad, continuing along lines securely laid down by English critics a century before. Surveying changes in Shakespeare criticism, Kenneth Muir observes that 'it would be wrong to assume that modern criticism supersedes that of early periods. Knight adds something to Bradley, but Bradley has still to be read.'[14] And in a more recent overview of Shakespeare criticism, John Drakakis, less indulgently, also stresses the continuities from Bradley to the 1980s:

But the Bradleian conception of dramatic character has remained very much at the centre of critical concern. . . . Although there have been minor changes of emphasis from time to time, this line of Shakespeare criticism remains firmly committed to the idealistic assertion that 'consciousness' precedes action, and that dramatic character constitutes axiomatically a unified subject of consciousness.[15]

There were one or two books on Shakespeare that challenged this approach, the best known being Arnold Kettle's 1964 collection *Shakespeare in a Changing World*, which claimed to be predicated on the materialist assumption that 'the nature and value of Shakespeare's work is inseparable from the myriad human developments—social, artistic, political, religious, scientific—of his time'.[16] However, such interventions remained marginal within university English literary culture, and they also made no discernible impression on the teaching of literature at schools. Examining Shakespeare's position in secondary education in the 1970s, Derek Longhurst concludes that '[c]ontrary to much academic opinion, A. C. Bradley is not dead; O and A-level examination papers still blend character assessment with analysis of imagery, themes and "theatrical effect"—all to be extracted from close reading of the texts.'[17]

At the end of the 1960s the critical consensus at British universities broke up under a combination of pressures. Universities became sites of conflict as a range of political movements—the women's movement, the anti-Vietnam War campaign, the Campaign for Nuclear Disarmament, and others—enjoyed sympathetic support among the expanding student body. The dissonance between these confrontational political discourses and those associated with the contemplation of literary classics was compounded by the fact that in the decades after the war the number of students had quadrupled, and these new students were drawn largely from outside the traditional élites. Often perceived by the institutions as 'inadequate', they placed fresh demands on the English literary establishment, as they responded ambivalently, and at times with hostility, to the received dispensation of great works.

The impact of these changes upon English studies in Britain might be conveyed by reference to two texts. Firstly, the response of the status quo is nicely captured in Dyson's editorial of the spring 1969 edition of *Critical Quarterly*:

If Arnold were to return in 1969 . . . he would be horrified to discover anarchy subverting the temple of culture itself. What would he make of the Jacobinism rampant in our educational theory, or of the spectacle of universities becoming the new home of the mob? What would he make of the inroads made by romantic egotism upon disciplined learning, or of the theory that 'self-fulfilment' is the chief end for which education exists?[18]

The fears of imminent anarchy were widely shared, and precipitated the rise of a new right hostile to the pluralist and democratic impulses announced by figures like Bateson. The principal forum for this revitalized fraction was the series of *Black Papers* published in the 1960s and 1970s, which argued in general for the reintroduction of élitist educational procedures that inducted a privileged few into the secluded contemplation of high culture.

However, this was not the only response, as there were many members of the mob identified by Dyson who did not see the impact of political protest on the teaching of English literature in quite the same way. The contributors to Trevor Pateman's 1972 collection *Counter Course* all experienced the atmosphere of rebellion as profoundly liberating. They insist on the connections between intellectual production in the universities and the reproduction of an exploitative socio-economic order, and further, that radical ideas democratically circulated in educational institutions have the capacity to transform existing hierarchies of exclusion in society. In the introduction to *Counter Course*, the euphoric editor argues:

our ideas, in so far as they show the mechanisms of production of ideology and the social functioning of higher education, could inform a wider struggle which does not accept to fight on a terrain defined by the boundaries of the higher educational institution, but rather aims at a society in which that boundary will itself be destroyed—which implies the destruction of the institution.[19]

And in the essay in the collection on English literature, Joe Spriggs vigorously attacks English faculties and departments for privileging the 'cultural patterns of the middle and upper classes . . . down to O-level size',[20] while at the same time ignoring the culture and achievements of the working classes. To break out of the élitism and obscurantism of traditional English studies, Spriggs recommends using a number of British socialist historians and critics, including George Thompson and Christopher Caudwell.

It was into this context that Barthes's ideas travelled in the 1970s, intersecting with other European currents of thought, and providing the British left with intellectual resources to supplement indigenous radical traditions. Raymond Williams's experience of encountering this long-invisible tradition of radical thought for the first time was typical:

I felt the excitement of contact with more new Marxist work: the later work of Lukács, the later work of Sartre, the developing work of Goldmann and Althusser, the variable and developing syntheses of Marxism and some forms of structuralism. At the same time, within this significant new activity, there was further access to older work, notably that of the Frankfurt School (in its most significant period of the twenties and thirties) and especially the work of Walter Benjamin; the extraordinarily original work of Antonio Gramsci; and, as a decisive element of a sense of the tradition, newly translated work of Marx and especially the *Grundrisse*.[21]

Journals like *Screen* and *New Left Review*, and critics like Williams, Terry Eagleton, Stuart Hall, and Terence Hawkes (via the New Accents series), played a central role in overseeing the popularization of this Continental theory, bringing out books and articles that made these ideas accessible to British undergraduates.[22]

The year 1968 has come to signal a point of fundamental transition: before 1968 the study of literature was organized by an Anglophile liberal fraction of the ruling class; after 1968 a new self-consciously heroic generation looked to Continental thought in order to challenge that hegemony. The editors of the Essex Conference in the 1970s and 1980s sought via their conferences to provide an 'international forum for left literary debate',[23] arguing in their publication *Literature, Politics and Theory* that the 'global conjuncture which has come to be known as "1968" . . . gave shape to the project represented by the essays in this volume' (p. ix). Colin McCabe, in his collection *Broken English*, draws together a selection of '[t]his brave new work',[24] and similarly identifies 1968 and the French thinkers associated with it as the 'original inspiration' (3) for continuing intellectual assaults in Britain on the traditional assumptions and practices of English studies. And most recently, Richard Wilson, in his introduction to *New Historicism and Renaissance Drama*, argues that Althusser and Foucault's relocating of 'the dynamo of history'[25] from economics to ideology and discourse was precipitated by the events of 1968 in Paris, and that this shift has since enabled a wealth of alternative Shakespeare criticism under the banner of new historicism.

In Renaissance studies, the challenge to canonical texts and readings was postponed slightly, with major studies drawing on the new critical alternatives only emerging in the 1980s. In Britain, the most influential texts have included Lisa Jardine's *Still Harping on Daughters*, Jonathan Dollimore's *Radical Tragedy*, Malcolm Evans's *Signifying Nothing*, and Catherine Belsey's *The Subject of Tragedy*, and collections edited by Drakakis (*Alternative Shakespeares*), and Dollimore and Sinfield (*Political Shakespeare*). Dollimore, in his introduction to *Political Shakespeare*, defines his project as pursued in the spirit of 'cultural materialism', understood as 'a combination of historical context, theoretical method, political commitment and textual analysis'.[26]

Sinfield argues, in *Faultlines*, that literature has been made politically agreeable by the following three strategies:

selecting the canon to feature suitable texts, interpreting these texts strenuously so that awkward aspects are explained away, and insinuating political implications as alleged formal properties (such as irony and balance). (21)

It is these strategies that have contributed to the creation of the establishment Shakespeare. There are, however, two ways of undermining this figure of authority. The first is indebted to Barthes's attack on the 'Author', and involves placing the text in its contexts:

thus [repudiating] the supposed transcendence of literature, seeking rather to understand it as a cultural intervention produced initially within a specific set of practices . . . and seeing it also as re-produced subsequently in other historical conditions. (22)

This strategy thus self-consciously undermines Shakespeare's claims to transcendent authority, offering instead historical explanations of how Shakespeare has over a long period been produced. The second strategy is to 'blatantly [rework] the authoritative text so that it is forced to yield, against the grain, explicitly oppositional kinds of understanding' (22). This should *not* be read as recovering the authentic Shakespeare; to make such a claim is simply to add to the authority of Shakespeare. What Sinfield undertakes rather is what he describes as 'an impudent anti-reading; a creative vandalism' (23).

A second British critic challenging received wisdoms about Shakespeare and English literature teaching in Britain is to be found in Malcolm Evans, in *Signifying Nothing*, which makes direct use of Barthes's arguments. In a chapter that ranges provocatively from *The Tempest* to Hegel's master–slave dialectic, to *Desert Island Discs*, to the Newbolt Report, and to post-structuralist theory, Evans contrasts Shakespeare the Great Author, 'the national and universal poet-hero who was simultaneously a voice of nature and law of hegemonic culture', and the Shakespeare text, 'the linguistic and semiotic *excess* which has been the occasion of innumerable interpretations, each performing its particular ideological closures'.[27] Hostile towards critics like David Lodge and Jonathan Culler who have ignored or domesticated the challenge of post-structuralist thought by turning it into 'safe, depoliticized forms of textual analysis' (206), Evans quotes with approval Barthes's insistence that in dealing with 'the essential enemy (the bourgeois norm)', semiology must 'be acknowledged as *semioclasm*' (209).

In travelling across the Channel, Barthes's theory of the Author has therefore had a mixed reception. On the one hand, it has been contained by the likes of Lodge using it as yet another way of approaching literary texts. Williams warns against this pattern of incorporation in his discussion of Marxism and structuralism: '[I]n so many of their actual tendencies they have been accommodated, or have accommodated themselves, *within* the paradigm, where they can be seen as simply diverse approaches to the same object of knowledge. They can then be taken as the guests, however occasionally untidy or unruly, of a decent pluralism.'[28] On the other hand, in work like that of Evans, Barthes's antipathy to authority and his desire to inscribe the reader in the production of meaning is echoed closely. Further, the philosophical sophistication of French semiotics, and later post-structuralism, is used as a critical purchase on Great English Authors like Shakespeare and the institutions that produce them.

From France to the USA

Before describing the translation of the ideas in Barthes's essay to the USA, the global ascendancy of the US model of English studies in the last twenty-five years must be noted. As economic and political hegemony has shifted westwards across the Atlantic in the post-war years, so the US has attained formidable cultural dominance, and Britain's status as primary exporter of cultural wares to the English-speaking colonies has declined. US cultural imperialism countersigns the hegemony of 'English', with prestigious US academic journals and publishing houses together making a significant impact on developments in the discipline in Britain. Alan Sinfield identifies the reinvention of modernism and the critical practices of New Criticism as being the most significant influences, and concludes that by the 1970s English studies in England was ultimately determined by its relation with the US: 'But since [the 1950s English studies in Britain] has been informed only residually by Leavis; its Englishness has been pressured not by imperial ambitions but by economic, political, military and cultural deference to the United States.'[29] The effects of this subordination were in general to shore up and prolong the more conservative impulses in English literary culture. New Criticism enforced an ahistorical formalism that demanded the study of individual texts unconnected to their own context and to the context in which they were being taught. Shakespeare was no exception to this pattern; indeed, according to Michael Bristol,[30] the US version of Shakespeare was, if anything, a more universal, transcendent source of cultural goodness than the English one.[31]

There are a number of versions of how French thought has travelled from Paris 1968 to US centres of learning. I refer to three of them. David Simpson focuses on how the emphasis on textuality is reworked by Paul de Man, arguing that de Man's reputation rests not on 'doing a milder version of what Roland Barthes and Walter Benjamin . . . had done much better',[32] effectively muting the radical energies of 1968–74 by discrediting 'the belief in any connection between textuality and a world in which difference and choice make a critical change' (726). For Simpson, de Man's project, while quoting Barthes with approval, is quite distinct, and altogether more conservative:

[de Man's] initiative was a quite different one, seeking to head off the credibility of a long tradition of European left-of-center culture criticism by claiming that 'literature is everywhere' . . . with the result that no differences can remain after the sceptical analysis: there is nothing that can withstand the deconstructive inspection and provide a place to stand. (725)

Edward Said is similarly dubious about the effects of transatlantic travel on French theory of the late 1960s. While '[t]he intellectual origins of literary theory in Europe were, I think it is accurate to say, insurrectionary', their radical edge was blunted in US academies, as 'American literary theory of the 1970s had retreated into the labyrinth of "textuality".'[33] Said connects this containment of European theory to the wider context as follows: '[I]t is no accident that the emergence of so narrowly defined a philosophy of pure textuality and critical noninterference has coincided with the ascendancy of Reaganism, or for that matter with a new cold war, increased militarism and defense spending, and a massive turn to the right on matters touching the economy, social services, and organized labour' (4).

More equivocal than Simpson and Said about the radical origins of Barthes's work in the Paris of the late 1960s, Aijaz

Ahmad none the less concedes that the work of Barthes and Claude Lévi-Strauss started 'first in fairly radical variants, in keeping with the temper of the times, and then [moved] in increasingly formalist, domesticated directions'.[34] In travelling to the US, the process of domestication has been accelerated, with theory understood as 'conversation' and being practised within the bounds of 'a peculiar American kind of pluralism ... albeit expressed in avant-gardist critical circles in the Barthesian language of "pleasure of the text", "free play of the Signifier"' (70). In becoming valued intellectual currency of US English departments, French theory—including Barthes's critique of the Author—functions as a commodity exchanged among privileged consumers:

One is now free to cite Marxists and anti-Marxists, feminists and anti-feminists, deconstructionists, phenomenologists, or whatever other theorist comes to mind, to validate successive positions within an argument, so long as one has a long list of citations, bibliographies, etc., in the well-behaved academic manner. Theory itself becomes a marketplace of ideas, with massive supplies of theory as usable commodity, guaranteeing consumers free choice and a rapid rate of obsolescence. (70)

What Ahmad also emphasizes is that in travelling from Europe to North America Western theory remained enclosed within its own privileged borders: 'important from the theoretical point of view—was the issue of the exclusive emphasis, in the Western academy, on the experience of Europe and North America' (63).[35]

Renaissance studies in the US have not been exempt from the influence of imported French theory. Critical works drawing on this newly available thought have been grouped under the title 'new historicism', and include Stephen Greenblatt's *Renaissance Self-Fashioning: From More to Shakespeare*, Jonathan Goldberg's *James I and the Politics of Literature: Jonson, Shakespeare, Donne and Their Contemporaries*, and Carolyn Lenz's collection *The Woman's Part: Feminist Criticism of Shakespeare*. There are differences between cultural materialism and new historicism,[36] though they share much in drawing on the new critical resources to challenge received readings of Elizabethan and Jacobean drama.

Perhaps the most influential of the new historicists has been Stephen Greenblatt, and his essay on *The Tempest* in *Shakespeare Negotiations* provides a good example of what happens to Shakespeare in this critical school. Focusing on how anxiety was aroused, manipulated, and contained in Jacobean England, Greenblatt analyses and compares meticulously the rhetorical strategies employed in the sermons of the martyred Protestant minister Hugh Latimer, in an unpublished letter about a shipwreck in the Caribbean of colonial entrepeneur William Strachey, and in *The Tempest* by William Shakespeare. In the final section of the essay, Greenblatt locates two senses of aesthetic representation in *The Tempest*, one which sees art as pure plenitude, and one which sees art as always involving loss. For Greenblatt, the name Shakespeare has since been transformed from being associated with the theatre to being associated with the institution of literature. The shift from stage to book, from playwright and actor to Author, signals a much larger shift from joint-stock company to modern corporation. None the less, what persists is 'the continued doubleness of Shakespeare in our culture: at once the embodiment of culture, freed from the anxiety of rule, and the instrument of empire' (161). An anecdote told by the explorer H. M. Stanley is used to tie up the argument about the double nature of Shakespeare in contemporary culture: in the anecdote, Stanley sacrifices his *Collected Shakespeare* in order to save his travel notes, which subsequent empire-builders would use to exploit the Congo region. Greenblatt concludes: 'What matters is the role Shakespeare plays in it, a role at once central and expendable—and in some obscure way, not just expendable but exchangeable for what really matters: the writing that more directly serves power' (163). As with Sinfield and Evans, Greenblatt attends both to the context in which Shakespeare wrote, and to his subsequent production as Great Author. What is less immediately apparent in Greenblatt's writing— though it might be implicit—is any attempt to connect the patterns of violent exclusion in Shakespeare to *contemporary* political events.

A second US critic who engages with French post-structuralism in great depth, and as such represents a useful comparison with Evans's contemporaneous encounter with

Barthes in Britain, is Jonathan Goldberg. In *Voice Terminal Echo*, he is concerned centrally with '[q]uestions about authorial self-representation and the nature of the book', and reads specific texts of Marvell, Spenser, Shakespeare, Herbert, and Milton, reflecting upon 'the status of representation within the book, the nature of characters as voices for the poet and re-presentations of the act of authoring'.[37] He describes his project thus:

[W]hat follows is not structured as an argument and resists such structures, eschewing (so far as possible) the critical impulse to totalize and the historical drive to historical closure. The voice on these pages is not singly determined to a procedure of logical dem-onstration. Multiple and fractured, it responds to texts and recounts them, pursuing and permitting disseminative practice. (4)

Goldberg's debt to Barthes is clear throughout the work, and in the section on George Herbert's *The Temple* he turns speci-fically to 'The Death of the Author' essay in considering the perennial question of the identity of the speaker in Herbert's poems. Deferring to Barthes's argument—thus demonstrating the life rather than the death of the Author Barthes—Goldberg summarizes 'that when the author has given himself over to the text he no longer is, except in the text' (107), Goldberg proceeds to focus in minute detail on Herbert's poems, un-covering the rhetorical strategies constituting and undoing the authorial presence. It is difficult to discern in these read-ings any vestige of the polemical extra-academic resonances of Barthes's original formulations.

What should finally be stressed in tracing these instances of theory travelling is that, in moving to Britain and the US, it moved into contexts dominated by a liberal–conservative consensus, a fact disguised by the energetic efforts of what remains an extremely small minority of literary critics teach-ing politics through literature. In the US, according to Ahmad, the great majority of teachers and critics function 'as if noth-ing much has changed since T. S. Eliot and "New Criticism"'; a significant minority pursues in a technicist fashion the the-oretical exposition of literary texts; and a small minority con-nected uneasily with this latter group attempt to fashion 'politically informed readings'.[38] Writing about Britain, Brian

Doyle makes a similar point, concluding from the arguments over the McCabe affair that

[t]he politics of English studies were revealed in a confrontation between a fundamentally right-wing educational policy and a countervailing defence of the need for plurality of emphasis. The defence of pluralism, however, was aligned to professional scholarship rather than a clearly formulated politics of education. Stephen Heath argued for McCabe's appointment on the grounds of the need to sustain the Cambridge English faculty as the 'greatest in the world'.[39]

The political ideals purported to be connected to theory—social critique, participation, respect for difference—were strategically suppressed, and in the interest of retaining some dubious and marginal left presence at Cambridge, banal arguments of professional élitism were wheeled out.

These criticisms of Western radical theory of the last twenty-five years—that it circulates as an intellectual commodity among an élite; that it operates only in the margins of what remains a conservative discipline; and that it relegates the non-European to its margins—of course do not disqualify all forms of such theory. There remain formidable resources of theoretical thought to be utilized in confronting the silences and exclusions of the Global English Studies Industry. However, these criticisms should induce some hesitancy on the part of those outside Anglo-American English departments who assume that in travelling South such theory will automatically serve democratizing impulses.

Travelling to South Africa

In travelling to South Africa, 'The Death of the Author' was destined for a context quite different to Britain and the USA. From Sharpeville in 1960 to the present, state authority and capital in South Africa have been challenged in direct and often violent ways.[40] Black South African schools in particular have been in turmoil, receptive spaces for revolutionary arguments about the contingent nature of authority.

France, Britain, and the US have continued to have extensive links with South Africa throughout this period. While both France and Britain have consistently supported investment in South Africa, the US in recent years has become South Africa's most important sponsor. Richard W. Hull records that after leaving the British Commonwealth in 1961, US businessmen 'richly capitalized on the loosening of Britain's hold on the South African economy and on growing anti-British feelings among important Afrikaner figures'.[41] The rationale for this interest is familiar: British companies in South Africa between 1967 and 1969 averaged profits of £76 million per year, and capital returns in South Africa of 20.6 per cent in 1966 for US multinationals were the highest in the world (investment in Japan, with returns of 12 per cent, was the next most lucrative). Although European and North American investment in South Africa has fluctuated, dipping noticeably after periods of political unrest—Sharpeville in 1960, Soweto in 1976, most of the country in 1985–6—it has continued to sustain local capital and the South African state.

In the 1970s foreign investment was increasingly directed towards manufacturing industries, which had become the major sector of the South African economy. The changing nature of the economy produced a demand for more 'skilled' labour, and the education system was reshaped to meet this need. Although the education system was slow in responding to this demand, there were none the less massive increases in the numbers of both black and white school pupils during this period: the total number of black students in primary and secondary schools doubled between 1960 and 1975 to 3,697,400, and the numbers of African pupils matriculating was 6,701 in 1975 compared to 397 in 1960; and the number of white matriculants rose from 26,097 in 1960 to 53,784 in 1975. These changes in the education system brought fresh pressures, as black students resisted incorporation as cheap labour into the apartheid state.

The Soweto Uprising forced the South African state to reconsider its separatist policies. Education again was one of the key areas focused for reform, as the state made an attempt to stabilize the black urban working class by offering them some stake in the status quo. Although severe repression continued, with states of emergency and large-scale detention without trial, there were also co-optive gestures. Measures (not hugely successful) designed to effect the project of limited co-option included: the reforms in labour relations initiated after the Wiehahn and Riekert Commissions in 1979; the establishment of a tricameral parliament with limited political suffrage offered to Coloureds and Indians; and the massive increases in black education spending, particularly after the De Lange Report of 1981. Like the other measures, De Lange represented in certain ways a shift away from the designs of grand apartheid, but again like the other measures, it threatened no major inroads on white hegemony: instead of an education system officially catering for the needs of different race groups, it set out to attune education more acutely to the national interest, understood quite clearly as the interests of the capitalist economy. What is particularly unoriginal about De Lange is the emphasis on technical education for black students, which in effect if not in as many words reinvents the division of Shakespeare for an élite and the three Rs and metalwork for the mass of students.[42]

In the 1980s, with increases in black unemployment and in the number of school-leavers (the number of African matriculants increased from 9,009 in 1975 to 86,873 in 1984), and with the education system continuing to function in inefficient, authoritarian, and racist fashion, black youth and students have been central in the struggle against the state. Notwithstanding the mistakes made and limitations of student politics in the 1980s, Nasson's concluding tribute seems accurate:

In Soweto, Atteridgeville, Alexandra and Mitchells Plain, rebellious children at the bottom of every unequal life distribution are not merely scrambling for educational ladders with which to make an individual, self-improving climb from poverty. For the molecular growth at a local level of an alternative educational culture represents the breaking-in of new kinds of community and class consciousness, opposed to the ladder image of bourgeois capitalist society.[43]

English literature teaching throughout this whole period, including the teaching of Shakespeare, did not adjust its procedures in response to the wider political and economic changes.[44] The new English syllabus for the Cape published

in 1973 merely repeated the requirements of the 1951 syllabus, with Shakespeare continuing as a compulsory set text.
Examinations continued to test the students' ability to recall
plot–theme–characterization, and to comment on poetic devices used by Shakespeare. For second-language English
speakers, the emphasis was far more strongly on memory-
and comprehension-type questions. Although there were
differences between the Shakespeare taught at the universities
and the Shakespeare of the education departments,[45] they were
still substantially the same Great Author, and to be approached
in similar reverent fashion: he was a timeless genius with
unique insight into universal human nature; the nature of his
relationship both to his own context and to the South Africa
of the 1970s was assumed to be of no concern to teachers and
students; and his plays were studied with a view to discovering the peculiarities of individual characters and the conservative themes encoded in the plot.

In the 1980s Shakespeare's place in school syllabuses was
debated more vigorously than before,[46] and some adjustments
have in recent years been made in terms of text selection, with
the inclusion of novels by African writers and of films as set
texts for examination. However, little change has occurred in
terms of the questions asked in the Shakespeare sections of
the current literature papers, with four categories for first-
language papers: rote recall; comprehension; assumptions and
deductions; and creative response.[47] For second-language
English speakers, the latter two types of question are absent,
with students still required to do little more than recall plot
details. This question from an English second-language examination on *Julius Caesar* is typical:

> 2. In an essay of about forty lines, trace the downfall of the con-
>   spirators as they desperately try to avoid the vengeance of
>   Mark Antony and his allies.[48]

Although the questions in the examination papers are similar in
the different education departments, there seem to be slightly
more 'creative response'-type questions in examinations set
by the Joint Matriculation Board, which reflect the influence
of 1960s British pupil-centred educational philosophies. This
tendency is symptomatic of a deeper division: encourage a

confident, critical relationship to texts among (predominantly white) middle-class students attending JMB schools; enforce via unquestioning rote-learning a deference to authoritative texts among (predominantly black) working-class students.

Reading only the syllabuses and examination papers for English at South African high schools does not of course convey the full picture. Students' experiences of being taught English were much more complicated, with English teachers and students at times successfully discovering in the plays a more interesting author than the one constructed by the education departments. Three examples illustrate this. Perhaps the most famous South African appropriation of Shakespeare is the one performed by Chris Hani, slain leader of the South African Communist Party and hero of the township youth. In a 1988 interview with the *Weekly Mail*, Hani observed that 'I was fascinated by Shakespeare's plays, especially *Hamlet*. . . . I want to believe I am decisive and it helps me to be decisive when I read *Hamlet*.'[49] The charismatic 'people's poet' Mzwakhe Mbuli also has very positive associations with Shakespeare. Mbuli compares his own relationship with his vast young audience to Shakespeare's relationship with his audience:

It is clear that this is one seed I was able to sow as a poetic farmer that will never be touched, that will obviously come out openly one day. When it happens like that, at its fertile stages, no-one will take it out. It cannot be devoured by the locusts of this world tomorrow. It is clear that I have managed—I want to believe—to become another Shakespeare of this era. This is evident in what people are saying.[50]

And most recently, John Matshikiza, director of a June 1994 production of *Julius Caesar*, has argued that 'Shakespeare doesn't belong to Margaret Thatcher and the British. His themes are universal, and can be made explicable wherever he's performed in the world.'[51] While conceding that '[t]he way Shakespeare is taught alienates students' (31), he none the less insists that Shakespeare can be reclaimed by relating the plays to South Africa in the 1990s. *Julius Caesar*, he argues,

is centrally about democracy . . . Four hundred years after its first performance in a monarchical society, democracy is an unresolved

question in South Africa—we've had an election of which we've
never seen the like. This is what makes Shakespeare such a great
teaching tool; and not only for English, but for history, sociology,
political science.   (31)

Notwithstanding these defences of Shakespeare, his continuing presence in South African schools, in whatever recoded
and democratized form, is not entirely secure. The reasons for
Shakespeare's vulnerability rests less in his capacity to change
his identity and start serving the new nation than in the difficulty of the language in the plays for second-language English
speakers. Even liberal educationalists have acknowledged this
to be a problem. In the most comprehensive survey of English
literature teaching at South African schools, Jane Reid defends
Shakespeare's universal value, but none the less concedes that
on the evidence of several surveys '[t]he average English-
speaking teenager finds the language of Shakespeare extremely
difficult to come to terms with; it must be almost insuperably
hard for those whose English is their second language'.[52]
In the years leading up to South Africa's first ever democratic elections, there were broadly two approaches to Shakespeare's fate in a post-apartheid educational dispensation. The
first was closely connected with the efforts of different anti-
apartheid bodies seeking to break with what they saw as a
reactionary, Eurocentric educational project. Michael Gardiner
of the National Education Crisis Committee (NECC), for
example, describes the concept of People's English as aimed
at helping students to

— understand the evils of apartheid and to think and speak in
  non-racial, non-sexist and non-elitist ways;
— determine their own destinies and to free themselves from
  oppression;
— play a creative role in the achievement of a non-racial democratic South Africa.[53]

Quite how these ambitions are to be realized is not elaborated
in detail, not least because 'the process of consultation' (160)
at the heart of People's Education is still in process, but Shakespeare does not feature directly in the list of possible texts to
be explored in People's English:

popular culture, biographies and life histories, oral literature including song, talks by people of the community and elsewhere,
written literature from the whole world (including translations) but
particularly from our time and place, newsletters, pamphlets, public
documents, speeches, essays, sermons and orations, material from
radio, television and film, texts from other subjects in the curriculum and the range of languages and dialects in South Africa [quot-
ing an NECC newsletter from 1986]. (163)

Indeed, Gardiner suggests the replacement of English studies
with cultural studies, a subject embracing this wide variety of
texts which would be taught by using non-hierarchical pedagogical practices.[54]

The second approach is best represented by the
Grahamstown-based Shakespeare Schools' Text Project. The
Project is funded by the Chairman's Fund of the Anglo-
American Corporation, enjoys the intellectual support of the
Shakespeare Society of Southern Africa, and is well positioned
to negotiate lucrative new deals with publishers for revised
school editions of the plays. Acknowledging that Shakespeare
has represented a substantial obstacle for English second-
language students, project director Andre Lemmer argues that
'a humanized response-centred methodology may provide a
sufficient pre-requisite for rendering any worthwhile literary
work (including Shakespeare) accessible and "relevant"'.[55] In
a longer report on the project, Lemmer dismisses 'the new
schools of "alternative" and "political" Shakespeare [as] too
recondite for application at school level',[56] and then proceeds
to argue the not unfamiliar case for installing in the schools a
revised Shakespeare capable of providing 'a bridge between
past and present and between one culture and another' (72).

Ideological differences aside, the stakes are very high in
the contest between these two visions of high-school English
studies. Susan Joubert identifies the strong centralization of
educational publishing:

[P]redictions among publishers are that a new national syllabus
will be introduced, a few subjects at a time, and not before 1993/4.
Seventy per cent of the various syllabi will be standard for all race
groups, under the new programme. Although a unified non-racial
education system is necessary, the consequences for all but the larg-
est publishing houses might be disastrous if textbook prescription

continues. Fewer texts, spread among more pupils, will mean that the profit to be made by those who get their books selected will be increased.[57]

More recently, in keeping with the general spirit of nation-building, compromise, and accommodation, these two different approaches seem to have drawn closer together. The 1994 ANC *Policy Framework for Education and Training* asserts that

[t]he curriculum of General Education will be committed to national development and social responsibility, to the development of a non-racial, non-sexist and democratic society and to the development of a national identity.[58]

The school core curriculum will include two or more South African languages, mathematics, science and technology, studies of society, art, music and drama, physical education, and life skills. There is in the Proposal a commitment to 'qualitative review of all existing textbooks' (98).

As regards English, the *English Guideline Document* (December 1993) drawn up by the Core Syllabus Committee for English defines the social mission of English in familiar terms: among other things, the study of English enriches students' 'personal and social lives by . . . contributing to their ethical and spiritual growth',[59] and, further, it will 'encourage learners to enjoy reading literature and to explore areas of universal human concern' (13). As to what texts will be taught, the document remains vague: 'An immensely wide range of English texts, from the local to the international, is available from which to choose appropriate stories, poems and plays to challenge inhumanity, prejudice and self-interest' (18). Whether Shakespeare is adequate to the task of 'challenging inhumanity' has yet to be decided.[60]

Travelling European theory has, not surprisingly, had a greater impact on the teaching of English literature at South African universities than it has at schools, though it has certainly not dislodged older paradigms.[61] Challenges to the traditional English studies model have relied on a variety of intellectual resources, with dissenting members of the profession questioning the practices of the discipline. In embryonic form, this dissent focused on the exclusion of South African writing from the syllabuses of the English departments, but disagreements were in general contained within a liberal consensus that never constituted any threat to the established canon or methods of critical analysis.[62] By the late 1970s strategic concessions had been made, and writers like Olive Schreiner, Alan Paton, and Pauline Smith were being studied.

The next stage is captured in Mike Kirkwood's influential essay 'The Colonizer: A Critique of the English South African Culture Theory'. Kirkwood focuses on Guy Butler as the pre-eminent representative of South African literary culture, and demonstrates the hypocrisy of the economically powerful English community (via Butler) depicting itself as embattled interlocutor between African and Afrikaner nationalism. Drawing extensively on Fanon, Memmi, and contemporaneous South African Marxist historians like Martin Legassick, Kirkwood argues that the only path forward for English-speaking South Africans is for them to relinquish their privileges and their connections with England, and to struggle towards a new (male) African identity: 'We argue that the White colonizer can only discover his true interest when he has discovered himself as a colonizer, and rejected that self.'[63] Kirkwood and the very small group of like-minded critics who attacked the South African critical establishment were emphatically opposed to white rule in South Africa and to English liberal virtues. Whereas the old Liberal Party was as far left as English lecturers conventionally ventured, this group defined themselves in unequivocal solidarity with black opposition struggles.

Kirkwood does not deal directly with English studies, but his arguments provide the basis for other critics, who make explicit the relation between English liberalism and literature teaching at the English departments of South African universities. In a special issue of *Critical Arts* on English studies in 1984, both Nic Visser and Michael Vaughan insist on their congruence. Vaughan argues:

The primary, or foundational concept is that of a universal aesthetic order. This then is built upon, interpreted or recognized, in the light of the values of liberal humanism. To this account we must add another factor: the *practical* or technical application of liberal humanist values and ideas to the recognition of the universal aesthetic order is achieved by means of a specific approach, or method. This method is 'practical criticism'.[64]

To reject the liberal humanist political and economic project therefore demanded intellectually a total rejection of the English studies cultural project in its practical-criticism form.

In order to challenge what Isabel Hofmeyr describes as the '[a]cademic complacency [and] genteel critical responses'[65] of traditional English studies, two categories of radical European thought were cultivated in South Africa: British social history and Continental critical theory, both loosely conceived in their Marxist forms. Of the two, the 'history from below' practices associated with *History Workshop* have taken root most firmly.

The main figure insisting on the recovery of neglected black South African literatures via the methods of social history was Tim Couzens.[66] Couzens argues that South African literary history 'is an open field where the critic can plough new ground rather than forge for the millionth time the conscience of a T. S. Eliot or a Jane Austen',[67] and he then goes on to suggest potential themes and areas for research. His one caveat is that professional standards be maintained: '[A] lot of hard work and commitment is essential' (25). Couzens's contributions, and those of colleagues Hofmeyr and Kelwyn Sole, frequently appeared in political rather than literary journals like *Africa Perspective* and *Work in Progress*, something which reflected their desire to seek out radical academics in other disciplines. Hofmeyr indicates as much in comparing South African English and history studies in the 1970s:

Since the early 70s, many scholars, responding to the growing complexity and crisis of the South African polity, rejected the 'conventional wisdom' of liberal studies. They felt that such an approach could not penetrate the surface of the South African social formation and opted instead for a more radical and historical approach that sought to explain the present in terms of the past, with the addendum that such an understanding would provide the guidelines in building alternatives for the future. . . . But in the field of literary studies, apart from a handful of praiseworthy exceptions, no such development took place. Instead, critics have continued on their path of 'original ignorance', using outdated methods that can explain nothing coherently.[68]

Whereas a significant number of South African historians were energetically and sometimes acrimoniously disagreeing at this time over whether E. P. Thompson or Louis Althusser represented a more appropriate model for analysing South African history,[69] South African literary critics remained divided between a massive liberal bloc and an embattled left minority. The appeal of switching disciplines was obvious, and both Hofmeyr and Couzens are currently employed outside English departments in African studies.

The second means of attacking the critical orthodoxies was with Continental critical theory, often in mediated Anglo-American form. Critical theory for certain critics represented a fresh vocabulary and mode of analysis which might at the same time explain cultural forms and discredit the liberal humanist project. Hofmeyr, for example, cites Raymond Williams and Francis Mulhern in justifying her plea that 'we need a theory of literature that includes the cultural products and practices of all classes';[70] Michael Green follows Althusser in arguing that 'the importance of critical theory . . . becomes obvious once the significance of no critical approach's being innocent is seen';[71] Sole, in writing about post-war black South African writers, footnotes Terry Eagleton and Althusser to support his contention that 'the class position of black writers in a specific period influenced what they wrote';[72] and Brenda Cooper similarly acknowledges her intellectual debt to Althusser and Nicos Poulantzas in her study of writer-intellectuals in independent Africa.[73]

One tendency in recent years has been for South African critics to look to US-packaged theory to import in preference to the British offerings. This reflects the increased status of US universities, as the route for postgraduates from South Africa to Oxbridge became less attractive, and the one to Columbia more so.[74] The central figure in this pattern is J. M. Coetzee,[75] who spent a long period living and studying in the US, and many South African critics now look to Jameson, Spivak, or Said rather than to Williams and Eagleton to secure their arguments. One example relevant to the history of South African English studies is Rory Ryan's essay on 'Literary-Intellectual Behavior in South Africa', which relies principally not on the British New Left to explain the English studies mission, but

on Americans William V. Spanos and Paul Bove.[76] Ryan endorses with particular zeal the anti-humanist sentiments
Spanos and Bove derive from the likes of Barthes.

How has travelling theory affected South African Shakespeare studies? Has Shakespeare been replaced with 'Shakespeare'? There have been two major projects in the past ten
years in South African Shakespeare studies. The first has been
referred to already, namely the work of the journal *Shakespeare in Southern Africa*. President of the Shakespeare Society
of Southern Africa, Guy Butler, defends the formation of the
Society, and launch of the journal in the first issue:

Some believe this is neither the time nor the place to be founding a
society to encourage the appreciation of a dramatist who was born
in a foreign land over four hundred years ago, and whose works are
written in an archaic form of English. South Africa has more important things to attend to. It certainly has; but that does not mean
long-term interests must be neglected. There are occasions when
urgent matters may properly benefit from our attending to matters
of permanent importance.[77]

Defending long-term interests involved in the first issues of
the journal a continuing investment in traditional English
Shakespeare critics, with names like Dover Wilson, Muir, and
Knights appearing most frequently in the endnotes.

There were (sometimes favourable) reviews of books by
cultural materialists, and new historicists, but the article that
best captures the journal's cautious attitude to Continental
theory is a short piece by Lawrence Wright, 'Shakespeare and
the Bomber Pilot: A Reply to Colin Gardner'. Opposed to the
kinds of political readings of Shakespeare performed by the
likes of Martin Orkin, Wright starts with an anecdote from T.
R. Henn's *The Apple and the Spectroscope* about a bomber pilot
who read a speech from *Macbeth* as related to flying aircraft.
He proceeds then to quote two passages from Barthes's *The
Pleasure of the Text* which emphasize the fecundity of readings
immanent in any text. Where Barthes develops this idea into
an argument for demystifying the figure of the Author and
endorsing the subjectivity of all readers in their encounters
with authoritative texts, Wright moves in the opposite direction. One paragraph after quoting Barthes, Wright observes

that 'we accept, as most literature teachers do, that some read-ings are truer than others',[78] and, two pages later, that '[w]ithout the ideal of objectivity, the entire academic enter-prise collapses' (86). Professional historical scholarship, exem-plified for Wright in Michael Echeruo's *The Conditioned Imagination from Shakespeare to Conrad*, will fix the meaning of the text in ways most useful to 'humanity in general' (87). The travelling theory in this case is acknowledged, but politely dismissed, as Wright develops here the critical complement to his and Lemmer's new school editions of the plays.

The second major work on Shakespeare in South Africa of the decade, Martin Orkin's *Shakespeare against Apartheid*, relies much more heavily on recent Renaissance criticism and theory from both Britain and the US to secure his argument. Con-ceived partly as a guide for undergraduates to radical read-ings of Shakespeare, and partly as an attack on conservative South African Shakespeare critics, Orkin's book sets out from the assumption that it is primarily the reader who determines the meaning of the text: '[w]e remain located in our world and the way in which we read will be significantly deter-mined by this fact.'[79] Institutional interpretations of Shake-speare in South Africa have encouraged conservative attitudes in students, but Orkin, in his readings of *Hamlet*, *Lear*, and *Othello*, argues ultimately that there is different and better Shakespeare to be salvaged:

If this book has any value at all it will be as a first step in the struggle to wrest the Shakespeare text from the conservative grasp of traditionalist critics. We need to work for the development of readings of the texts that will free them from ruling class appropria-tion, from their present functions as instruments of hegemony. In so doing we may pave the way for a new educational dispensation, a dispensation that will include one day, amongst many more impor-tant things, the emergence, perhaps, of a people's Shakespeare. (184)

On this line, although the instability of the text is noted, the Author is wounded rather than dead. In a similar argument to that of Matshikiza, Shakespeare emerges from behind the innumerable reactionary readings of his plays to confirm him-self as the sensitive and politically astute Master ready to instruct anxious South African students. In locating such value in Shakespeare, Orkin forestalls the option, which might arise in a post-apartheid South Africa, of choosing a different set of texts.[80]

Conclusion

The problem of radical theory travelling and changing over time and space is not new. The words of Karl Marx on the opening page of *The Eighteenth Brumaire of Louis Bonaparte* warn against establishing as paradigmatic the vocabulary and analyses of prior revolutionary moments, and then reading subsequent or even contemporary events in their anachronistic terms:

The tradition of the dead generations weighs like a nightmare on the minds of the living. And, just when they appear to be engaged in the revolutionary transformation of themselves and their material surroundings, in the creation of something which does not yet exist, precisely in such epochs of revolutionary crisis they timidly conjure up the spirits of the past to help them; they borrow the names, slogans and costumes so as to stage the new world-historical scene in this venerable disguise and borrowed language. Luther put on the mask of the apostle Paul; the Revolution of 1789–1814 draped itself alternately as the Roman republic and the Roman Empire; and the revolution of 1848 knew no better than to parody at some points 1789 and at others the traditions of 1793–5.[81]

That we must be enslaved to the categories of past revolutions, however, is not the only alternative envisaged by Marx. Referring to the English Revolution, he observes that past revolutions can also inspire and instruct:

In these revolutions, then, the resurrection of the dead served to exalt the new struggles, rather than to parody the old, to exaggerate the given task in the imagination, rather than to flee from solving it in reality, and to recover the spirit of the revolution, rather than to set its ghost walking again. (148)

For Marx, no theory is inherently revolutionary. Whether a particular theory challenges authority will be determined by its use and its context; invoking the names of earlier revolutionary thinkers might as easily be a token of incorporation as of subversion. Accordingly, South African English critics and teachers might appropriate travelling theory in one of two ways. They might 'timidly conjure up the spirits of the past' in order to protect existing intellectual and institutional practices. Or, they might use the knowledge, memories, and theories of past revolutions in order to 'exalt the new struggles'. This study has tried to follow the latter path.

Afterword

Rereading the closing paragraphs of the last chapter, I am struck by the combative tone. It is a tone that in the post-election, post-apartheid South Africa sounds pious and anachronistic: to write of exalting new struggles appears at odds with the often-moving gestures of forgiveness being made in the euphoria of building the new nation.

None the less, there are at least two reasons why I have not rewritten these paragraphs, or the many others that reflect the urgency of struggle rather than the pathos of reconciliation. The first is an extension of a basic premiss of this study, namely that there is a connection between historical context and intellectual production. The historical context of this study has changed enormously in the four years I have been working on it: in 1989 South Africa's white minority regime ruled by states of emergency and mass detention, with the country's legitimate leaders in prison; since April 1994 a democratically elected government of national unity has ruled by a fragile consensus, with Nelson Mandela inaugurated as President. To pretend to have sustained through this period a unity and consistency of vision would involve claiming an authority, a sense of authorship, which transcends material social practices. I prefer to think of my writing in different terms: as constituted by the contradictory historical conditions, as *part of* those historical conditions; yet at the same time as a strategic intervention within those conditions.

Insisting upon authorial agency, the capacity to make strategic interventions, is the necessary condition for the second, and more substantial, reason for retaining the language of struggle in this argument. In short, there remains much to struggle *for*, much to be angry *about*, in the institutions and practices of English studies in post-1994 South Africa. Most urgently, the question of access to the study of English must be addressed: in a population of about 35 million, between 9 and 12 million South Africans above the age of 15 are illiterate.[1] Addressing statistics of this scale is never easy, but they stand as a challenge to those protecting existing educational structures and practices. To continue gazing to Oxbridge and Columbia for intellectual inspiration, and to continue teaching Shakespeare as before to relatively small numbers of students, seems particularly unlikely to make a positive impression on these statistics, on these entrenched patterns of exclusion.

As regards the reception of my arguments, I would again stress the context where they will be disseminated. The place of a critique such as this in South Africa is less certain than it might have been in the past. Before 1990 my arguments would have found a natural place as part of a wider left analysis of the institutions of the apartheid state. But South African left intellectuals can no longer write against the state and capital with the same unequivocal anger and certainty; 'the enemy' is no longer so easy to identify, and many formidable radical intellectuals have been drawn into positions of central state power, assuming responsibility for correcting the nation's injustices. There are two possible responses to this: that the ANC left has 'sold out', and that the new state should therefore be opposed as vigorously as the old one had been; or that the left at last enjoy the recognition and influence their talents deserve, and that the new state should therefore be supported in its efforts to meet the needs of its electorate.[2] In the context of English studies, this would mean: continuing outside state education policy forums (this might be enforced), and identifying the authoritarian tropes of new canons, syllabuses, and critical approaches; or seeking control of the new centres of power in order to try and install educational practices more democratic and empowering. Will this history of Shakespeare in South Africa be read exclusively as critique, as located *outside* the formations of the discipline of English studies? Or will it be incorporated *within* a reformulated version of English studies, and read as a contribution towards the forging of a 'People's English'?[3]

My own hopes for this study are that it will make some impact on at least four distinct audiences. Much of the writing was completed in England, and my arguments in the first instance were addressed to what I perceived to be a sympathetic, but detached, audience based at British and US universities. At all times though, imagined South African readers asserted their presence, both those from the academy—the personnel of English studies, and the academic left—and Shakespeare teachers at South African high schools.

The final audience is South African students I have taught Shakespeare. My impulse to write this book developed in three years of teaching English to adults at a night school in Wynberg, Cape Town. This book stands as a long answer to those students, many of whom were Xhosa-speaking, who struggled to pass their examinations on the Shakespeare plays. I hope that though they are unlikely to buy and read the book, these arguments, in some form or another, reach them; that they might come to see support for the view that their 'failures' with Shakespeare are part of much larger histories of imperial violence, in which the Bard plays a central and deeply compromised role.

Notes

INTRODUCTION

1. R. Nixon, 'Caribbean and African Appropriations of *The Tempest'*, *Critical Inquiry*, 13 (1987), 558. Subsequent references in the text.
2. K. Marx and F. Engels, *The German Ideology* (London, 1970), 47.
3. E. Said, 'Opponents, Audiences, Constituencies and Community', (*Critical Inquiry*), 9 (1982), 2.
4. In *The World, the Text, and the Critic* (London, 1983), 47, Said refers with approval to the method of *The German Ideology* and places Foucault in the same tradition. Aijaz Ahmad, in *In Theory* (London, 1992), provides a critical discussion of Said's relation to Marx. I return in detail to these issues in Ch. 4.
5. K. Marx, *The Eighteenth Brumaire of Louis Bonaparte*, in *Surveys from Exile*, ed. D. Fernbach (Harmondsworth, 1973), 146.
6. R. Williams, 'The Uses of Cultural Theory', *New Left Review*, 158 (1986), 20.
7. On the contingent meaning of 'men', see e.g. Jacques Derrida's critical discussion of Jean-Paul Sartre in *Margins of Philosophy* (Hemel Hempstead, 1982): in Sartre's work, Derrida argues, 'the history of the concept of man is never examined. Everything occurs as if the sign "man" had no origin, no historical, cultural, or linguistic limit' (116). Derrida returns to the dangers of transcendental 'man' in 'Onto-theology of National Humanism', *Oxford Literary Review*, 14 (1992), 3–23, where he argues that Marx in *The German Ideology* is rightly critical of 'the claim by one country or nation to the privilege of "representing", "embodying", "identifying with the universal essence of man" ' (17). In 'Spectres of Marx', *New Left Review*, 205 (1994), Derrida invokes Marx's attack on Stirner in *The German Ideology*, as he criticizes Francis Fukuyama's elevation of 'the *transhistorical and natural* criterion of man as *man*' (48).
8. Two recent examples of work that combines an engagement with theory and a commitment to historical method are, in the context of English studies, Gauri Viswanathan's *Masks of Conquest* (New York, 1989) and, in the context of South African historiography, Clifton Crais's *The Making of the Colonial Order* (Johannesburg, 1992).
9. J. Dollimore, *Radical Tragedy* (Hemel Hempstead, 1989), p. xli.
10. The phrase is used by Raymond Williams in *Writing in Society* (London, 1983), 196.
11. W. Benjamin, *Illuminations* (New York, 1968), 257.

CHAPTER 1

1. A preliminary word of definition is necessary. Literature during this period included types of writing like scientific reports and political tracts. My discussion uses the term in its more modern sense to refer to imaginative writing. Raymond Williams, in *Keywords* (London, 1983), 183–8, traces the shifts in the meaning of 'literature'.

2. Albie Sachs, 'Preparing ourselves for Freedom', in Ingrid de Kock and Karen Press (eds.), *Spring is Rebellious* (Cape Town, 1990), 19.

3. Three recent works discussing in detail the political, economic, and cultural histories of the Cape Colony in the first half of the 19th cent. are Jean and John Comaroff's *Of Revelation and Revolution* (Chicago, 1991), Clifton Crais's *The Making of the Colonial Order* (Johannesburg, 1992), and Noel Mostert's *Frontiers* (London, 1992). There is a useful review of Crais and Mostert by Martin Legassick in 'The State, Racism and the Rise of Capitalism in the Nineteenth-Century Cape Colony', *South African Historical Journal*, 28 (1993), 329–68.

4. This survey of mission schooling in the first half of the 19th cent. in the Cape Colony is drawn from early and more recent histories. The two principal early sources are the *Preliminary Report on the State of Education in the Colony of the Cape of Good Hope, by Donald Ross* (the Ross Report) (Cape Town, 1883), and the British *Special Reports on Educational Subjects*, v (the Muir Report) (London, 1901). The more recent sources include: M. Ashley, 'Universes in Collision' *Journal of Theology for Southern Africa*, 32 (1980), 28–38; J. Comaroff, 'Images of Empire, Contests of Conscience', *American Ethnologist*, 16/4 (1989), 661–85; L. de Kock, ' "History", "Literature", and "English"' *English Academy Review*, 9 (1992), 1–21; E. Elbourne, 'A Question of Identity'; C. T. Keto, 'Pre-industrial Education Policies and Practices in South Africa' in M. Nkomo (ed.), *Pedagogy of Domination* (Trenton, 1990); F. Molteno, 'The Historical Foundations of the Schooling of Black South Africans', in P. Kallaway (ed.), *Apartheid and Education* (Braamfontein, 1984); and D. Taylor, *The Role of Missionaries in Conquest* (Cumberwood, 1986), 68–9, 135–8.

5. E. G. Malherbe provides this statistic in *Education in South Africa* (Cape Town, 1925), 98.

6. Elizabeth Jay emphasizes the redemptive dimension of missionary work in her study *The Religion of the Heart* (Oxford, 1979): 'The Evangelicals did not see the relief of suffering as their main objective. Though they attempted to relieve it, suffering chiefly moved them to intensify their battle against its cause, the evil rooted in men's souls' (173).

7. Quoted in Ashley, 'Universes in Collision', 33.

8. Quoted in I. Michael, *The Teaching of English from the Sixteenth Century to 1870* (Cambridge, 1987), 221.

9. J. Sales, *Mission Stations and the Colonial Communities of the Eastern Cape 1800–1852* (Cape Town, 1975), 42.

10. See Mary Penrith's MA thesis 'A Historical and Critical Account of the Teaching of English Language and Literature in English-Medium Universities in South Africa', University of Cape Town, 1972, 24–36, for a more detailed account of the personal biographies of these early teachers.

11. A Well Wisher to the Youth of this Colony, Open Letter, *Cape of Good Hope Literary Gazette*, 2/11 (1832), 391. The *Gazette* ran from 1830 to 1835

under the editorship of A. J. Jardine. Jardine's strict Presbyterian up-
bringing predisposed him against theatre and imaginative literature, and
there were very novel reviews in the journal. See A. M. Lewin Robinson,
None Daring to Make us Afraid (Cape Town, 1962), 126–244, for a detailed
history of the *Gazette*.

12. Doreen Rosman in ch. 8 of her study *Evangelicals and Culture* (London,
    1984), surveys Evangelical literary criticism in England at this time. She
    pays particular attention to Shakespeare criticism, which was for the
    most part extremely hostile (177–8).
13. 'Fiction', *Cape Town Mirror*, 1/14 (5 Dec. 1848), 107.
14. N. J. Merriman, *On the Study of Shakespeare* (Grahamstown, 1857), 1.
    Gauri Viswanathan in *Masks of Conquest* (New York, 1989) refers to mis-
    sionaries in India who proceeded from the same assumption. She quotes
    the Revd William Keane, who argues, like Merriman, that 'Shakespeare
    . . . is full of the common sense principles which none but Christian men
    can recognize' (80).
15. Merriman, *On the Study of Shakespeare*, 2.
16. N. J. Merriman, *Shakespeare as Bearing on English History* (Grahamstown,
    1857), 3.
17. Merriman's suspicion of Byron is consistent given the latter's cynicism
    about the uncritical Bardolatory of his contemporaries. Jonathan Bate, in
    Shakespeare and the English Romantic Imagination (Oxford, 1986) describes
    Byron's critique of Romanticism as 'an essential antidote to the attitudes
    and practices' (223) of his more conservative contemporaries like
    Coleridge.
18. Merriman, *On the Study of Shakespeare*, 15.
19. This summary of the early history of Cape schooling is drawn from J.
    Sturgis, 'Anglicisation at the Cape of Good Hope in the Early Nine-
    teenth Century', *Journal of Imperial and Commonwealth History*, 11/1 (1982),
    5–32; Muir Report, 11–19; M. Ashley, 'The British Influence on Education
    in South Africa' in André de Villiers (ed.), *English Speaking South Africa
    To-day* (Cape Town, 1976); and E. G. Pells, *The Story of Education in South
    Africa* (Cape Town, 1938), 26–35.
20. Muir Report, 14.
21. Pells, *The Story of Education in South Africa*, 27.
22. Viswanathan, *Masks of Conquest*, 46.
23. J. S. Mill, *Mill's Essays on Literature and Society* (London, 1965), 58.
24. J. Fairbairn, 'On Literary and Scientific Societies', *South African Journal*,
    1/1 (1824), 54. For the history of Thomas Pringle and John Fairbairn's
    endeavours with the *Journal*, see Lewin Robinson, *None Daring to Make
    us Afraid*, 9–66.
25. Mill, for example, in 'The Spirit of the Age', writes: 'It is right that every
    man should attempt to understand his interest and his duty. It is right
    that he should follow his reason as far as his reason will carry him, and
    cultivate the faculty as highly as possible. But reason itself will teach
    most men that they must, in the last resort, fall back upon the authority
    of still more cultivated minds, as the ultimate sanction of the convictions
    of their reason itself' (*Essays*, 44).
26. The letter is reproduced in W. T. Ferguson and R. F. M. Immelman
    (eds.), *Sir John Herschel and Education at the Cape 1834–1840* (Cape Town,
    1961), 46.

27. Quoted in A. E. du Toit, *The Earliest South African Documents on the Education and Civilisation of the Bantu* (Pretoria, 1963), 84.
28. Quoted in R. Johnson, 'Educational Policy and Social Control in Early Victorian England', *Past and Present*, 49 (1970), 101.
29. R. Johnson, 'Educating the Educators', in A. P. Donajgrodzki (ed.), *Social Control in Nineteenth Century Britain* (London, 1977), 94.
30. Quoted in A. E. du Toit, *The Earliest British Document on Education for the Coloured Races* (Pretoria, 1962), 27–9. It is not coincidental that Kay Shuttleworth's memorandum was published for the first time in South Africa in the 1960s, at a time when industrial training for black South Africans was being enforced by the Department of Bantu Education.
31. See P. Curtin, *The Image of Africa* (Madison, 1964), 425–7; B. Holmes (ed.), *Educational Policy and the Mission Schools* (London, 1967), 25–30; and C. H. Lyons, 'The Educable African', in V. M. Battle and C. H. Lyons (eds.), *Essays in the History of African Education* (New York, 1970), 13–23 for more detail on the history of English missionary endeavours with regard to education in Africa in the 19th cent.
32. The official history of Lovedale is by R. H. W. Shepherd: See also *Lovedale, South Africa 1824–1955* (Lovedale, 1971). See also De Kock's interesting ' "History", "Literature", and "English" ', and M. Ashley, 'Features of Modernity', *Journal of Theology for Southern Africa*, 38 (1982), 56–8, for the details of this shift.
33. In Ferguson and Immelman (eds.), *Sir John Herschel*, 47.
34. 'Literature, Science and Art', *Cape of Good Hope Literary Magazine*, 1/1 (1847), 107. The *Magazine* was produced by James Long Fitzpatrick, and sought to explore a wider range of subjects than its short-lived predecessors.
35. Gary Taylor, in *Reinventing Shakespeare* (London, 1989), 164–73 summarizes the main contributions of this period.
36. 'On the Sources of Shakespeare's Plots', *Cape of Good Hope Literary Magazine*, 2/10 (1848), 572.
37. J. Fairbairn, 'On the Writings of Wordsworth', part 1, *South African Journal*, 1/1 (1824), 15.
38. Ibid., part 2, *South African Journal*, 1/2 (1824), 107.
39. 'Poetry', *Cape of Good Hope Literary Gazette*, 1/2 (1830), 23.
40. 'Literature, Science, and Art', part 1.1, 103.
41. A more precise distinction might be made here between the internal function of literature, a *national* position, and the external function, an *imperial* position. Gauri Viswanathan, in 'Raymond Williams and British Colonialism', *Yale Journal of Criticism*, 4/2 (1991), 47–66, summarizes the dangers of privileging the former position; I have chosen here to include the 'national' within the term 'imperial' in order to emphasize the presence of the colonies in defining 'domestic' English thought.
42. 'The English Language', *Cape of Good Hope Literary Gazette*, 2/10 (1832), 372–3.
43. Quoted in H. Caygill, *Art of Judgement* (Oxford, 1989), 65.
44. 'Popular Literature', *Cape Town Mirror*, 1/1 (1848), 3.
45. Details of these early Shakespeare productions are provided by W. R. Quince in his Ph.D. thesis 'Shakespeare in South Africa', University of Southern Illinois, 1987, 10–14.
46. This merging of positions should be read in the light of shifts in cultural thought in England. Raymond Williams, in the chapter 'Mill on Bentham

and Coleridge', in *Culture and Society 1780–1950* (Harmondsworth, 1961), traces how Mill enlarged the early utilitarian thought of Bentham by supplementing it with romantic conceptions of culture derived from Coleridge.

47. 'Literature, Science and Art', part 1.4, 465.
48. J. C. Adamson, *Modern Literature* (Cape Town, 1844), 4.
49. Albie Sachs, 'Preparing Ourselves for Freedom', in Ingrid de Kock and Karen Press (eds.), *Spring is Rebellious* (Cape Town, 1990), 21.

CHAPTER 2

1. L. O'Dowd, intro. to Albert Memmi, *The Colonizer and the Colonized* (London, 1990), 33.
2. R. Young, *White Mythologies* (London, 1990), 124.
3. See e.g. C. Baldick, *The Social Mission of English Criticism 1848–1932* (Oxford, 1983), 18–58, and W. V. Spanos, 'The Appollonian Investment of Modern Humanist Education', *Cultural Critique*, 1 (1985), 17–29.
4. M. Arnold, 'Introduction: Democracy', in *The Collected Prose Works*, ii (Ann Arbor, 1962), 28.
5. M. Arnold, 'The Future of Liberalism', ibid., ix (Ann Arbor, 1973), 140.
6. Arnold, 'Introduction: Democracy', 21.
7. M. Arnold, 'The Twice Revised Code', ibid., ii. 227–8.
8. M. Arnold, *Report of 1880* (Harmondsworth, 1973), 59–60.
9. M. Arnold, 'An Eton Boy', in *The Collected Prose Works of Matthew Arnold*, x: *Philistinism in England and America*, ed. R. H. Super (Ann Arbor, 1974), 43.
10. Eric Stokes in *The English Utilitarians and India* (Oxford, 1959) makes a similar point about John Stuart Mill: liberal ideas on government apply only within Britain; Indians were not 'sufficiently advanced in civilization to be capable of settling their affairs by rational discussion' (298).
11. The best overviews of the education system in the Cape Colony during this period are the the Ross Report, and the the Muir Report.
12. L. Dale, quoted in the Muir Report, 71.
13. L. Dale, *The Philosophy of Method* (Cape Town, 1877), 20.
14. L. Dale, 'Imagination: An Essay', *South African Magazine*, 3 (1869), 109.
15. Cameron's essay is discussed with warm approval by A. C. Partridge in 'English Scholarship', *English Studies in Africa*, 1/1 (1958), 1–9, and more critically by R. Ryan in 'Literary-Intellectual Behavior in South Africa', *Boundary 2*, 15/3 (1988), 283–304.
16. The educative value of the classics at the Cape at this time was also debated before a wider audience by J. D. Coley in 'The Advantages of a Classical Education', *South African College Union Annual*, 1 (1888), 23–4. Coley's main argument is the same as that of Cameron: 'a Classical education has been found from experience to be the best general training, and to furnish the most solid foundation for any superstructure of a technical kind that may afterwards be reared upon it. It affords the best means for enlarging the mind, and developing the reasoning faculty. In a word, it makes a boy think' (23).
17. J. Cameron, 'Classical Studies and their Relation to Colonial Education',

in R. Noble (ed.), *The Cape and its People and Other Essays* (Cape Town, 1869), 297.

18. J. G. Greenwood, 'On the Languages and Literatures of Greece and Rome', in *Introductory Lectures on the Opening of Owens* College (Manchester, 1852), 35.

19. Quoted in W. H. Chaloner, *The Movement and Extension of Owens College, Manchester 1863–1873* (Manchester, 1973), 2.

20. Greenwood, 'On the Languages and Literatures of Greece and Rome', 26.

21. J. G. Greenwood, 'On Some Relations of Culture to Practical Life', in Balfour Stewart and A. W. Ward (eds.), *Essays and Addresses, by Professors and Lecturers of Owens College, Manchester* (London, 1874), 5–6.

22. J. W. Hales, 'The Teaching of English', in F. W. Farrar (ed.), *Essays on a Liberal Education* (London, 1867), 306.

23. Cameron, 'Classical Studies and their Relation to Colonial Education', 301–2.

24. W. G. Clark, 'General Education and Classical Studies', in *Cambridge Essays* (London, 1855), 293.

25. M. Legassick, 'The Frontier Tradition in South African Historiography', in S. Marks and A. Atmore (eds.), *Economy and Society in Pre-industrial South Africa* (London, 1980), 55.

26. D. M. Schreuder, in 'The Cultural Factor in Victorian Imperialism', *Journal of Imperial and Commonwealth History*, 4/3 (1976), 283–317, provides a careful analysis of the ideas expressed by colonial officials in the administration of the Eastern Cape frontier in Britain and South Africa in the 1870s and 1880s, and confirms this distinction: 'In contrast to the . . . official mind in London, the "administrative mind" in the colonial periphery would appear to reveal aspects of social engineering—drawn from cultural hubris and "civilising zeal"—more purposeful and crudely energetic than the muted outlook of its Whitehall counterpart' (284).

27. This discussion of Britain's economic and political history is drawn from E. J. Hobsbawm, *Industry and Empire* (Harmondsworth, 1969), 109–54; C. Leys, *Politics in Britain* (London, 1983), 38–51; B. Simon, *Education and the Labour Movement 1870–1920* (London, 1965), 165–75; T. Nairn, *The Break-up of Britain* (London, 1981), 19–24; S. Hall and B. Schwarz, 'State and Society 1880–1930', in M. Langan and B. Schwarz (eds.), *Crises in the British State* (London, 1985); and M. Barratt Brown, 'Away with all the Great Arches', *New Left Review*, 167 (1988), 22–51. They obviously differ on a number of points; it is difficult to go into those differences in detail here, but I have referred to them where I have thought necessary.

28. K. Brehony, 'Popular Control or Control by Experts?', in Langan and Schwarz (eds.), *Crises in the British State*, 260.

29. The precise nature of the British ruling class has been the subject of considerable debate in the British left. Barratt Brown, in 'Away with all the Great Arches', sees the division in the English ruling class being between 'the practice of practical men in industry, technology *and* in banking and commerce and . . . the philosophy of the academics in education, science and government' (41); Perry Anderson, in 'The Figures of Descent', *New Left Review*, 161 (1987), 20–77, argues that the land-owning aristocracy never relinquished control of the means of production to the

rising middle classes, who 'remained junior partners in the natural order of things, without compelling economic motives or collective social resources to transform it' (40); and E. P. Thompson, in *The Poverty of Theory* (New York, 1978), argues that no aristocratic interest remained, that as the old landowners they were 'like the staff at an elaborate and prestigious hotel who could in no way influence the comings and goings of clientele' (265), and that in all but the question of manners the emergent bourgeoisie was therefore the dominant fraction of the ruling class. These are important arguments because they shed light on official education policies in both England and the colonies.

30. S. J. Maclure, *Educational Documents 1816 to the Present Day* (London, 1979), 94.

31. Quoted in D. Shayer, *The Teaching of English in Schools 1900–1970* (London, 1972), 94. The full title of the Cross Report was *Report of the Royal Commission on the Elementary Education Acts*. The full details and background to the report are summarized by Maclure, in *Educational Documents*, 128–39.

32. Taunton Report, 525. The Taunton Report was known officially as the *Report of the Royal Commission known as the Schools Inquiry Commission*. It in fact made no immediate impact on legislation governing education in Britain. See Maclure, *Educational Documents* 89–97.

33. R. Altick, *The English Common Reader* (Chicago, 1957), 158.

34. Gauri Viswanathan, in *Masks of Conquest* (New York, 1989), describes the establishment of English literature examinations in India in detail (23–44).

35. *University of London Calendar 1860*, p. clxv.

36. The history of the public service examinations is described by D. J. Palmer, *The Rise of English Studies* (London, 1965), 45–50; B. Doyle, *English and Englishness* (London, 1989), 25–7; Baldick, *The Social Mission of English Criticism* 70–5; and Altick, *The English Common Reader*, 183–6.

37. Taunton Report, 521.

38. *Shakespeare's 'Othello'*, ed. H. Roscoe (London, 1883), 175–6.

39. *Shakespeare's Tragedy of 'Hamlet'*, ed. L. C. Maxy (Boston, 1892), p. v.

40. *Shakespeare's Tragedy of 'Hamlet'* (Rugby, 1870), p. vi.

41. The theme of physical courage is also encoded in Thomas Parry's ed. of *Julius Caesar* (London, 1882), which describes the play as 'an excellent introduction to a more extended study of Shakespeare, as the scaling of Snowdon is good training for the scaling of Mont Blanc' (p. vi). For more detail on public school culture at this time, see J. A. Mangan, *The Games Ethic and Imperialism* (New York, 1986), and E. J. Hobsbawm, *The Age of Empire 1875–1914* (London, 1987), 174–9.

42. *Shakespeare's 'Tempest'*, ed. J. M. D. Meiklejohn (London, 1880), 4.

43. *Shakespeare's 'The Tempest'*, ed. Revd D. Morris (London, 1875), 10.

44. A. Davin, 'Mind that you Do as you are Told', in G. Weiner and M. Arnot (eds.), *Gender under Scrutiny* (London, 1987), 144–5. See also Davin's more detailed discussion of relations between women and empire in the late 19th cent. in 'Imperialism and Motherhood', *History Workshop*, 5 (1978), 9–64.

45. C. Dyhouse, 'Social Darwinistic Ideas and the Development of Women's Education in England', *History of Education*, 5/1 (1976), 54.

46. Exaggerating Bradley's originality also diminishes the formidable influence of Edward Dowden, who not only influenced Bradley, but at the

time of his death had thirty former students who were professors of English. (See T. Brown, *Ireland's Literature: Selected Essays* (Mullingar, 1988), 40).

47. See E. H. Carr's *What is History?* (Harmondsworth, 1964), 8–20.

48. A. C. Bradley, *Shakespearean Tragedy* (New York, 1905), 7.

49. Terence Hawkes, in *That Shakespeherian Rag* (London, 1986), 27–8, emphasizes Bradley's initial marginalization *within* Oxford. Such marginalization did not, however, translate into doubts about his (privileged) relation to the world *outside* Oxford.

50. J. Dollimore, *Radical Tragedy* (Hemel Hempstead, 1989), 260.

51. J. J. van Helten, in 'British Capital, the British State and Economic Investment in South Africa', 1–17, records that British exports to South Africa had increased from £9,819,033 in 1890 to £14,778,017 in 1900, whereas they had decreased dramatically in other markets as a result of protective tariffs and competition.

52. D. M. Schreuder, *The Scramble for Southern Africa 1877–1895* (Cambridge, 1980), 317.

53. For further detail on the economic and political history of the Western Cape in the late 19th cent., see V. Bickford Smith's 'A "Special Tradition of Multi-racialism"?', in W. G. James and M. Simons (eds.), *The Angry Divide* (Cape Town, 1989), 49; and A. Mabin's 'The Underdevelopment of the Western Cape 1850–1900', in James and Simons (eds.), *The Angry Divide*, 93–4.

54. Even more radical accounts of this period, like S. Trapido's 'The Friends of the Natives', in Marks and Atmore (eds.), *Economy and Society in Pre-industrial South Africa*, tend to homogenize the differences within the English bourgeoisie at the Cape (see particularly his conclusion, 267–8).

55. On English racism in the Colony, see Atmore and Marks, 'The Imperial Factor' 114; and P. Brantlinger, in 'Victorians and Africans', *Critical Inquiry*, 12 (1985), 194. H. Giliomee, in 'Aspects of the Rise of Afrikaner Capital', in James and Simons (eds.), *The Angry Divide*, provides an excellent analysis of the material basis of the Afrikaner farmer–English merchant difference in the Cape during this period.

56. The *Report of the Education Commission* (Cape Town, 1912) complacently notes that '[t]he most striking change which has been made since 1891 is the separation of the European and coloured children. No strong feeling about this had been manifested before 1891, but the change, which was strongly urged by Sir Langham Dale in 1891, has certainly commended itself to public opinion—at any rate, among the Europeans' (7). It records that in 1891 there were about 10,000 white children in third-grade mission schools, and in 1910 there were less than 550. For a useful discussion of these developments, and the struggles to resist them, see G. Lewis's *Between the Wire and the Wall* (Cape Town, 1987), 30–4.

57. See W. Ritchie, *The History of the South African College 1829–1918* (Cape Town, 1918), E. A. Walker, *The South African College and the University of Cape Town* (Cape Town, 1929), and the *Report of the University Commission* (Cape Town, 1914), 18–23, for the official histories of the university. (There is a new history of Cape Town University by Howard Phillips due out soon.) M. Boucher in *The Examining Boards and the Examining University* (Pretoria, 1969) distils the defining ethos of its founding: 'The creation of the University of the Cape of Good Hope . . . cannot be fully

understood without some reference to that confident Victorian belief in the efficacy of written examination and of examining institutions. Examination was discovered to be a ready method of ensuring good professional standards and of classifying ability; examining universities and boards could operate in the spirit of Benthamite liberal utilitarianism as impartial bodies, non-sectarian in character, capable of securing what Darwin was in 1859 to call "the survival of the fittest" and able to foster the spirit of competition in an age dedicated to the ideal of free trade, opening the door to the advancement of the capable, irrespective of social standing or church affiliation' (2). He might have added that they were also useful for closing the door to those not capable in quite the prescribed way.

58. The history of South Africa's private schools is traced by Peter Randall in *Little England on the Veld* (Johannesburg, 1982). For details of their beginnings in the Western Cape, see 55–65.

59. Ross Report, 12.

60. E. G. Malherbe in *Education in South Africa* (Cape Town, 1925), 95–8, provides details of the 1865 Act, which was to regulate education in the Colony for the next forty years. He sums up its dominant ethos as follows: 'The political philosophy underlying this system of state aid is more akin to the *laissez faire* policy propounded by J. S. Mill and Herbert Spencer than to a system of benevolent paternalism' (117).

61. Barry Report, 23. The Commission of Enquiry into the Educational System of the Cape Colony under the chairmanship of Sir J. D. Barry investigated *inter alia* school attendance, the need for facilities, language policy, and African education. The Commission did not lead to immediate legislation, but had some influence on Dale's successor, Sir Thomas Muir.

62. See M. Boucher, *The Examining Boards and the Examining University* (Pretoria, 1969), 22–3, for details of the first woman and black students in the Cape. The number of students at school in the Cape increased steadily during the period, with a particularly sharp acceleration after the mineral discoveries in the 1870s. Malherbe provides the following statistics:

Year	Total pupils	White pupils
1853	9,811	c. 5,000
1870	40,412	c.18,000
1890	104,291	c.42,000
1900	144,340	58,471

63. 'A Lady', 'A Plea for Colonial Girls', *Cape Monthly Magazine*, 10 (1875), 320.

64. Viswanathan, *Masks of Conquest*, 164.

65. Ross Report, 41.

66. *The Calendar of the University of the Cape of Good Hope 1897–1898*, 13–14.

67. *The Calendar of the University of the Cape of Good Hope 1887–1888*, 72.

68. C. Carter, 'Macho School partly to Blame for Racist Killing', *South*, 7–13 Mar. 1991, 4.

69. 'Dale Boy's Dad Points Finger at Headmaster', *Weekend Argus*, 9 Mar. 1991, 6.

70. 'Dale College Boys: Why did they Do It?', *Weekend Argus*, 9 Mar. 1991, 12.

71. P. Candido, 'Dale Supporters Protect School', *Cape Argus*, 23 Feb. 1991, 4.

72. M. Bothma, '"System" to Blame for Killing by Dale Boys', *Cape Times*, 1 Apr. 1991, 4.

73. F. Bridgland, 'Bloodsport on the Playing Fields', *Sunday Telegraph* (24 Feb. 1991), 19.

74. 'Dale College Boys'. Alan Sinfield describes the opposition of athletes and aesthetes in England and the USA in *Faultlines* (London, 1992), 272–9.

75. A. Lemmer, 'Upgrading the Study of Shakespeare in Southern African Secondary Schools', *Shakespeare in Southern Africa*, 2 (1988), 72. For more detail on the project, see Lemmer's 'ESL Shakespeare in Schools and Colleges', *NESLATT Journal*, 4 (1989), 22–7.

76. 'Kids Live out ANC Dad's Schoolboy Dream', *Cape Times*, 14 Feb. 1991, 3.

77. A. Sinfield, 'Tennyson and the Cultural Politics of Prophecy', *ELH* 57/1 (1990), 179.

CHAPTER 3

1. S. T. Plaatje, 'A South African's Homage', in I. Gollancz (ed.), *A Book of Homage to Shakespeare* (Oxford, 1916), 339.

2. For the background to Plaatje's tribute, see S. Gray, 'Plaatje's Shakespeare', *English in Africa*, 4/1 (1977), 1–6, and B. Willan, *Sol Plaatje: A Biography* (Johannesburg, 1984), 193–4, 331.

3. These are not the only possible ways of reading Plaatje; there is, for example, a feminist reading by Myrtle Hooper, which emphasizes the sympathetic treatment of the eponymous Mhudi in Plaatje's novel.

4. See D. Chanaiwa's 'African Humanism in Southern Africa', in A. T. Mugomba and M. Nyaggah (eds.), *Independence without Freedom* (Santa Barbara, Calif., 1980), for a valuable overview of this generation of African intellectuals.

5. The period 1870–1930 has received much attention from South African economic historians. See e.g. the valuable work of S. Marks and R. Rathbone, Introduction, in *Industrialisation and Social Change in South Africa* (London, 1982); S. Marks and S. Trapido, 'Lord Milner and the South African State', *History Workshop*, 8 (1979), 50–80; M. Fransman and R. Davies, 'The South African Social Formation in the Early Capitalist Period', in T. Adler (ed.), *Perspectives on South Africa* (Johannesburg, 1977); J. J. van Helten, 'Milner and the Mind of Imperialism', *The Societies of Southern Africa in the Nineteenth and Twentieth Centuries*, 10 (1981), 42–57; B. Magubane, *The Political Economy of Race and Class in South Africa* (New York, 1980), esp. ch. 8; and B. Bozzoli, *The Political Nature of a Ruling Class* (London, 1980). I. Wallerstein, in 'The Three Stages of African Involvement in the World Economy', in C. W. Gutkind and I. Wallerstein (eds.), *The Political Economy of Contemporary Africa* (London, 1976), connects economic developments in South Africa to those in the rest of Africa.

6. *Mhudi*, with its explorations of nationhood, has in recent years received increasing amounts of critical attention. See e.g. the range of readings of Plaatje in the University of Bophuthatswana Institute of African Studies, *A Collection of Solomon Plaatje Memorial Lectures* (Bophuthatswana, 1993).

7. Sol Plaatje, *Native Life in South Africa* (Harlow, 1987), 162–3.

8. 'In the Editor's Sanctum', *Educational Journal*, 1/1 (1915), 4.

9. 'A Luxury of Life', *Educational Journal*, 2/5 (1916), 8.

10. *Hamlet*, ed. An Examiner (Dublin, 1920), p. xiv.

11. *Othello*, ed. R. Gopal and P. R. Singarachari (Bangalore, 1928), p. iv.

12. W. L. Courtney, *Tercentenary Programme for 'Julius Caesar'* (London, 1916), foreword.

13. A. Quiller-Couch, *Historical Tales from Shakespeare* (London, 1899), p. xi.

14. W. Raleigh, *Shakespeare's England* (Oxford, 1916), 45. Terence Hawkes, in *That Shakespeherian Rag* (London, 1986), 35–41 discusses Raleigh's attitude to the Germans in detail.

15. Francis Colmer, *Shakespeare in Time of War* (London, 1916), p. xii.

16. Israel Zangwill, 'The Two Empires', in Gollancz (ed.), *A Book of Homage to Shakespeare*, 248.

17. *Johannesburg Shakespeare Tercentenary Celebration* (Johannesburg, 1916), 2.

18. 'The Greatest Son of England', *Cape Times*, 25 Apr. 1916, 7.

19. *Johannesburg Shakespeare Tercentenary Celebration*, prologue.

20. 'The Greatest Son of England', 8.

21. Quoted in W. J. de Kock and D. W. Kruger (eds.), *Dictionary of South African Biography*, ii (Cape Town, 1972), 469.

22. Another piece of South African Shakespeare criticism from this period, H. Austin's *An Hour with Shakespeare* (Claremont, 1908) is similarly dominated by the ideas of English critics, and particularly those of Raleigh. Austin also places primary emphasis on Shakespeare's capacity to produce memorable and life like characters. The most scholarly work of criticism, however, was Arnold Wynne's *The Growth of English Drama* (Oxford, 1914). Wynne was a junior lecturer in Cape Town, who was killed in France during the First World War.

23. John Clark, *Aristotle's Poetics and Shakespeare's Tragedies* (Cape Town, 1912), 21.

24. A. C. Bradley, *Shakespearean Tragedy* (New York, 1905), 36.

25. Not all members of the Colony's English-teaching fraternity were as steadfast in their gaze towards England. A. S. Kidd, of Rhodes College in Grahamstown, writes with regret that the situation in the Cape is in fact very different to England. In his essay 'The English Language and Literature in South Africa', he argues since 'the colonial mind . . . cannot realise the conditions of life in the Homeland' (159), there should be a closer union of the teaching of English and history: 'When studying a special period of Literature or a special book, the student should study the whole historical setting of that period or book, and by history I do not mean merely chronology, but political, social, economic, religious history also' (161). However, even Kidd, who sounds like an early cultural materialist from this passage, sacrificed his radical intentions in his actual teaching, directing his energies to the protection of traditional standards of English usage by *inter alia* exhorting students to resist the corrosive influence of Afrikaans.

26. University of the Cape of Good Hope, *Examination Papers* (Cape Town, 1916).

27. 'The Shakespeare Tercentenary', *Education Gazette*, 15/24 (27 Apr. 1916), 1022.

28. F. H. Sykes, 'The Teaching of English', *Education Gazette*, 5/33 (7 June 1906), 791.

29. 'The New Syllabus in English', *Educational News*, 26/5 (1916), 70.

30. H. Redfern Loades, 'The English High School Syllabus', *Educational News*, 26/10 (1916), 160.

31. H. Redfern Loades, 'The Teaching of English', *Educational News*, 26/12 (1916), 194.

32. *The Tempest*, ed. S. J. Newns (Cape Town, 1913), 8.

33. Z. K. Matthews, *Freedom for my People* (Cape Town, 1981), 24.

34. F. Fanon, *The Wretched of the Earth* (Harmondsworth, 1967), 178–9.

35. F. Fanon, *Towards the African Revolution* (Harmondsworth, 1970), 191.

36. F. Fanon, *Black Skin, White Masks* (London, 1986), 30.

37. Henry Louis Gates Jr., in 'Critical Fanonism', *Critical Inquiry*, 17 (1991), 457–70, provides an interesting discussion of Memmi's relation to Fanon (468–70). He also summarizes more recent engagements with Fanon.

38. A. Cabral, 'Culture, Colonization and National Liberation', in A. de Bragança and I. Wallerstein (eds.), *The African Liberation Reader*, i (London, 1982), 160–1.

39. A. Cabral, 'National Liberation and Culture', in *Unity and Struggle* (London, 1980), 140.

40. Albert Memmi, *The Colonizer and the Colonized* (London, 1990), 149.

41. *The C. L. R. James Reader*, ed. A. Grimshaw (Oxford, 1992), 327.

42. A. Césaire, *Discourse on Colonialism* (New York, 1972), 14–15.

43. R. Nixon summarizes the anti-imperialist readings of *The Tempest*. See my discussion of Nixon in Ch. 1. It should be added that there also were positive readings of Caliban in England before the 1960s. For an excellent discussion of late 19th-cent. readings of *The Tempest*, see Trevor Griffiths's '"This Island's Mine": Caliban and Colonialism', *Yearbook of English Studies*, 13 (1984), 159–80.

44. R. F. Retamar, 'Caliban. Notes towards a Discussion of Culture in our America', *Massachusetts Review*, 15 (1974), 62.

45. For detailed discussion of Marx's writings on India, see A. Ahmad, *In Theory* (London, 1992), 221–42, and B. Chandra, 'Karl Marx: His Theories of Asian Societies and Colonial Rule', in *Sociological Theories* (Paris, 1980).

46. K. Marx, 'The British Rule in India', in *On Colonialism* (Moscow, 1959), 41.

47. K. Marx, 'The Future Result of British Rule in India', in *On Colonialism* (Moscow, 1959), 81.

48. K. Marx, 'Marx to V. I. Zasulich in St Petersburg', in *Marx–Engels Selected Correspondence* (Moscow, 1955), 339.

49. K. Marx, 'Marx to the Editorial Board of the *Otechestvenniye Zapiski*', in *Marx–Engels Selected Correspondence* (Moscow, 1955), 313.

50. A. Brewer, in *Marxist Theories of Imperialism* (London, 1990), 108–17, argues that although it is by far the most famous Marxist text on imperialism, Lenin's *Imperialism, the Highest Stage of Capitalism* (Moscow, 1917) in fact makes no original contribution to the Marxist legacy since it does little more than summarize the work of Hobson, Hilferding, and Bukharin.

51. Lenin, *Imperialism, the Highest Stage of Capitalism*, 74–5.
52. The continuing concern in Marxist theories of imperialism with the economic as the ultimate key to social analysis is reflected in the question put by Tom Kemp in 'The Marxist Theory of Imperialism', in R. Owen and B. Sutcliffe (eds.), *Studies in the Theory of Imperialism* (London, 1972): 'The nub of the question is really this. Given the scope and power of the technological drives of advanced capitalism, represented by powerful firms and financial institutions which owned and controlled the main means of production, the sources of wealth and power, can it really seriously be maintained that the determining and decisive role in world development was played by those forces which Marxists call superstructural?' (25).
53. M. Barratt Brown, 'A Critique of Marxist Theories of Imperialism', in Owen and Sutcliffe (eds.), *Studies in the Theory of Imperialism*, 38.
54. A. Sivanandan, *Communities of Resistance* (London, 1990), 164.
55. P. Anderson, *Considerations on Western Marxism* (London, 1976), 42.
56. Martin Jay, for example, in *Marxism and Totality* (Cambridge, 1984), observes: 'Western Marxists remained true to Marx's expectation that a genuine socialist revolution could succeed in only the most advanced capitalists. . . . And though they staunchly supported the process of decolonization, few believed global revolution could be led by the emerging Third World' (6). Robert Young, in *White Mythologies: Writing History and the West* (London, 1990), provides a critique of the Eurocentrism of Western Marxism. His most telling insights, however, are frequently drawn from figures like Ahmad, who would disagree sharply with his claims for a non-imperialist, post-structuralist history writing.
57. There are, of course, anti-imperialist writers from Africa who attack Marxism for being no different from other Western political thought systems. The most bitter attack on 'Marxist imperialism' is the one delivered by Ayi Kwei Armah in 'Masks and Marx', *Présence Africaine*, 131 (1984), 35–65.
58. K. Nkrumah, *Class Struggle in Africa* (London, 1970), 12.
59. H. J. and R. E. Simons, *Class and Colour in South Africa* (London, 1969), 429.
60. Willan, in his article 'Sol Plaatje, De Beers and an Old Tram Shed', *Journal of Southern African Studies*, 4/2 (1978), 195–215, discusses this passage from *Class and Colour* in greater detail (196–7).
61. The main figures are Tim Couzens, Brian Willan, and Stephen Gray. Their considerable work on Plaatje is listed in the bibliography.
62. T. Couzens, 'Criticism of South African Literature', *Work in Progress*, 2 (1977), 45–6.
63. E. P. Thompson, *The Making of the English Working Class*, 12.
64. Willan, *Sol Plaatje*, p. vii.
65. T. Couzens, *The New African* (Johannesburg, 1985), p. xv.
66. S. Biko, *I Write what I Like* (London, 1978), 29.
67. Willan, in his biography of Plaatje, refers to a letter written by Plaatje to the Secretary of De Beers in Aug. 1918, in which he complains of the threat to harmonious race relations on the mines posed by 'these black Bolsheviks of Johannesburg' (224). This chapter of *Sol Plaatje* captures more than any other the sense of Plaatje as mediator between quite irreconcilable class interests, with the discourse of individual liberal accommodation unable to cover up deep social antipathies.

68. T. Couzens, 'The Dark Side of the World', *English Studies in Africa*, 14/ 2 (1971), 202. In 'Solomon Plaatje's Vision of a Just South Africa', in *A Collection of Solomon T. Plaatje Memorial Lectures* (Bophuthatswana, 1993), Couzens sets out more directly what Plaatje means for contemporary South Africa: '[Platjes *Mhudi*] advocates South Africanism, a common society, a common (though not enforced) culture, where all the citizens are equal before the law, are free to meet, to express their opinions, to record their vote' (118).

69. T. Couzens and B. Willan (eds.), *English in Africa*, Special issue on Sol Plaatje, 3/2 (1976), 6 (first ellipsis in the original).

70. Writing in a context of neo-colonialism rather than decolonization, Ngugi wa Thiong'o repeats the same themes and concerns as Fanon and Cabral. His image of the first generation of black middle-class intellectuals is at least as hostile as that of Fanon, and he too places great stress on the cultural dimension of the colonial mission. In *Homecoming* (London, 1972), for example, like Retamar he uses the exchange between Prospero and Caliban to establish the context: 'Prospero, the stranger on the island, comes with the soft voice of the serpent. He is at first friendly to Caliban, and flatters him, but all the time he is learning the secrets of the island. To him Caliban has no culture or meaningful past. He has even given *his* language to Caliban. And before Caliban knows it, Prospero has taken his land, has set up a one-man government, and turns Caliban into a slave labourer' (9). Having destroyed the material base of African society and dismantled traditional social and political structures, the colonizers created 'an elite who took on the tongue and adopted the style of the conquerors' (10). In *Writers in Politics* (London, 1981), he expands on how this occurred, emphasizing the role of Western literature. As a result of reading and being taught Western literature, African students come to accept 'the image of the European bourgeois with all its narrow-mindedness, bigotry and spiritual wasteland as "the universal man"' (16). Ngugi stresses that 'the effect of that kind of literature was to produce an African permanently injured by a feeling of inadequacy, a person who would look up with reverent awe to the achievements of Europe' (23). And, as Fanon does, he identifies reverence for European culture as the inevitable correlative of political bankruptcy and betrayal: the reader of Shakespeare is not easily distinguished from the 'national middleman of international industrial and finance monopoly capitalism' (23). The urgency of Ngugi's polemic contrasts sharply with the much more careful arguments of his colonial discourse contemporaries writing in the West.

71. For an excellent overview of the different intellectual histories of current colonial discourse theory, see P. Williams and L. Chrisman, *Colonial Discourse and Post-colonial Theory* (Brighton, 1993). They are especially useful in identifying the 20th-cent. Marxist theorists of imperialism and culture. Another valuable survey is A. Dirlik's 'The Postcolonial Aura: Third World Criticism in the Age of Global Capitalism', *Critical Inquiry*, 20 (1994), 328–56. Dirlik criticizes 'postcolonialism's diversion of attention from contemporary problems of social, political, and cultural domination' (331), and argues further that in challenging the universalistic pretensions of Marxism, it 'ends up not with its dispersion into local

vernaculars but with a return to another First World language with universalistic pretensions' (342).

72. See M. A. Skura's 'Discourse and the Individual', *Shakespeare Quarterly*, 40/1 (1989), 42–69, whose first footnote provides a summary of the most recent work on *The Tempest*. See also A. Loomba's *Gender, Race, Renaissance Drama* (Manchester, 1989), a full-length study of the deployment of Shakespeare in India that draws substantially on current Western critical theory.

73. D. Simpson, 'Literary Criticism and the Return to "History" ', *Critical Inquiry*, 14 (1988), 722.

74. E. Said, 'Intellectuals in the Post-colonial World', *Salmagundi*, 70–1 (1986), 52.

75. H. L. Gates Jr., Editor's Introduction, *Critical Inquiry*, 12 (1985), 6.

76. A. JanMohamed and D. Lloyd, 'Introduction: Minority Discourse', *Cultural Critique*, 7 (1987), 12.

77. F. Barker *et al.* (eds.), *Europe and its Others*, i (Colchester, 1984), preface.

78. B. Parry, 'Problems in Current Theories of Colonial Discourse', *Oxford Literary Review*, 9 (1987), 29.

79. E. Said, *Orientalism* (Harmondsworth, 1985), 24.

80. H. Bhabha, 'Representation and the Colonial Text', in F. Gloversmith (ed.), *The Theory of Reading* (Brighton, 1984), 95.

81. G. C. Spivak, *In Other Worlds* (London, 1988), 204.

82. H. Bhabha, *'The Location of Culture* (London, 1994), 67.

83. E. Said, *Culture and Imperialism* (London, 1993), 70.

84. I discuss this problem in detail in 'Importing Metropolitan Post-colonials', *Current Writing*, 6/1 (1994), 73–85. A closely related variation on the tendency of First World colonial discourse theorists to silence Third World voices is identified by Ania Loomba in her acute discussion of contemporary explanations of 'sati' in 'Dead Women Tell No Tales', *History Workshop*, 36 (1993), 209–27. Focusing on Gayatri Spivak's relation to Indian feminists in India, Loomba argues convincingly that many First World feminist theorists who insist on how subaltern subjects are determined and thus silenced by neo-colonial discourses fail to acknowledge or address the struggles of Third World feminists in their own countries (218–20).

CHAPTER 4

1. N. Ndebele, *Rediscovery of the Ordinary* (Johannesburg, 1991), 115.

2. A. Thompson and H. Wilcox (eds.), *Teaching Women* (Manchester, 1989), 2. On the impact of feminism on English studies in the US, see A. Kolodny, 'Dancing through a Minefield', in D. Spender (ed.), *Men's Studies Modified* (New York, 1981). Also interesting in the context of the US is N. McKay's 'Reflections on Black Women Writers', in C. Farnham (ed.), *The Impact of Feminist Research in the Academy* (Bloomington, Ind., 1987).

3. A. Sinfield, *Faultlines* (London, 1992), 294.

4. A. JanMohamed, 'Humanism and Minority Literature', *Boundary 2*, 12/3–13/1 (1984), 282.

5. Gayatri Spivak reflects on locating the 'centre' of contemporary English studies in the US when she first positions herself as an 'outsider' in relation to the discipline, but then asks, 'where is the inside?' (*In Other Worlds*, 102). Her response is to commit herself to 'a way of reading that would continue to break down these distinctions, never once and for all, and *actively* interpret "inside" and "outside" as texts for involvement as well as for change' (102).

6. G. Orwell, 'The Frontiers of Art and Propaganda', in *The Collected Letters*, ii (Harmondsworth, 1970), 152.

7. My summary of the British state, economy, and polity in the 1930s is drawn from E. J. Hobsbawm, 'Between the Wars', in D. Potter (ed.), *Society and the Social Sciences* (London, 1981); C. Leys, *Politics in Britain* (London, 1983), 52–7; and P. Anderson, 'The Figures of Descent', *New Left Review*, 161 (1987), 44–6.

8. Certain English socialists, like George Orwell in his novel *Burmese Days* and his early essays, insisted on the importance of the colonies in maintaining British living standards, but they were few and far between.

9. G. Wilson Knight, *The Imperial Theme* (London, 1951), p. v.

10. Henderson's chapter summarizes arguments developed in more detail by Soviet critic A. A. Smirnov, in *Shakespeare: A Marxist Interpretation* (New York, 1936).

11. P. Henderson, *Literature and a Changing Civilisation* (London, 1935), 52.

12. F. R. Leavis, *For Continuity* (Cambridge, 1933), 13–15.

13. R. Williams, *Politics and Letters* (London, 1981), 245.

14. L. C. Knights, *Drama and Society in the Age of Jonson* (London, 1937), 9.

15. Even Knights, the most 'materialist' of the three, alludes to Shakespeare with reverence when he explains his choice of dramatists: 'If Ben Jonson appears to have a disproportionate amount of space, it is because he seems to me so immeasurably superior to all his contemporaries—with the one obvious exception—and because his greatness as a poet makes clear the value of the popular tradition' (150).

16. In a letter to the *UC Tattle*, 'Literary Society Criticised', *UC Tattle*, 7 June 1940, 8, for example, 'Brutus' complains: 'At the last meeting on T. S. Eliot, it achieved the massive audience of twelve. This is a pity, because so much could be made of it. A sad commentary on the "good work" of the Society when more students go to hear a native choir than a cultural group discussing T. S. Eliot' (8).

17. Penrith, in 'A Historical and Critical Account', MA thesis, University of Cape Town, 1972, provides biographical details of several of the figures discussed below: Sewell, 125; Mackie, 99–103; Doughty, 119–23; and Kolbe, 63–5 and 81.

18. H. A. Reyburn, Prologue, 1.

19. P. Duncan, 'Hamlet', *Critic*, 1/1 (1932), 3.

20. In fairness to Mackie, he also edited *A Book of English Verse for South African Readers* (London, 1935).

21. A. M. Lewin Robinson, *Catalogue of Theses and Dissertations Accepted for Degrees by the South African Universities* (Cape Town, 1943).

22. W. S. Mackie, Preface, in *Symposium on Practical Criticism* (Cape Town, 1948), 1.

23. W. A. Sewell, 'Shakespeare', *University of Cape Town Quarterly*, 14 (1931), 10.

24. Another of the first South African critics to reflect the influence of the more contemporary English critics was Doris Greenberg, who 'In Defence of Literary Criticism', *Groote Schuur*, 2/1 (1941), 56–9, put forward the *Scrutiny* case for a committed cultural vanguard in South Africa.

25. A. J. Friedgut, 'The Rise of the Caliban Drama', *Critic*, 5 (1939), 1.

26. F. C. Kolbe, *Shakespeare's Way* (Cambridge, 1930), p. vii. As I have been stressing the recruitment of 'outsiders' to the expanding profession of English studies, Kolbe's position as a determined African and as a Catholic priest should be mentioned. In an earlier piece, *The National Crisis* (Pretoria, 1915), he concedes that he cannot speak Afrikaans well, but none the less protests that 'if I am an Afrikander, why may I not at least try to talk my own language' (6).

27. Wilson Knight, *The Imperial Theme*, p. viii.

28. Kolbe, *Shakespeare's Way*, p. ix.

29. The first South African-trained critics from Cambridge only took up posts at the end of the decade—both Alan Warner at Rhodes and Geoffrey Durrant at Stellenbosch returned infused with the spirit of Leavis in 1939—and their work is therefore discussed in the next chapter.

30. The earliest Shakespeare criticism by a South African woman I have come across is a light-hearted piece by E.M.C. entitled 'Shakespeare's References to the Modern Wheel' published in the *Huguenot Seminary Annual* (Cape Town, 1900).

31. A. Milligan, 'A Shakespearean Study: Lady Macbeth', *African Monthly*, 2/7 (1907), 31.

32. M. Anglin, 'His Infinite Variety', *Cape Times*, 24 April 1916, 9.

33. The constituency of the journal was defined as follows by E. Schreiner in 'A Debt of Honour', *Bluestocking*, 1/3 (1931), 4–5: 'The constitution of our federation recognises no barriers of creed, class or colour. Any member of any state who has attained a certain of education and passed through the liberalising and humanising influences of university life is welcomed into the ranks' (5).

34. G. Newman, 'The Fairy Lore in *A Midsummer Night's Dream*', *Bluestocking*, 5/2 (1935), 6.

35. M. E. Wright, 'The English Literature Syllabus', *Educational News of South Africa*, (Dec. 1937), 264.

36. *Syllabus for Senior Certificate* (Cape Town, 1930), 67.

37. Quoted in Wright, 'The English Literature Syllabus', 264.

38. M. M. Miller *et al.* 'The English Literature Course', *Educational News of South Africa* (Dec. 1937), 264.

39. Mrs M. Drennan, 'The Teaching of English', *Bluestocking*, 7/3 (1937) 3.

40. L. Gordon, *Shared Lives* (Cape Town, 1992), 47–8.

41. E. Schreiner, 'A Debt of Honour', 4.

42. For example, in the same edition of the *Bluestocking*, C. Williamson argues: 'In South Africa the white community could exist without a native population, but further north the material prosperity of the whites is inseparably bound up with that of the blacks'. And further: 'We feel white culture and race purity matter more to us than justice to a more primitive race' 'Imperial African Native Policy (in Relation to South Africa)', *Bluestocking*, 1/3 (1931), 28 and 29.

43. The history of the *rapprochement* in the 1930s between white English liberals and members of a small black urban élite is recorded by R.

Elphick, 'Mission Christianity and Interwar Liberalism', in Jeffrey Butler *et al.* (eds.), *Democratic Liberalism in South Africa* (Cape Town, 1987); T. Couzens, *The New African* (Johannesburg, 1985), 99–114; and P. Rich, *White Power and the Liberal Conscience* (Johannesburg, 1984), 10–53.

44. Dhlomo's criticism has been collected in a special ed. of *English in Africa* (4/2 (1977)), ed. N. W. Visser. The piece on African drama and poetry discussed below is repr. in this collection.

45. H. I. E. Dhlomo, 'African Drama and Poetry', *South African Outlook*, 1 Apr. 1939, 89.

46. B. W. Vilikazi, To the Editor, *South African Outlook*, 1 July 1939, 166.

47. For excellent analyses of the Newbolt Report, see C. Baldick, *The Social Mission of English Criticism* (Oxford, 1983), 92–106, and B. Doyle, *English and Englishness* (London, 1989), 41–67. Gargi Bhattacharyya's essay 'Cultural Education in Britain', *Oxford Literary Review*, 13 (1991), 4–19, charts the connections between attempts to incorporate the working classes into the nation in the 1920s with recent attempts in multicultural education to assimilate immigrant communities.

48. Newbolt Report, *The Teaching of English in England* (London, 1921), p. xii.

49. J. H. Fowler, *The Art of Teaching English* (London, 1932), 94.

50. *Hamlet* ed. J. Hampden (London, 1930), p. v.

51. *Othello* ed. G. Boas (London, 1934), 153.

52. *The Tempest* ed. E. Thompson (London, 1934), p. x.

53. This overview is drawn from S. Dubow, *Racial Segregation and The Origins of Apartheid in South Africa* (London, 1989), D. Yudelman, *The Emergence of Modern South Africa* (Westport, 1983), 249–62, and R. Davies *et al.* 'Class Struggle and the Periodisation of the State in South Africa', *Review of African Political Economy*, 7 (1976), 13–20.

54. Education was a beneficiary, and this was reflected in the 25 per cent increase in budget allocation, which rose from £3,278,981 in 1931 to £4,343,832 in 1939. The greatest percentage was, of course, allocated to white education: £2,785,966 for 158,975 white pupils; £631,631 for 122,029 Coloured pupils; and £451,309 for 202,763 black pupils. These figures are from the Reports of the Superintendent General of Education in the Cape of Good Hope in 1930 and 1939.

55. 'Humanism in the Schools', *Educational News of South Africa*, Jan. 1933, 3.

56. A factor contributing to the new urgency regarding the cultural mission of the schoolteacher was the advent of the cinema, which by the 1930s had precipitated in South Africa a reduction in the dramatic productions of Shakespeare. Quince notes this tendency: 'The increasing popularity of the cinema, particularly after the advent of the "talkies" in 1929, resulted in a dearth of productions in the 1930s. Shakespeare was kept alive by the schools, the University of Cape Town, and the amateur societies' (24).

57. L. Herman, 'The Appreciation of Literature in School', *Educational News of South Africa*, (Aug. 1930), 324.

58. Greig's work is discussed in more detail by C. M. W. Doherty in his study 'A Genealogical History of English Studies in South Africa', MA thesis, University of Natal, 96–102.

59. R. W. Watson, The Teaching of English Literature in Secondary Schools', B.Ed. thesis, University of Cape Town, 1939, 20.

60. 'Cape Town', *1820*, 27.

61. Examiner's Report, *Education Gazette*, 29/5 (1930), 179.
62. Cape of Good Hope, Department of Public Education, *Senior Certificate English Higher Examination 1930*, Paper 1.
63. It is of course important not to exaggerate the degree of freedom of expression allowed in the context of examinations. John Bowen, in 'Practical Criticism, Critical Practice', *Literature and History*, 13/1 (1987), 77–94, acutely summarizes the complex tyranny of the 'personal response' in writing about I. A. Richards: 'What is exemplary about Richards is the explicitness with which he seeks to reproduce an impossible, impossibly sincere "personal response" and equally an impossible consensus of socially produced evaluations. It is between those two poles, these two impossible demands, that students of English have had to pick their way ever since, condemned to a plausible ventriloquism, which is offered back to them, assessed, as their response' (91).
64. Cape of Good Hope, Department of Public Education, *Syllabus for Senior Syllabus 1930* (Cape Town, 1930), 44.
65. Cape of Good Hope, Department of Public Education, *Senior Certificate English Higher Examination 1939*, Paper 2.

CHAPTER 5

1. K. Marx, *Grundrisse. Foundations of the Critique of Political Economy* (Harmondsworth, 1973), 331.
2. See A. Sinfield, *Literature, Politics and Culture in Postwar Britain* (Oxford, 1989), 6–22; A. Calder, *The People's War* (London, 1969), 501–23; and C. Barnett, *The Audit of War* (London, 1987), 11–37.
3. Barnett, *The Audit of War*, 11.
4. G. Durrant, *Propaganda and Public Opinion* (Johannesburg, 1944), 1.
5. Williams's final chapter of *The Long Revolution* (Harmondsworth, 1965), entitled 'Britain in the 1960s', sets out a programme for socialist intervention in cultural production, with suggestions for how reorganizing cinema, broadcasting, publishing, and drama might stimulate 'a healthy cultural growth' (375). Williams's confession in *Politics and Letters* (London, 1981) that his *Long Revolution* plan was misconceived applies with even greater force to Durrant's plan: 'What I was wrong about was to assume that a cultural and educational programme alone could revitalise the left, [an error caused by] a radical underestimate of the capitalist state' (364).
6. Durrant, *Propaganda and Public Opinion*, 30.
7. G. Durrant, 'Prospero's Wisdom', *Theoria*, 7 (1955), 58.
8. Durrant argued the case for practical criticism with great vigour in *English Studies and the Community* (Pietermaritzburg, 1945), 'The Teaching of Poetry', in *Proceedings of the First Conference of University Teachers of English* (Johannesburg, 1946) and 'The Place of Practical Criticism in the University Curriculum', in W. S. Mackie (ed.), *Practical Criticism* (Cape Town, 1948). His arguments are summarized by Penrith, 'A Historical and Critical Account of the Teaching of English Language and Literature in English-Medium Universities in South Africa', MA thesis, University of Cape Town, 1972, 115–7, and Doherty, 'A Genealogical History of English

Studies in South Africa', MA thesis, University of Natal, 1989, 104–8. What Doherty emphasizes is Durrant's efforts to introduce the teaching of South African literature in South African English departments.

9. Durrant, *English Studies and the Community*, 3.

10. Quoted in P. Rich, *White Power and the Liberal Conscience* (Johannesburg, 1984), 118.

11. W. H. Gardner, in 'Practical Criticism', in *Proceedings of the Second Conference of University Teachers of English* (Pietermaritzburg, 1949), reproduces Durrant's ambitions for English studies in South Africa, and then makes the only reference to contemporaneous political events in all the academic literary criticism of the period I have surveyed: 'Our immediate aim is to produce mentally alert, humane and spiritually progressive citizens, and, in particular well-equipped teachers for the schools.... I began my First Year tutorials with a frontal attack on the debased cultural values, taking as my text, as it were, the first forty lines of Eliot's *The Waste Land*.... I went on to read Roy Campbell's poem called *The Zulu Girl*. By the method of oral question and answer I tried to make the students feel how, in that apparently simple poem, the smothered fury and repressed aspirations of the African natives are presented as ethnological and psychological realities; and as the Durban riots had taken place barely six weeks earlier, the prophetic insight of the poem needed no labouring' (24).

12. D. R. C. Marsh, *The Recurring Miracle* (Pietermaritzburg, 1962), p. v.

13. As a student at the time in Pietermaritzburg, Graham Pechey recalls the elaborate lengths he had to go to obtain Left Book Club publications. The general indifference on the part of South African English lecturers to Marxism is indicated by Philip Segal, in 'Practical Criticism and Critical Practice', in *Essays and Lectures* (Cape Town, 1973), where he sneers at the Marxist habit of treating poetry as 'a chemical "product" of struggles' (22), and then concludes that 'Marxist criticism [is] sometimes valuable, sometimes thoroughly mediaeval in its tendency to look upon every book as an allegory on the salvation of the proletarian soul' (24).

14. The most dogged perpetrator of this myth was Guy Butler. For discussion of Butler and the limitations of his thought, see M. Kirkwood, 'The Colonizer: A Critique of the English South African Culture Theory', in P. Wilhelm and J. Polley (eds.), *Poetry 74* (Johannesburg, 1976), and E. Williams, 'Guy Butler and South African Culture', MA thesis, University of Cape Town, 1989.

15. I am grateful to Graham Pechey for his English II lecture notes, from which the quoted passage is taken.

16. A. Paton, *Cry, the Beloved Country* (Harmondsworth, 1958), 125, 149.

17. There is a short biography of van Heyningen in J. A. Berthoud and C. O. Gardner's introduction to *The Sole Function* (Pietermaritzburg, 1969), a collection of essays dedicated to her.

18. C. van Heyningen, *On the Printed Page* (Cape Town, 1969), 3.

19. C. van Heyningen, 'Christian National Education', *African South*, 4/3 (1960), 52.

20. C. van Heyningen, 'Afrikaans Translations of Shakespeare', *Vista*, 1 (1950), 17.

21. e.g. A. C. Partridge's *The Humanities and English Studies* (Johannesburg, 1956), R. G. Howarth's 'The Life of Literature', *Southerly*, 3 (1958), 1–12,

Guy Butler's *The Republic and the Arts* (Johannesburg, 1964), and A. G. Woodward's *Aspects of Literary Experience* (Johannesburg, 1966).

22. A. C. Partridge, in his editorial for the first edition of *English Studies in Africa* (1958), sets out the journal's function thus: 'The task of *English Studies in Africa* will be to serve the English language on this Continent, and to promote the study of the best English literature, wherever it is written. A great tradition in the hands of a minority group, as the English-speaking people happen to be in Africa, must give tangible evidence of the will of the group to survive' (1). A typical edition, presumably evincing the group's will to survive, included essays on Shakespeare and Italy; Chesterton and St Thomas; poetry; Secundum Iohannem Maundvyle; Congreve and Ann Bracegirdle; the Self in Hopkins; Pre-Raphaelitism; the teaching of English in the Congolese Republic; and book reviews. (This is the table of contents of the Sept. 1961 edn.)

23. Doherty, 'A Genealogical History of English Studies in South Africa', 104–5, summarizes these statistics, and makes the additional point that the practical criticism teaching method, with its tutorial-size classes, at times was at odds with burgeoning student numbers.

24. Quoted in M. Cross and L. Chisolm, 'The Roots of Segregated Schooling in Twentieth Century South Africa', in M. Nkomo (ed.), *Pedagogy of Domination* (Trenton, 1990), 54.

25. Quoted in H. Bernstein, 'Schools for Servitude', in Alex La Guma (ed.), *Apartheid* (London, 1972), 46.

26. The major work on the period, Deborah Posel's *The Making of Apartheid 1948–1961* (Oxford, 1991), explores with great care the connections between capital and the apartheid state. The relation between capital and state education is described in P. Kallaway (ed.), *Apartheid and Education* (Braamfontein, 1984), and Nkomo (ed.), *Pedagogy of Domination* (Trenton, 1990).

27. Peter Kallaway in 'From Bantu Education to People's Education in South Africa', in *Handbook of Educational Ideas and Practices* (London, 1990), insists that 'Bantu Education, far from being a unique form of schooling, was simply a locally specific form of mass schooling under capitalism, that had the eccentric feature of identifying working-class children by the colour of their skin' (235). The need to look beyond apartheid definitions in studying education in South Africa is also stressed by Bill Nasson in 'Perspectives on Education in South Africa', in S. Burman and P. Reynolds (eds.), *Growing up in a Divided Society* (Johannesburg, 1986): 'For the sake of clarity, writers, the present included, have dealt in segregationist labelling: white education, black education, liberal (white) educational history, radical (black) educational history, and so on. Without such perspectives, educational differences would naturally be impossible to define, and comparisons and contrasts regarding such factors as expenditure, pupil-teacher ratios, and drop-out rates, impossible to make. But over and above such considerations, there is a compelling need to consider a type of analysis more accommodating to the idea of education having a single and inclusive pattern of action' (96).

28. D. Yudelman, *The Emergence of Modern South Africa* (Westport, Conn., 1983), 13–14.

29. The record of British and US investment in South Africa is described by R. First, J. Steele, and C. Gurney, *The South African Connection* (London,

1972), and M. Legassick, 'The Record of British Firms in South Africa', *South African Labour Bulletin*, 2/1 (1975), 7–36.

30. The statistics on education cited in the para. below are drawn from Elaine Unterhalter, 'Changing Aspects of Reformism in Bantu Education', in E. Unterhalter *et al.* (eds.), *Apartheid Education and Popular Struggles* (Johannesburg, 1991), and Ken Hartshorne, *Crisis and Challenge* (Cape Town, 1992). The most comprehensive source for statistics on education under apartheid are the Annual Reports of the South African Institute for Race Relations edited by Muriel Horrell.

31. 'Proposed Syllabus in English as a First Language', *Education Gazette*, 50/1 (1951), 759.

32. Union of South Africa, Department of Education, *English First Language Senior Certificate 1952*, Paper 1.

33. Cape of Good Hope, Department of Education, *English First Language Senior Certificate 1958*, Paper 1.

34. *Macbeth*, ed. J. L. du Plooy and V. H. Vaughan (London, 1960), p. xiii.

35. *A Midsummer Night's Dream*, ed. P. de Munnik (Johannesburg, 1967), p. x.

36. *The Tempest*, ed. H. J. Oldendorf and H. Arguile (Cape Town, 1956), p. 4.

37. *The Tempest*, ed. de Munnik, p. xxviii.

38. *The Tempest*, ed. I. S. Middleton and V. H. Vaughan (Johannesburg, 1964), p. xxiii.

39. *The Tempest*, ed. de Munnik, p. viii.

40. *Macbeth*, ed. Du Plooy and Vaughan, p. v.

41. *The Tempest*, ed. Middleton and Vaughan, p. vi.

42. I. J. Kriel, 'English Teaching in South African Schools', *Trek*, 14/10 (1950), 25.

43. J. B. Gardener, ' The English-Speaking Pupil and South African Set-Books', *English Studies in Africa*, 13/1 (1970), 26.

44. Union of South Africa, Department of Bantu Education, *English Second Language Examination Standard VI 1952*.

45. End of an Educational Era', *Ikhwesi Lomso*, Feb. 1959, 3.

46. D. N. Young, 'An Approach to the Teaching of Shakespeare's Plays', *Bantu Education Journal*, 14/6 (1968), 31.

47. D. N. Young, 'The Teaching of Shakespeare in the Classroom: II', *Bantu Education Journal*, 14/8 (1968), 32.

48. Many have argued that Shakespeare has special resonances for black students. Ken Hartshorne, in 'Literature across Cultures', *English Studies in Africa*, 13/1 (1970), 67–79, for example, concludes that Shakespeare in some ways appeals more to black than to white students: 'The idea of Kingship, that golden thread running through so much of Shakespeare, he finds far easier to accept and understand than his White counterpart' (67). At this stage, my point is to establish that whether certain black students liked Shakespeare or not, his presence in black schools in the 1950s did not seriously impair the imposition of Bantu Education.

49. *Maynardville Tenth Anniversary Programme* (Cape Town, 1964), 11.

50. 'The Bard—Kids Love him Nowadays', *Cape Times*, 1 May 1969, 5.

51. 'Council Row on Maynardville Show Audiences', *Cape Times*, 28 Oct. 1965, 3.

52. The *Drum* writers have received a substantial amount of critical attention.

The fullest treatment is that of D. Rabkin, 'Drum Magazine 1951–1961', Ph.D. thesis, University of Leeds, 1975, but see also K. Sole, 'Class, Continuity and Change in Black South African Literature', in B. Bozzoli, Labour Townships and Protest (Johannesburg, 1979), M. Chapman (ed.), The 'Drum' Decade (Pietermaritzburg, 1985), and P. Gready, 'The Sophiatown Writers of the Fifties', Journal of Southern African Studies, 16/1 (1990), 139–64.

53. P. Abrahams, Tell Freedom (London, 1954), 48.

54. C. Themba, 'Through Shakespeare's Africa', New African, 2/8 (1963), 150.

55. B. Modisane, Blame me on History (Craighall, 1986), 143.

56. In Modisane's short story 'The Situation', Black Orpheus, 12 (1964), 10–16, the protagonist Caiaphus is forced at gunpoint by the gangster Deadwood Dick to perform Mark Antony's speech from Julius Caesar. In this story, Shakespeare is identified at the same time with élite English culture (Caiaphus' intimate knowledge of Shakespeare separates him from the gangsters), and with the street culture of Sophiatown (the gangsters know and enjoy the speech from seeing the movie version with Marlon Brando). My thanks to Mark Sanders for directing me to this short story.

57. Joe Ka Nelani reviews King of the Bastards in the Torch, 5/7 (1950), 6. Commenting on the glowing foreword provided by J. C. Smuts, the reviewer concludes: 'Reading the novel reveals not only the emptiness of Smuts's encomiums, not only his profound ignorance of South African history, but also Sarah Gertrude Millin's artistic barrenness and smallness as a writer, largely due to her neurotic preoccupation with the colour of people's skins' (6). Much of the review is taken up refuting Millin's version of South African history.

58. Albert Thomas, in 'The Good Woman of Setzuan: Little Theatre Production a Fraud', Citizen, 3/5 (1958), 9, is very critical of the élitist context of the production: 'The UCT drama school is just what it is and in no way capable of fulfilling the basic function of the Brechtian aesthetic: Theatre for the people!'

59. Carter Ebrahim in later years became Minister of Education in the House of Representatives, presiding with very little popular support over the 1985–6 school boycotts in the Western Cape. One of the student slogans of 1985 was 'We won't barter with Carter'. For more on post-war radical politics in the Western Cape, see Bill Nasson, 'Opposition Politics and Ideology in the Western Cape', in G. Moss and I. Obery (eds.), South African Review 5 (Johannesburg, 1989), and Gavin Lewis's Between the Wire and the Wall (Cape Town, 1987), 245–71.

60. C. Ebrahim, 'The Drama and Society', Discussion, 1/6 (1952), 27.

61. 'Impressed', Review of Episode, by Harold Bloom, Torch, 11/12 (1956), 6.

62. Michael Harmel wrote a four-part commentary on Schreiner in New Age, 1/20 (1955), 7, emphasizing the relevance of her anti-racist commitments to Verwoerd's South Africa, and also her sympathy for Marxism.

63. The article by J.C., entitled 'Robert Tressell and his Book', Guardian, 15/49 (3 Jan. 1952), 2, reviews F. C. Ball's biography of Tressell, and focuses on the effect on Tressell of his time spent in South Africa. The article concludes by quoting the optimistic ending to The Ragged Trousered Philanthropists cut by earlier editors.

64. Stanley Uys reviews Gordimer's novel A World of Strangers, praising her

ability to satirize northern-suburbs Johannesburg, but criticizing severely the plausibility of her protagonist and her depiction of shebeen life.

65. Ezekiel Mphahlele, in 'Negro Poet: Trumpet at his Lips', *Fighting Talk*, 15/11 (1961), 12–13, favourably reviews Hughes's poetry, praising in particular Hughes's ability to transcend the limits of 'outlived dead-pan protest' (13).

66. Bennie Bunsee, in *Fighting Talk*, 17/2 (1963), 10–11 reviews Paton's play *Sponono*, comparing it unfavourably to works by Alex la Guma and Richard Rive, and concluding with a criticism of Paton's liberalism: 'Much as I admire Paton's humanism and know him to be a man of the utmost sincerity and honesty and integrity, yet his Christianity with the charity bowl only bolsters up reaction. His Christianity is good for those who practise it but not for the millions who find it used to protect vested interests' (11).

67. S. Kahn, 'Poets of Reaction', *Advance*, 14 Jan. 1954, 4.

68. W. Soyinka, *Myth, Literature and the African World* (Cambridge, 1976), 127.

CHAPTER 6

1. E. Said, *The World, the Text, and the Critic* (London, 1983), 241–2.

2. V. Dhareshwar, in 'Toward a Narrative Epistemology of the Postcolonial Predicament', *Inscriptions*, 5 (1989), suggests that Said's travelling theory would need to be rethought when it moves outside the relatively unified space of Europe (Budapest to Paris to Cambridge). Difficult questions must be faced: 'The task of making theory travel *to* postcolonial spaces (rather than confining oneself to "representing" the latter) thus requires an examination of the relationship between the object of theory and the political objectives of postcolonial intellectuals working within the field of theory' (145).

3. A. Rich, 'Notes towards a Politics or Location', in *Blood, Bread and Poetry* (New York, 1986), 210–1.

4. Another influential essay reflecting on the limits of Western feminism is Chandra Mohanty's 'Under Western Eyes: Feminist Scholarship and Colonial Discourses', *Boundary* 2, 12/3–13/1 (1984), 333–57. In an articulate attack on Western feminist thought, Mohanty stresses in particular the tendency of Western thinkers to homogenize distinct Third World struggles and identities: 'And it is in the production of this "Third World Difference" that Western feminisms appropriate and "colonize" the fundamental complexities and conflicts which characterise the lives of women of different classes, religions, cultures, races and castes in these countries. It is in this process of homogenization and systematization of the third world that power is exercised in much of recent Western feminist discourse, and this power needs to be defined and named' (335).

5. C. Lockett, 'Feminism(s) and Writing in English in South Africa', *Current Writing*, 2/1 (1990), 2.

6. S. Maqagi, 'Who Theorises?', *Current Writing*, 2/1 (1990), 23.

7. M. Orkin, *Shakespeare against Apartheid* (Craighall, 1987), 11.

8. L. Wright, Review of *Shakespeare against Apartheid*, *Shakespeare in Southern Africa*, 1 (1987), 73.

9. R. Barthes, 'The Death of the Author', in *Image Music Text* (London, 1977), 146.

10. Several qualifications are necessary regarding this use of Barthes. First, his 'Death of the Author' essay is itself a stopover rather than main terminal for travelling theory; it is a selective appropriation of ideas disseminated principally from Germany: Husserl's theory of the sign; Nietzsche's cultural criticism; Freud's procedures of interpretation and decoding; and Marx's concept of ideology as signification. Second, Barthes's work is *not* a moment of authentic radical dissent; indeed, in his own elaborate performances-as-author, Barthes himself appears as critical authority providing the academy with exhaustive readings of selected texts, an irony that undercuts his anti-authoritarian claims. Third, this particular Barthes essay is used strategically, metonymically, standing in for Theory; in itself, it has not been especially influential in South Africa.

11. P. Anderson, 'Components of the National Culture', *New Left Review*, 50 (1968), 6. There are a number of obvious exceptions to Anderson's intellectual history, not least the influence of Marx himself on the British left. Further, Anderson's division of British common sense and European theory is also somewhat artificial. None the less, the broad contours of his argument remain plausible.

12. Leavis's own theoretical impoverishment, as well as his ambivalent radicalism, have been elaborated at length. See e.g. Anderson, 'Components of the National Culture', 50–6; F. Mulhern, *The Moment of Scrutiny* (London, 1981), 305–31; and T. Eagleton, *Literary Theory* (Oxford, 1983), 30–43.

13. Quoted in B. Doyle, *English and Englishness* (London, 1989), 111. For further detail on the journals and institutions governing English studies in the post-war period, see ibid. 94–132 and S. Laing, 'The Production of Literature', in A. Sinfield (ed.), *Society and Literature 1945–1970* (London, 1983), 144–53. Doyle is particularly useful in two areas: in summarizing the important initiatives that emerged outside Oxbridge, and in demonstrating the deeply entrenched and continuing conservatism of English studies.

14. K. Muir, 'Changing Interpretations of Shakespeare', in *The Pelican Guide to English Literature*, ii (Harmondsworth, 1955), 299.

15. J. Drakakis (ed.), *Alternative Shakespeares* (London, 1985), 10–11.

16. A. Kettle, *Shakespeare in a Changing World* (London, 1964), 12.

17. D. Longhurst, 'Reproducing a National Culture: Shakespeare and Education', 12–13. A. Sinfield, in 'Give an Account of Shakespeare and Education', in J. Dollimore and A. Sinfield (eds.), *Political Shakespeare* (Manchester, 1985), looks at more recent developments in secondary school literature teaching, reinforcing Longhurst's assessment of Shakespeare's function in secondary education: 'The examination papers construct Shakespeare and the candidate in terms of individuated subjectivity through their stress upon Shakespeare's free-standing genius, their emphasis on characterisation, and their demand for the candidate's personal response' (140). Sinfield demonstrates not only the continuity with

Bradley, but also the limitations of the more recent progressivist, pupil-centred approaches to English teaching which emerged in the 1960s.

18. *Critical Quarterly* (1969), preface.
19. T. Pateman (ed.), *Counter Course* (Harmondsworth, 1972), 7.
20. J. Spriggs, 'Doing Eng. Lit.', in Pateman (ed.), *Counter Course*, 238.
21. R. Williams, *Marxism and Literature* (Oxford, 1977), 4.
22. See S. Hall, 'A Critical Survey of the Theoretical and Practical Achievements of the Last Ten Years', in *Literature, Society and the Sociology of Literature* (Colchester, 1976); P. Widdowson (ed.), *Re-reading English* (London, 1982); and A. Sinfield, 'Literary Theory and the Crisis in English Studies', *Critical Quarterly*, 3 (1983), 35–47, for more detail on this new work. Anthony Easthope, in *British Post-structuralism since 1968* (London, 1988), describes in detail the impact of French thought on the British intellectual left in the late 1960s and 1970s. A recent work that discusses the genesis and initial context of Barthes's essay is Sean Burke's *The Death and Return of the Author* (Edinburgh, 1992).
23. F. Barker *et al.* (eds.), *Literature, Politics and Theory* (London, 1986), p. xii.
24. C. McCabe (ed.), *Broken English* (Manchester, 1988), 3.
25. R. Wilson and R. Dutton (eds.), *New Historicism and Renaissance Drama* (London, 1992), 2.
26. Dollimore and Sinfield (eds.), *Political Shakespeare*, p. vii.
27. M. Evans, *Signifying Nothing* (Hemel Hempstead, 1989), 102–3.
28. R. Williams, *Writing in Society* (London, 1983), 196.
29. A. Sinfield, *Literature, Politics and Culture in Postwar Britain* (Oxford, 1989), 198.
30. M. Bristol, *Shakespeare's America, America's Shakespeare* (London, 1990), 16.
31. The relation between British and US literary criticism since the war is also described by Eagleton, *Literary Theory*, 44–53, and A. Ahmad, *In Theory* (London, 1992), 46–64. They both concur with Sinfield as regards the conservatism of New Criticism, with Ahmad acutely extending his discussion to current critical fashion, but they do not place as much emphasis on the influence of US patterns on English studies in Britain.
32. D. Simpson, 'Literary Criticism and the Return of "History"', *Critical Inquiry*, 14, (1988), 725.
33. Said, *The World, the Text, and the Critic*, 3.
34. Ahmad, *In Theory*, 60.
35. This is a controversial assertion. Robert Young, in *White Mythologies* (London, 1990), for example, argues that French post-structuralists have a deep insight into the contradictions of cultural imperialism. (See esp. his favourable commentary on Helene Cixous in Ch. 1.)
36. There is already a substantial amount of criticism on the relation between British and US Renaissance work of the last ten years. Wilson and Dutton (eds.), *New Historicism and Renaissance Drama*, contains a selection of the better-known articles, as well as an introduction and postscript detailing areas of convergence and disagreement. For a range of views on the politics of Renaissance studies in the 1980s and 1990s, see J. Goldberg, 'The Politics of Renaissance Literature', *ELH* 49 (1982), 514–42; J. E. Howard, 'The New Historicism in Renaissance Studies', *English Literary Renaissance* 16 (1983), 13–43; L. Montrose, 'Renaissance Literary Studies and the Subject of History', *English Literary Renaissance*, 16 (1986), 5–12; W. Cohen, 'Political Criticism of Shakespeare', in J. E. Howard and

M. O'Connor (eds.), *Shakespeare Reproduced* (New York, 1986); D. E. Wayne, 'Power, Politics and the Shakespearean Text', in Howard and O'Connor (eds.), *Shakespeare Reproduced*; G. Taylor, *Reinventing Shakespeare* (London, 1989), 298–372; J. Holstun, 'Ranting at the New Historicism', *English Literary Renaissance*, 19 (1989), 189–225; C. Porter, 'History and Literature: "After the New Historicism"', *New Literary History*, 21 (1990), 253–72; Dollimore and Sinfield (eds.), *Political Shakespeare*, 2–17; and J. Dollimore, 'Culturalism, Feminism and Marxist Humanism' *New Literary History*, 21 (1990), 471–92.

37. J. Goldberg, *Voice Terminal Echo* (London, 1986), 2.

38. Ahmad, *In Theory*, 56–7.

39. Doyle, *English and Englishness*, 132.

40. In providing a sense of South African history of the past twenty-five years, I have drawn on the following sources: for a record of foreign investment, R. First, J. Steele, and C. Gurney, *The South African Connection* (London, 1972), 9–40; R. W. Hull, *American Enterprise in South Africa* (New York, 1990), 242–359; and M. Legassick, 'The Record of British Firms in South Africa', *South African Labour Bulletin*, 2/1 (1975), 7–36; for a general economic history, S. Terreblanche and N. Nattrass, 'A Periodization of the South African Economy from 1910', in N. Nattrass and E. Ardington (eds.), *The Political Economy of South Africa* (Oxford, 1990), 14–23; B. Magubane, *The Political Economy of Race and Class in South Africa* (New York, 1980), 193–220; and M. Hartwig and R. Sharp, 'The State and the Reproduction of Labour Power in South Africa', in P. Kallaway (ed.), *Apartheid and Education* (Braamfontein, 1984), 318–40; for the conflict between the state and political opposition, T. Lodge, *Black Politics in South Africa* (Johannesburg, 1983), 321–62; J. Saul and S. Gelb, *The Crisis in South Africa* (London, 1986), 9–44; H. Wolpe, *Race, Class and the Apartheid State* (London, 1988), 71–110; and A. Callinicos, *South Africa between Reform and Revolution* (London, 1988), 59–126; for the struggles in education, J. Davies, 'Capital, State and Educational Reform in South Africa', in Kallaway (ed.), *Apartheid and Education*; L. Chisolm, 'Redefining Skills', in Kallaway (ed.), *Apartheid and Education*; E. Unterhalter, 'Changing Aspects of Reformism in Bantu Education', in Unterhalter *et al.* (eds.), *Apartheid Education and Popular Struggles* (Johannesburg, 1991); B. Nasson, 'Redefining Inequality', in B. Nasson and J. Samuel (eds.), *Education* (Cape Town, 1990); J. Hyslop, 'State Education Policy and the Social Reproduction of the Urban African Working Class', *Journal of Southern African Studies*, 14/3 (1988), 453–76, and 'Schools, Unemployment and Youth', in Nasson and Samuel (eds.), *Education*; C. Bundy, 'Action, Comrades, Action!', in W. G. James and M. Simons (eds.), *The Angry Divide* (Cape Town, 1989); B. Hirson, *Year of Fire, Year of Ash* (London, 1979), 40–75; M. Cross and L. Chisolm, 'The Roots of Segregated Schooling', in M. Nkomo (ed.), *Pedagogy of Domination* (Trenton, 1990), 53–74; P. Kallaway, 'From Bantu Education to People's Education', in *Handbook of Educational Ideas and Practices* (London, 1990), 149–62; and G. Trotter, 'Education and the Economy', in Nattrass and Ardington (eds.), *The Political Economy of South Africa*. These divisions are not absolute, as many of these commentators make suggestive connections between economics, politics, and education.

41. Hull, *American Enterprise in South Africa*, 257.

42. Commentators like Nasson, in 'Redefining Inequality', and P. Kallaway in 'Privatisation and the Educational Politics of the New Right', in G. Moss and I. Obery (eds.), *South African Review 5* (Johannesburg, 1989), emphasize the increased intervention in recent years on the part of capital in the education system. Kallaway (155–8) notes in particular the privatization of sections of South African education, inspired by Thatcher's similar policies in Britain.

43. Nasson, 'Redefining Inequality', 78.

44. Ahmed Essop, in his short story 'The Nightingale and the Dove', from the collection *Noorjehan and Other Stories* (Johannesburg, 1990), has the narrator reflecting on the desperate poignancy of teaching Keats's 'Ode to a Nightingale' at a Soweto high school after 1976. The narrator sees a dying wood-dove in the road on his way home from the school, and ponders: 'I sat there for a while with the dead wood-dove in my hand. I thought of the nightingale in the "Ode". Both birds were dead. And the children whose hearts the soldier's hearts had riven—they were dead too' (108).

45. Orkin, for example, distinguishes in 'Holofernes and the Transvaal Senior Schools Certificate', *Crux*, 16/3 (1982), 27–36, between the 'Shakespeare who is taught because he has profound things to say about the human condition [and] the Shakespeare of the Transvaal Senior Schools Certificate' (27), the latter being a dull figure diminished by a process of fragmentation into examinable parts.

46. The main contributors to the arguments in *Crux* were: M. J. Black, 'A Case for Shakespeare', *Crux*, 16/2 (1982), 31–2; P. Edmunds, 'Perseverance Keeps Honour Bright', *Crux*, 19/1 (1985), 9–13; C. Morton, 'A Case against Shakespeare', *Crux*, 15/3 (1981), 33–5; Orkin, 'Holofernes and the Transvaal Senior Schools Certificate'; J. Sherman, 'Cultural Despotism and the Shakespeare Treadmill', *Crux*, 19/3–4 (1985), 65–71, and 'No Literature for Anybody', *Crux*, 18/2 (1984), 3–8; and J. Unterslak and D. Ricci, 'Shakespeare for Enjoyment and Instruction', *Crux*, 19/2 (1985), 51–5. They are summarized by S. Bock in 'Teaching *Macbeth* to the 1988 Matriculation Class at SACHED, Grahamstown', BA (Hons.) thesis, Rhodes University, 1988.

47. See P. N. Mullineux, 'An Examination of the Use of the Contextual Question in Examining Shakespeare's Plays', MA thesis, Rhodes University, 1988, 38–48, for further analysis and examples of examination papers from the Cape Education Department.

48. This was an examination paper set by the Department of Education and Culture for third-year Afrikaans-speaking Coloured students training to be primary school teachers. These tortured descriptions of exactly where particular examination papers come from are a consequence of the apartheid education system, which created over fifteen education departments for different provinces and state-constituted race groups. See Bock, 'Teaching *Macbeth*', 3–14, for a summary of the English Second Language requirements for the literature examination.

49. *Weekly Mail*, 6–10 June 1988.

50. Sol Makgabutlane, 'The Pied Piper', *Tribute* (June 1990), 25. My thanks to Duncan Brown for directing me to this article.

51. G. Willoughby, 'Friends, Schoolchildren . . . Lend me your Ears!', *Weekly Mail*, 10/23 (10–16 June 1994), 31.

52. J. Reid, *English Literature in South African Senior Schools* (Cape Town, 1982), 78.

53. M. Gardner, 'Liberating Language', in Nasson and Samuel (eds.), *Education*, 162.

54. There has in the last five years been an enormous amount of work on post-apartheid language policy, and the teaching of English has figured centrally. On language policy generally, see: N. Alexander, *Language Policy and National Unity in South Africa* (Cape Town, 1989), and National Education Crisis Committee, 'Towards a Language Policy for a Post-apartheid South Africa', in *Readings from a Workshop Held in Harare* (Harare, 1990). On the teaching of English specifically, see N. Ndebele, *Rediscovery of the Ordinary* (Johannesburg, 1991), 91–118; R. Aitken, 'Masks as Cultural Defence', *English Academy Review*, 4 (1987), 215–26; and A. Potter, 'The Role of So-called "English" Departments in English Studies in South Africa', *Journal for Language Teaching*, 21/2 (1987), 1–7.

55. A. Lemmer, 'ESL Shakespeare in Schools and Colleges', *NESLATT Journal*, 4 (1989), 25.

56. A. Lemmer, 'Upgrading the Study of Shakespeare in Southern African Secondary Schools', *Shakespeare in Southern Africa*, 2 (1988), 68.

57. S. Joubert, 'Publishing in Another South Africa', *African Book Publishing Record*, 17/1 (1991), 10.

58. ANC Education Department, *A Policy Framework for Education and Training*, 98.

59. Core Syllabus Committee for English, *English Guideline Document* (n.p., 1993), 10.

60. In discussions with a number of education planners, the general impression is that Shakespeare is likely to continue in high schools for the foreseeable future. Two factors are emphasized: the perception among black students of Shakespeare as representing a necessary acquisition for upward mobility, and the conservatism of the teaching profession, who 'know how to do Shakespeare', and are wary of change. I am grateful to Joan Ashworth, Zubeida Desai, Peter Kallaway, Jeanne Prinsloo, and Lorraine Singh for spending time discussing this issue with me.

61. The full history of this period of turbulent debate in South African English studies remains to be written. Important contributions have included: T. Couzens, 'The ABC of Research', *Africa Perspective*, 4 (1976), 21–6, and 'Criticism of South African Literature', *Work in Progress*, 2 (1977), 44–52; M. Green, 'The Manifesto and the Fifth Column', *Critical Arts*, 3/2 (1984), 9–19; E. Harber, 'South Africa: The White English-Speaking Sensibility', *Journal of Commonwealth Literature*, 11/1 (1976), 57–71; G. Haresnape, 'The Battle for the Books', *English Studies in Africa*, 31/1 (1988), 41–9; I. Hofmeyr, 'Problems of Creative Writers', *Work in Progress*, 2 (1977), 31–7, and 'The State of South African English Criticism', *English in Africa*, 6/2 (1979), 39–50; E. Mphahlele, 'Prometheus in Chains', *English Academy Review*, 2/1 (1984), 89–104; R. Ryan, 'Literary-Intellectual Behavior in South Africa', *Boundary* 2 (1988), 283–304; K. Sole, 'Problems of Creative Writers in South Africa', *Work in Progress*, 1 (1977), 4–25; M. Vaughan, 'A Critique of the Dominant Ideas in Departments of English in the English-Speaking Universities of South Africa', *Critical Arts*, 3/2 (1984), 35–51; A. Van der Hoven, 'Planning the Future of English Studies in South

Africa', *Theoria*, 68 (1986), 107–18; N. Visser, 'The Critical Situation and the Situation of Criticism', *Critical Arts*, 3/2 (1984), 2–8; and C. Wilhelm, 'Trends in Recent English Fiction and Criticism in South Africa', *English in Africa*, 5/2 (1978), 17–27.

62. C. Doherty, in 'A Genealogical History of English Studies in South Africa' MA thesis, University of Natal, 1989, discusses these early attempts to include South African literature in English syllabuses in detail (159–65).

63. M. Kirkwood, 'The Colonizer', in P. Wilhelm and J. Polley (eds.), *Poetry 74* (Johannesburg, 1976), 125.

64. Vaughan, 'A Critique of the Dominant Ideas', 38.

65. Hofmeyr, 'The State of South African Literary Criticism', *English in Africa*, 6/2 (1979), 41.

66. Also energetic in this direction were Stephen Gray, Brian Willan, and Nic Visser. There is more detailed discussion of their work in Ch. 4.

67. Couzens, 'The ABC of Research', 20.

68. Hofmeyr, 'The State of South African Literary Criticism', 41.

69. These disagreements are summarized by C. Bundy, *Re-making the Past* (Cape Town, 1986), 1–7; C. Saunders, *The Making of the South African Past* (Cape Town, 1988), 165–91; and K. Smith, *The Changing Past* (Johannesburg, 1988), 155–228.

70. Hofmeyr, 'The State of South African Literary Criticism', 44.

71. Green, The Manifesto and the Fifth Column', 10.

72. K. Sole, 'Class, Continuity and Change in Black South African Literature', in B. Bozzoli (ed.), *Labour, Townships and Protest* (Johannesburg, 1979), 144.

73. B. Cooper, 'Some Generalisations about the Class Situation of the Writer-Intellectual from Independent in Africa', *African Perspective*, 16 (1980), 78.

74. See M. Nkomo's essay 'Foreign Policy and Scholarship Programmes for Black South Africans', in Nkomo (ed.), *Pedagogy of Domination* (Trenton, 1990) on US scholarship programmes for black South Africans for valuable insights into the politics of student funding.

75. The interviews with Coetzee in D. Atwell's edited collection of Coetzee's essays, *Doubling the Point*, are illuminating in this regard.

76. It has become the norm for articles in South African literary journals to cite critical theory, with the pattern particularly marked in the *Journal of Literary Studies*, *Current Writing*, and *Pretexts*. The exchanges in the 1990 edn. of *Pretexts* between Visser, Sole, and Atwell seem to be in part about whether British socialist or US deconstructive critical practices serve the forging of a democratic intellectual culture in South Africa more effectively. My hesitations about *any* Western theory, and particularly US theory, travelling to South Africa are set out above, but I would none the less resist privileging either (as would the three critics above, I assume).

77. G. Butler, 'Editorial'.

78. L. Wright, 'Shakespeare and the Bomber Pilot', *Shakespeare in Southern Africa*, 2 (1988), 84.

79. Orkin, *Shakespeare against Apartheid*, 14.

80. One question beyond the scope of this chapter is the extent to which theory travels *within* Southern Africa. Clearly universities have greater

cultural capital, and disseminate theory throughout the subcontinent, while schools and colleges receive theory. In a useful, though now slightly out-of-date, survey of English department policy-makers, Patricia Marzo observes that those academics at South African universities enjoying the greatest influences at schools were all educated at white South African universities or at Oxbridge, and include Guy Butler, Peter Haworth, Helen Gardner, and F. R. Leavis.

81. K. Marx, *The Eighteenth Brumaire*, in *Surveys from Exile*, ed. D. Fernbach (Harmondsworth, 1973), 146–7.

AFTERWORD

1. J. Godden, *Overcoming Adult Literacy* (London, 1991), 1.
2. These positions, and several others, as regards the role of the left in the new South Africa have been given fullest expression in (the now extinct) *Work in Progress*. See e.g. J. Cronin, 'We Need more than Group Therapy', *Work in Progress*, 89 (1993), 13–15; C. Bundy, 'Theory of a Special Type', *Work in Progress*, 89 (1993), 16–19, 'Middle Road or Cul de sac', *Work in Progress*, 91 (1993), 37–8; L. Harris, 'One Step Forward . . .', *Work in Progress*, 89 (1993), 20–2; E. Laclau, 'Socialism Goes off the Beaten Track', *Work in Progress*, 90 (1993), 33–6; and P. Hudson and S. Louw, 'Beware the Shining Path!', *Work in Progress*, 90 (1993), 37–9.
3. There are no such clear alignments in South African English studies; rather, there is a common anxiety over the future of the discipline. The titles of recent inaugural lectures by Chairs of English betray this anxiety: A. Brink, *Why Literature?* (Grahamstown, 1980); M. van Wyk Smith, *What Literature?* (Grahamstown, 1981); A. E. Voss, *Living in a Critical Community* (Pietermaritzburg, 1984); M. Chapman, *Literary Studies in South Africa* (Pietermaritzburg, 1985); and Johan Gouws, *The Pursuit of Poetry* (Grahamstown, 1990). The anxiety is explained by Alex Potter in 'The Role of So-called "English" Departments in English Studies in South Africa' as a question of economics: 'I wonder how much it costs in real terms to sensitise a few hundred privileged students . . . to literature each year, so that they can go out and perpetuate the system, so using up more and more scarce national resources' (4).

Bibliography

ABRAHAMS, PETER, *Tell Freedom* (London: Faber & Faber, 1954).

ABRAMS, PHILIP, 'History, Sociology, Historical Sociology', *Past and Present*, 87 (1980), 3–16.

ADAMSON, JAMES CONSTANTINE, *Modern Literature: An Address Delivered at the Fifteenth Annual Meeting of the Subscribers to the Public Library* (Cape Town: J. H. Collard, 1844).

AHMAD, AIJAZ, *In Theory: Classes, Nations, Literatures* (London: Verso, 1992).

AITKEN, RICHARD, 'Masks as Cultural Defence: Reflections on "English" as a Discipline in a Black Context', *English Academy Review*, 4 (1987), 215–26.

'A Lady', 'A Plea for Colonial Girls', *Cape Monthly Magazine*, 10 (May 1875), 320.

ALEXANDER, NEVILLE, *Language Policy and National Unity in South Africa* (Cape Town: Buchu Books, 1989).

ALTICK, RICHARD D., *The English Common Reader* (Chicago: University of Chicago Press, 1957).

'A Luxury of Life', *Educational Journal*, 2/5 (June 1916), 8.

ANC EDUCATION DEPARTMENT, *A Policy Framework for Education and Training (Draft)* (Braamfontein, Jan. 1994).

ANDERSON, PERRY, 'Components of the National Culture', *New Left Review*, 50 (1968), 3–57.

—— *Considerations on Western Marxism* (London: New Left Books, 1976).

—— 'The Figures of Descent', *New Left Review*, 161 (1987), 20–77.

ANGLIN, MARGARET, 'His Infinite Variety', *Cape Times*, 24 Apr. 1916, 9.

ARMAH, AYI KWEI, 'Masks and Marx', *Présence Africaine*, 131 (1984), 35–65.

ARNOLD, MATTHEW, *Culture and Anarchy*, in *The Collected Prose Works of Matthew Arnold*, v: *Culture and Anarchy*, ed. R. H. Super (Ann Arbor: University of Michigan Press, 1965).

—— 'An Eton Boy', in *The Collected Prose Works of Matthew Arnold*, x: *Philistinism in England and America*, ed. R. H. Super (Ann Arbor: University of Michigan Press, 1974).

—— 'The Function of Criticism at the Present Time', in *The Collected*

Prose Works of Matthew Arnold, iii: *Lectures and Essays in Criticism*, ed. R. H. Super (Ann Arbor: University of Michigan Press, 1962).

—— 'The Future of Liberalism', in *The Collected Prose Works of Matthew Arnold*, ix: *English Literature and Irish Politics*, ed. R. H. Super (Ann Arbor: University of Michigan Press, 1973).

—— 'Introduction: Democracy', in *The Collected Prose Works of Matthew Arnold*, ii: *Democratic Education*, ed. R. H. Super (Ann Arbor: University of Michigan Press, 1962).

—— *Report of 1880*, in *Matthew Arnold on Education*, ed. Gillian Sutherland (Harmondsworth: Penguin, 1973).

—— 'The Study of Poetry', in *The Collected Prose Works of Matthew Arnold*, ix: *English Literature and Irish Politics*, ed. R. H. Super (Ann Arbor: University of Michigan Press, 1973).

—— 'The Twice Revised Code', in *The Collected Prose Works of Matthew Arnold*, ii: *Democratic Education*, ed. R. H. Super (Ann Arbor: University of Michigan Press, 1962).

ASHLEY, MICHAEL, 'The British Influence on Education in South Africa', in André de Villiers (ed.), *English Speaking South Africa To-day* (Cape Town: Oxford University Press, 1976).

—— 'Features of Modernity: Missionaries and Education in South Africa 1850–1900', *Journal of Theology for Southern Africa*, 38 (1982), 49–58.

—— 'Universes in Collision', *Journal of Theology for Southern Africa*, 32 (1980), 28–38.

ATMORE, A., and S. MARKS, 'The Imperial Factor in South Africa in the Nineteenth Century: Towards a Reassessment', *Journal of Imperial and Commonwealth History*, 3/1 (Oct. 1974), 105–39.

ATTWELL, DAVID, 'Political Supervision: The Case of the 1990 Wits History Workshop', *Pretexts*, 2/1 (1990), 78–85.

AUSTIN, H., *An Hour with Shakespeare* (Claremont: Progressive Printing and Publishing, 1908).

A WELL WISHER TO THE YOUTH OF THIS COLONY, Open Letter, *Cape of Good Hope Literary Gazette*, 2/11 (Nov. 1832), 391–2.

BALDICK, CHRIS, *The Social Mission of English Criticism 1848–1932* (Oxford: Basil Blackwell, 1983).

'The Bard—Kids Love him Nowadays', *Cape Times*, 1 May 1969, 5.

BARKER, FRANCIS, PETER HULME, MARGARET IVERSON, and DIANA LOXLEY (eds.), *Europe and its Others* (Colchester: University of Essex, 1984).

—— *Literature, Politics and Theory* (London: Methuen, 1986).

BARNETT, CORELLI, *The Audit of War* (London: Papermac, 1987).

BARRATT BROWN, MICHAEL, 'A Critique of Marxist Theories of Imperialism', in Owen and Sutcliffe, *Studies in the Theory of Imperialism*.

—— 'Away with all the Great Arches: Anderson's History of British Capitalism', *New Left Review*, 167 (1988), 22–51.

Barry Report. See *First Report and Proceedings* . . .

BARTHES, ROLAND, 'The Death of the Author', in *Image Music Text*, trans. Stephen Heath (London: Fontana, 1977).

BATE, JONATHAN, *Shakespeare and the English Romantic Imagination* (Oxford: Oxford University Press, 1986).

BELSEY, CATHERINE, *The Subject of Tragedy: Identity and Difference in Renaissance Drama* (London: Methuen, 1985).

BENJAMIN, WALTER, *Illuminations* (New York: Harcourt Brace Jovanovich, 1968).

BERNSTEIN, HILDA, 'Schools for Servitude', in Alex La Guma (ed.), *Apartheid* (London: Lawrence & Wishart, 1972).

BERTHOUD, J. A., and C. O. GARDNER (eds.), *The Sole Function* (Pietermaritzburg: University of Natal Press, 1969).

BHABHA, HOMI K., *The Location of Culture* (London: Routledge, 1994).

—— 'Representation and the Colonial Text: A Critical Exploration of Some Forms of Mimeticism', in Frank Gloversmith (ed.), *The Theory of Reading* (Brighton: Harvester Press, 1984).

BHATTACHARYYA, GARGI, 'Cultural Education in Britain: From the Newbolt Report to the National Curriculum', *Oxford Literary Review*, 13 (1991), 4–19.

BICKFORD SMITH, VIVIAN, 'A "Special Tradition of Multi-racialism"? Segregation in Cape Town in the Late Nineteenth and Early Twentieth Centuries', in James and Simons (eds.), *The Angry Divide*.

BIKO, STEVE, *I Write What I Like* (London: Heinemann, 1978).

BLACK, M. J., 'A Case for Shakespeare', *Crux*, 16/2 (1982), 31–2.

BOCK, SUSANNE, 'Teaching *Macbeth* to the 1988 Matriculation Class at SACHED, Grahamstown', BA (Hons.) thesis, Rhodes University, 1988.

BOTHMA, MIKE, ' "System" to Blame for Killing by Dale Boys', *Cape Times*, 1 Apr. 1991, 4.

BOUCHER, M., *The Examining Boards and the Examining University* (Pretoria: Communications of the University of South Africa, 1969).

BOWEN, E. E., 'On Teaching by Means of Grammar', in Farrar (ed.), *Essays on a Liberal Education*.

BOWEN, JOHN, 'Practical Criticism, Critical Practice: I. A. Richards and the Discipline of "English" ', *Literature and History*, 13/1 (Spring 1987), 77–94.

BOZZOLI, BELINDA, *The Political Nature of a Ruling Class: Capital and Ideology in South Africa 1890–1933* (London: Routledge & Kegan Paul, 1980).

BRADLEY, A. C., *Shakespearean Tragedy*, 2nd edn. (New York: Macmillan, 1905).

BRANTLINGER, PATRICK, 'Victorians and Africans: The Genealogy of the Myth of the Dark Continent', *Critical Inquiry*, 12 (Autumn 1985), 166–203.

BREHONY, KEVIN, 'Popular Control or Control by Experts? Schooling between 1880 and 1902', in Langan and Schwarz (eds.), *Crises in the British State*.

BREWER, ANTHONY, *Marxist Theories of Imperialism*, 2nd edn. (London: Routledge, 1990).

BRIDGLAND, FRED, 'Bloodsport on the Playing Fields', *Sunday Telegraph*, 24 Feb. 1991, 19.

BRINK, ANDRÉ, *Why Literature?* (Grahamstown: Rhodes University, 1980).

BRISTOL, MICHAEL, *Shakespeare's America, America's Shakespeare* (London: Routledge, 1990).

BROWN, TERRENCE, *Ireland's Literature: Selected Essays* (Mullingar: Lilliput Press, 1988).

'BRUTUS', 'Literary Society Criticised', *UC Tattle*, 7 June 1940, 8.

BUNDY, COLIN, '"Action, Comrades, Action!" The Politics of Youth-Student Resistance in the Western Cape 1985', in James and Simons (eds.), *The Angry Divide*.

—— *Re-making the Past: New Perspectives in South African History* (Cape Town: Department of Adult Education and Extra-mural Studies, University of Cape Town, 1986).

—— 'Middle Road or Cul de sac', *Work in Progress*, 91 (Aug.–Sept. 1993), 37–8.

—— 'Theory of a Special Type', *Work in Progress*, 89 (June 1993), 16–19.

BUNSEE, BENNIE, 'Paton and *Sponono*', *Fighting Talk*, 17/2 (1963), 10–11.

BURKE, SEAN, *The Death and Return of the Author* (Edinburgh: Edinburgh University Press, 1992).

BUTLER, GUY, Editorial, *Shakespeare in South Africa*, 1 (1987), pp. iv–v.

—— *The Republic and the Arts* (Johannesburg: Witwatersrand University Press, 1964).

CABRAL, AMILCAR, 'Culture, Colonization and National Liberation', in Aquino de Bragança and Immanuel Wallerstein (eds.), *The African Liberation Reader* (London: Zed, 1982).

—— 'National Liberation and Culture', in *Unity and Struggle* (London: Heinemann, 1980).

CALDER, ANGUS, *The People's War* (London: Jonathan Cape, 1969).

CALLINICOS, ALEX, *South Africa between Reform and Revolution* (London: Bookmarks, 1988).

CAMERON, JAMES, 'Classical Studies and their Relation to Colonial Education', in Noble (ed.), *The Cape and its People*.

CANDIDO, PAT, 'Dale Supporters Protect School', *Cape Argus*, 23 Feb. 1991, 4.

CAPE OF GOOD HOPE, DEPARTMENT OF PUBLIC EDUCATION, *Examination Papers* (Cape Town: Department of Education: 1930, 1939, 1952, 1958).

—— —— *Syllabus for Senior Certificate 1930* (Cape Town: Department of Public Education, 1930).

'Cape Town: A Place in the Sun when you Retire', *1820*, 27/3 (Aug. 1933).

CARR, E. H., *What is History?* (Harmondsworth: Penguin, 1964).

CARTER, CHIARA, 'Macho School partly to Blame for Racist Killing', *South*, 7–13 Mar. 1991, 4.

CAYGILL, HOWARD, *Art of Judgement* (Oxford: Basil Blackwell, 1989).

CÉSAIRE, AIMÉ, *Discourse on Colonialism* (New York: Monthly Review Press, 1972).

CHALONER, W. H., *The Movement for the Extension of Owens College, Manchester 1863–1873* (Manchester: Manchester University Press, 1973).

CHANAIWA, DAVID, 'African Humanism in Southern Africa: The Utopian, Traditionalist, and Colonialist Worlds of Mission Educated Elites', in Aggrippah T. Mugomba and Mougo Nyaggah (eds.), *Independence without Freedom: The Political Economy of Colonial Education in Southern Africa* (Santa Barbara Calif.: ABC-Clio, 1980).

CHANDRA, BIPAN, 'Karl Marx: His Theories of Asian Societies and Colonial Rule', in *Sociological Theories: Race and Colonialism* (Paris: Unesco, 1980).

CHAPMAN, MICHAEL (ed.), *The 'Drum' Decade: Stories from the 1950s* (Pietermaritzburg: University of Natal, 1989).

—— *Literary Studies in South Africa: Contexts of Value and Belief* (Pietermaritzburg: University of Natal Press, 1985).

CHISOLM, LINDA, 'Redefining Skills: Black Education in South Africa in the 1980s', in Kallaway (ed.), *Apartheid and Education*.

CLARK, JOHN, *An Ode on the Occasion of the Visit to South Africa of the Prince of Wales* (Cape Town: Townshend, Taylor & Snashall, 1924).

—— *Aristotle's Poetics and Shakespeare's Tragedies* (Cape Town: Townshend, Taylor & Snashall, 1912).

CLARK, WILLIAM GEORGE, 'General Education and Classical Studies', in *Cambridge Essays* (London: John W. Parker, 1855).

COETZEE, J. M., *Doubling the Point: Essays and Interviews*, ed. David Attwell (Cambridge, Mass.: Harvard University Press, 1992).

COHEN, WALTER, 'Political Criticism of Shakespeare', in Howard and O'Connor (eds.), *Shakespeare Reproduced*.

COLEY, J. D., 'The Advantages of a Classical Education', *South African College Union Annual*, 1 (18 Dec. 1888), 23–4.

COLMER, FRANCIS, *Shakespeare in Time of War: Excerpts from the Plays Arranged with Topical Allusion* (London: Smith, Elder, 1916).

COMAROFF, JEAN and JOHN, *Of Revelation and Revolution: Christianity, Colonialism, and Consciousness in South Africa*, i (Chicago: University of Chicago Press, 1991).

COMAROFF, JOHN L., 'Images of Empire, Contests of Conscience: Models of Colonial Domination in South Africa', *American Ethnologist*, 16/4 (1989), 661–85.

COOPER, BRENDA, 'Some Generalisations about the Class Situation of the Writer-Intellectual from Independent in Africa', *Africa Perspective*, 16 (1980), 60–79.

CORE SYLLABUS COMMITTEE FOR ENGLISH, 'English Guideline Document (Final Draft)', 1993.

'Council Row on Maynardville Show Audiences', *Cape Times*, 28 Oct. 1965, 3.

COURTNEY, W. L., *Tercentenary Programme for 'Julius Caesar'* (London: Macmillan, 1916), foreword.

COUZENS, TIM, 'The ABC of Research', *Africa Perspective*, 4 (1976), 21–6.

—— 'Criticism of South African Literature', *Work in Progress*, 2 (Nov. 1977), 44–52.

—— 'The Dark Side of the World: Sol Plaatje's *Mhudi*', *English Studies in Africa*, 14/2 (1971), 187–203.

—— *The New African: A Study of the Life and Work of H. I. E. Dhlomo* (Johannesburg: Ravan, 1985).

—— 'Solomon Plaatje's Vision of a Just South Africa', in *A Collection of Solomon T. Plaatje Memorial Lectures* (Bophuthatswana: Institute of African Studies, Unibop, 1993).

—— and BRIAN WILLAN (eds.), *English in Africa*, special issue on Sol Plaatje, 3/2 (Sept. 1976).

CRAIS, CLIFTON, *The Making of the Colonial Order: White Supremacy and Black Resistance in the Eastern Cape 1770–1865* (Johannesburg: Witwatersrand University Press, 1992).

CRONIN, JEREMY, 'We Need more than Group Therapy', *Work in Progress*, 89 (June 1993), 13–15.

CROSS, MICHAEL, and LINDA CHISOLM, 'The Roots of Segregated Schooling in Twentieth Century South Africa', in Nkomo (ed.), *Pedagogy of Domination*.

CURTIN, PHILIP D., *The Image of Africa: British Ideas and Action 1780–1850* (Madison: University of Wisconsin Press, 1964).

'Dale Boy's Dad Points Finger at Headmaster', *Weekend Argus*, 9 Mar. 1991, 12.

'Dale College Boys: Why did they Do It?', *Weekend Argus*, 9 Mar. 1991, 12.

DALE, LANGHAM, 'Education', in Noble (ed.), *The Cape and its People*.
—— 'Imagination: An Essay', *South African Magazine*, 3 (1869), 108–
11; 4 (1869), 156–9; 5 (1869), 299–303.
—— *The Philosophy of Method* (Cape Town: J. C. Juta, 1877).
DAVIES, JOHN, 'Capital, State and Educational Reform in South
Africa', in Kallaway (ed.), *Apartheid and Education*.
DAVIES, ROBERT, DAVID KAPLAN, MIKE MORRIS, and DAN O'MEARA,
'Class Struggle and the Periodisation of the State in South Africa',
Review of African Political Economy, 7 (1976), 4–30.
DAVIN, ANNA, 'Imperialism and Motherhood', *History Workshop*,
5 (Spring 1978), 9–64.
—— ' "Mind that you Do as you are Told": Reading Books for Board
School Girls 1870–1902', in Gaby Weiner and Madeleine Arnot
(eds.), *Gender under Scrutiny* (London: Hutchinson Education, 1987).
DE KOCK, INGRID, and KAREN PRESS (eds.), *Spring is Rebellious*.
(Cape Town: Buchu Books, 1990).
DE KOCK, LEON, ' "History", "Literature", and "English": Reading
the Lovedale Missionary Record within South Africa's Colonial
History', *English Academy Review*, 9 (1992), 1–21.
DE KOCK, W. J., and D. W. KRUGER (eds.), *Dictionary of South African
Biography*, ii (Cape Town: Tafelberg, 1972).
—— *The Tempest* (Johannesburg: Voortrekkerpers, 1963).
DERRIDA, JACQUES, *Margins of Philosophy*, trans. Alan Bass (Hemel
Hempstead: Harvester, 1982).
—— 'Onto-theology of National Humanism (Prolegomena to a Hy-
pothesis)', *Oxford Literary Review*, 14 (1992), 3–23.
—— 'Spectres of Marx', *New Left Review*, 205 (1994), 31–58.
DHARESHWAR, VIVEK, 'Toward a Narrative Epistemology of the
Postcolonial Predicament', *Inscriptions*, special issue, 5, *Traveling
Theory, Traveling Theorists* (1989), 135–57.
DHLOMO, HERBERT, 'African Drama and Poetry', *South African Out-
look*, 1 Apr. 1939, 88–90.
DIRLIK, ARIF, 'The Postcolonial Aura: Third World Criticism in
the Age of Global Capitalism', *Critical Inquiry*, 20 (Winter 1994),
328–56.
DOHERTY, CHRISTOPHER MALCOLM WILLIAM, 'A Genealogical His-
tory of English Studies in South Africa, with Special Reference to
the Responses of South African Academic Literary Criticism to
the Emergence of an Indigenous South African Literature', MA
thesis, University of Natal, 1989.
DOLLIMORE, JONATHAN, 'Culturalism, Feminism and Marxist Humanism', *New Literary History*, 21 (1990), 471–93.
—— 'Introduction: Shakespeare, Cultural Materialism and the New
Historicism', in Dollimore and Sinfield (eds.), *Political Shakespeare*.
—— *Radical Tragedy: Religion, Ideology and Power in the Drama of*

Shakespeare and his Contemporaries, 2nd edn. (Hemel Hempstead: Harvester Wheatsheaf, 1989).

—— and ALAN SINFIELD (eds.), *Political Shakespeare: New Essays in Cultural Materialism* (Manchester: Manchester University Press, 1985).

DOYLE, BRIAN, *English and Englishness* (London: Routledge, 1989).

DRAKAKIS, JOHN (ed.), *Alternative Shakespeares* (London: Methuen, 1985).

DRENNAN, Mrs Max, 'The Teaching of English', *Bluestocking*, 7/3 (Oct. 1937), 3–4.

DUBOW, SAUL, *Racial Segregation and the Origins of Apartheid in South Africa 1919–36* (London: Macmillan, 1989).

DUNCAN, PATRICK, 'Hamlet', *Critic*, 1/1 (Sept. 1932), 3–19.

DURRANT, GEOFFREY, *English Studies and the Community* (Pietermaritzburg: Natal Witness, 1945).

—— 'The Place of Practical Criticism in the University Curriculum', in W. S. Mackie (ed.), *Practical Criticism* (Cape Town: University of Cape Town, 1948).

—— *Propaganda and Public Opinion*, South African Affairs Pamphlets, 5 (Johannesburg: Society of the Friends of Africa, 1944).

—— 'Prospero's Wisdom', *Theoria*, 7 (1955), 50–8.

—— 'The Teaching of Poetry', in *Proceedings of the First Conference of University Teachers of English* (Johannesburg: University of Witwatersrand, 1946).

DU TOIT, A. E., *The Earliest British Document on Education for the Coloured Races* (Pretoria: Communications of the University of South Africa, 1962).

—— *The Earliest South African Documents on the Education and Civilisation of the Bantu* (Pretoria: Communications of the University of South Africa, 1963).

DYHOUSE, CAROL, 'Social Darwinistic Ideas and the Development of Women's Education in England 1880–1920', *History of Education*, 5/1 (1976), 41–58.

DYSON, A. E., 'Culture and Anarchy 1869, 1969', *Critical Quarterly*, 11 (1969), preface.

EAGLETON, TERRY, *Literary Theory: An Introduction* (Oxford: Basil Blackwell, 1983).

EASTHOPE, ANTHONY, *British Post-structuralism since 1968* (London: Routledge, 1988).

EBRAHIM, CARTER, 'The Drama and Society', *Discussion*, 1/6 (Dec. 1952), 21–31.

EDMUNDS, P., 'Perservance Keeps Honour Bright: A Plea to Retain Shakespeare', *Crux*, 19/1 (1985), 9–13.

ELBOURNE, ELIZABETH, 'A Question of Identity: Evangelical Culture and Khoisan Politics in the Early Nineteenth Century Eastern Cape', *The Societies of Southern Africa in the Nineteenth and Twentieth Centuries*, 18 (1992), 14–30.

ELPHICK, RICHARD, 'Mission Christianity and Interwar Liberalism', Jeffrey Butler, Richard Elphick, and David Welsh (eds.), *Democratic Liberalism in South Africa* (Cape Town: David Philip, 1987).

E.M.C., 'Shakespeare's References to the Modern Wheel', *The Huguenot Seminary Annual 1900* (Cape Town: 1900).

'End of an Educational Era: Shakespeare Banned?', *Ikhwesi Lomso*, Feb. 1959, 3.

'The English Language', *Cape of Good Hope Literary Gazette*, 2/10 (1832), 372–3.

ESSOP, AHMED, *Noorjehan and Other Stories* (Johannesburg: Ravan, 1990).

EVANS, MALCOLM, *Signifying Nothing*, 2nd edn. (Hemel Hempstead: Harvester Wheatsheaf, 1989).

Examiner's Report, *Education Gazette*, 29/5 (1930), 179.

FAIRBAIRN, JOHN, 'On Literary and Scientific Societies', *South African Journal*, 1/1 (1824), 50–5.

—— 'On the Writings of Wordsworth', *South African Journal*, 1/1 (1824), 12–16; 1/2 (1824), 107–17.

FANON, FRANTZ, *Black Skin, White Masks* (London: Pluto, 1986).

—— *Towards the African Revolution* (Harmondsworth: Penguin, 1970).

—— *The Wretched of the Earth* (Harmondsworth: Penguin, 1967).

FARRAR, F. W. (ed.), *Essays on a Liberal Education* (London: Macmillan, 1867).

FERGUSON, W. T., and R. F. M. IMMELMAN (eds.), *Sir John Herschel and Education at the Cape 1834–40* (Cape Town: Oxford University Press, 1961).

'Fiction', *Cape Town Mirror*, 1/14 (5 Dec. 1848), 107.

First Report and Proceedings with Appendices of a Commission Appointed to Enquire into and Report upon Certain Matters Connected with the Educational System of the Colony (the Barry Report) (Cape Town: Cape of Good Hope, 1891).

FIRST, RUTH, JONATHAN STEELE, and CHRISTABEL GURNEY, *The South African Connection: Western Investment in Apartheid* (London: Temple Smith, 1972).

FOWLER, J. H., *The Art of Teaching English* (London: Macmillan, 1932).

FRANSMAN, MARTIN, and ROB DAVIES, 'The South African Social Formation in the Early Capitalist Period *circa* 1870–1939: Some Views on the Question of Hegemony', in T. Adler (ed.), *Perspectives on South Africa: A Collection of Working Papers* (Johannesburg: University of Witwatersrand African Studies Institute, 1977).

FRIEDGUT, A. J., 'The Rise of the Caliban Drama', *Critic*, 5 (1939), 1–12.

GARDENER, J. B., 'The English-Speaking Pupil and South African Set-Books', *English Studies in Africa*, 13/1 (1970), 21–36.

GARDINER, MICHAEL, 'Liberating Language: People's English for the Future', in Nasson and Samuel (eds.), *Education*.

GARDNER, W. H., 'Practical Criticism', in *Proceedings of the Second Conference of University Teachers of English* (Pietermaritzburg: University of Natal, 1949).

GATES, HENRY LOUIS Jr., 'Critical Fanonism', *Critical Inquiry*, 17 (Spring 1991), 457–70.

—— Editor's Introduction: 'Writing "Race" and the Difference it Makes', *Critical Inquiry*, 12 (Autumn 1985), 1–20.

GILIOMEE, HERMANN, 'Aspects of the Rise of Afrikaner Capital and Afrikaner Nationalism in the Western Cape 1870–1915', in James and Simons (eds.), *The Angry Divide*.

GODDEN, JONATHAN, *Overcoming Adult Literacy* (London: RESA, 1991).

GOLDBERG, JONATHAN, 'The Politics of Renaissance Literature: A Review Essay', *ELH* 49 (1982), 514–42.

—— *Voice Terminal Echo: Postmodernism and English Renaissance Texts* (London: Methuen, 1986).

GOLLANCZ, ISRAEL (ed.), *A Book of Homage to Shakespeare* (Oxford: Oxford University Press, 1916).

GORDON, LYNDALL, *Shared Lives* (Cape Town: David Philip, 1992).

GOUWS, JOHAN, *The Pursuit of Poetry: A Defence* (Grahamstown: Rhodes University, 1990).

GRAY, STEPHEN, 'Plaatje's Shakespeare', *English in Africa*, 4/1 (1977), 1–6.

GREADY, PAUL, 'The Sophiatown Writers of the Fifties: The Unreal Reality of their World', *Journal of Southern African Studies*, 16/1 (1990), 139–64.

'The Greatest Son of England: Mr Merriman's Tribute to Shakespeare', *Cape Times*, 25 Apr. 1916, 7–8.

GREEN, MICHAEL, 'The Manifesto and the Fifth Column', *Critical Arts*, 3/2 (1984), 9–19.

GREENBLATT, STEPHEN, *Renaissanse Self-Fashioning: From More to Shakespeare* (Chicago: University of Chicago Press, 1980).

—— *Shakespeare Negotiations: The Circulation of Social Energy in Renaissance England* (Oxford: Oxford University Press, 1988).

GREENBERG, DORIS, 'In Defence of Literary Criticism', *Groote Schuur*, 2/1 (1941), 56–9.

GREENWOOD, J. G., 'On the Languages and Literatures of Greece and Rome', in *Introductory Lectures on the Opening of Owens College* (Manchester, 1852).

—— 'On Some Relations of Culture to Practical Life', in Balfour Stewart and A. W. Ward (eds.), *Essays and Addresses, by Professors and Lecturers of Owens College, Manchester* (London: Macmillan, 1874).

GREIG, J. Y. T., 'Literature in the Machine Age', in *Our Changing World View: Ten Lectures on Recent Movements in Science, Economics, Education, Literature, and Philosophy* (Johannesburg: Witwatersrand University Press, 1932).

GRIFFITHS, TREVOR, ' "This Island's Mine": Caliban and Colonialism', *Yearbook of English Studies*, 13 (1984), 159–80.

HALES, J. W., 'The Teaching of English', in Farrar (ed.), *Essays on a Liberal Education*.

HALL, STUART, 'A Critical Survey of the Theoretical and Practical Achievements of the Last Ten Years', in *Literature, Society and the Sociology of Literature* (Colchester: Essex Conference, 1976).

—— and BILL SCHWARZ, 'State and Society 1880–1930', in Langan and Schwarz (eds.), *Crises in the British State*.

HARBER, ERIC, 'South Africa: The White English-Speaking Sensibility', *Journal of Commonwealth Literature*, 11/1 (1976), 57–71.

HARESNAPE, GEOFFREY, 'The Battle for the Books: The Evolution of Academic Criticism of South African Literature in English 1956–1976', *English Studies in Africa*, 31/1 (1988), 41–9.

HARMEL, MICHAEL, 'Olive Schreiner—Fearless Fighter against Injustice', *New Age*, 1/20 (10 Mar. 1955), 7.

HARRIS, LAURENCE, 'One Step Forward . . .', *Work in Progress*, 89 (June 1993), 20–2.

HARTSHORNE, KEN, *Crisis and Challenge: Black Education 1910–1990* (Cape Town: Oxford University Press, 1992).

—— 'Literature across Cultures: English Literature in Bantu Schools', *English Studies in Africa*, 13/1 (1970), 67–79.

HARTWIG, MERVYN, and RACHEL SHARP, 'The State and the Reproduction of Labour Power in South Africa', in Kallaway (ed.), *Apartheid and Education*.

HAWKES, TERENCE, 'Swisser-Swatter: Making a Man of English Letters', in Drakakis (ed.), *Alternative Shakespeares*.

—— *That Shakespeherian Rag* (London: Methuen, 1986).

HENDERSON, PHILIP, *Literature and a Changing Civilisation* (London: Bodley Head, 1935).

HERMAN, LOUIS, 'The Appreciation of Literature in School', *Educational News of South Africa*, Aug. 1930, 324–5; Oct. 1930, 383–6.

HIRSON, BARUCH, *Year of Fire, Year of Ash* (London: Zed, 1979).

HOBSBAWM, E. J., *The Age of Empire 1875–1914* (London: Weidenfeld & Nicolson, 1987).

—— 'Between the Wars', in David Potter (ed.), *Society and the Social Sciences* (London: Routledge & Kegan Paul, 1981).

HOBSBAWM, E. J., *Industry and Empire* (Harmondsworth: Penguin, 1969).

HOFMEYR, ISABEL, 'Problems of Creative Writers: A Reply', *Work in Progress*, 2 (1977), 31–7.

—— 'The State of South African Literary Criticism', *English in Africa*, 6/2 (1979), 39–50.

HOLMES, BRIAN (ed.), *Educational Policy and the Mission Schools: Case Studies from the British Empire* (London: Routledge, 1967).

HOLSTUN, JAMES, 'Ranting at the New Historicism', *English Literary Renaissance*, 19 (1989), 189–225.

HOOPER, MYRTLE, 'Rewriting History: The "Feminism" of *Mhudi*', *English Studies in Africa*, 35/1 (1992), 68–79.

HOWARD, JEAN E., 'The New Historicism in Renaissance Studies', *English Literary Renaissance*, 16 (1983), 13–43.

—— and MARION O'CONNOR (eds.), *Shakespeare Reproduced* (New York: Methuen, 1986).

HOWARTH, R. G., 'The Life of Literature', *Southerly*, 3 (1958), 1–12.

HUDSON, PETER, and STEPHEN LOUW, 'Beware the Shining Path!', *Work in Progress*, 90 (July–Aug. 1993), 37–9.

HULL, RICHARD W., *American Enterprise in South Africa* (New York: New York University Press, 1990).

'Humanism in the Schools', *Educational News of South Africa*, Jan. 1933, 3–4.

HYSLOP, JONATHAN, 'Schools, Unemployment and Youth: Origins and Significance of Student and Youth Movements 1976–1987', in Nasson and Samuel (eds.), *Education*.

—— 'State Education Policy and the Social Reproduction of the Urban African Working Class: The Case of the Southern Transvaal 1955–1976', *Journal of Southern African Studies*, 14/3 (1988), 446–76.

'IMPRESSED', Review of *Episode*, by Harry Bloom, *Torch*, 11/12 (29 May 1956), 6.

'In the Editor's Sanctum', *Educational Journal*, 1/1 (May 1915), 4.

JAMES, C. L. R., *The C. L. R. James Reader*, ed. Anna Grimshaw (Oxford: Blackwell, 1992).

JAMES, WILMOT G., and MARY SIMONS (eds.), *The Angry Divide: Social and Economic History of the Western Cape* (Cape Town: David Philip, 1989).

JANMOHAMED, ABDUL R., 'Humanism and Minority Literature: Toward a Definition of Counter-hegemonic Discourse', *Boundary 2*, 12/3–13/1 (1984), 281–99.

—— and DAVID LLOYD, 'Introduction: Minority Discourse: What is to Be Done?', *Cultural Critique*, 7 (Fall 1987), 5–17.

JARDINE, LISA, *Still Harping on Daughters: Woman and Drama in the Age of Shakespeare* (Brighton: Harvester, 1983).

JAY, ELIZABETH, *The Religion of the Heart: Evangelicism and the Victorian Novel* (Oxford: Oxford University Press, 1979).

JAY, MARTIN, *Marxism and Totality: The Adventures of a Concept from Lukács to Habermas* (Cambridge: Polity, 1984).

J.C., 'Robert Tressel and his Book', *Guardian*, 15/49 (3 Jan. 1952), 2.

Johannesburg Shakespeare Tercentenary Celebration (Johannesburg, 1916).

JOHNSON, DAVID, 'Importing Metropolitan Post-colonials', *Current Writing*, 6/1 (1994), 73–85.

JOHNSON, RICHARD, 'Educating the Educators: "Experts" and the State 1833–1839', A. P. Donajgrodzki (ed.), *Social Control in Nineteenth Century Britain* (London: Croom Helm, 1977).

—— 'Educational Policy and Social Control in Early Victorian England', *Past and Present*, 49 (1970), 96–119.

—— ' "Really Useful Knowledge": Radical Education and Working-Class Culture 1790–1848', in John Clarke Chas Critcher, and Richard Johnson (eds.), *Working-Class Culture* (London: Hutchinson, 1979).

JONES, GARETH STEDMAN, 'History: The Poverty of Empiricism', in Robin Blackburn (ed.), *Ideology in the Social Sciences* (London: Fontana, 1972).

JOUBERT, SUSAN, 'Publishing in Another South Africa', *African Book Publishing Record*, 17/1 (1991), 9–15.

KALLAWAY, PETER (ed.), *Apartheid and Education* (Braamfontein: Ravan, 1984).

—— 'From Bantu Education to People's Education in South Africa', in *Handbook of Educational Ideas and Practices* (London: Routledge, 1990).

—— 'Privatisation and the Educational Politics of the New Right', in Moss and Obery (eds.), *South African Review 5*.

KAHN, SAM, 'Poets of Reaction', *Advance*, 14 Jan. 1954, 4.

KA NELANI, JOE, Review of *King of the Bastards*, *Torch*, 5/7 (24 Apr. 1950), 6.

KEMP, TOM, 'The Marxist Theory of Imperialism', in Owen and Sutcliffe (eds.), *Studies in the Theory of Imperialism*.

KETO, C. TSEHLOANE, 'Pre-industrial Education Policies and Practices in South Africa', in Nkomo (ed.).

KETTLE, ARNOLD (ed.), *Shakespeare in a Changing World* (London: Lawrence & Wishart, 1964).

KIDD, A. S., 'The English Language and Literature in South Africa', in *Report of the Seventh Annual Meeting of the South African Association for the Advancement of Science held in Bloemfontein, 27 August– 2 September 1909* (Cape Town: South African Association for the Advancement of Science, 1910).

'Kids Live out ANC Dad's Schoolboy Dream', *Cape Times*, 14 Feb. 1991, 3.

KIRKWOOD, MIKE, 'The Colonizer: A Critique of the English South African Culture Theory', in Pieter Wilhelm and James Polley (eds.), *Poetry 74* (Johannesburg: AD Donker, 1976).

KNIGHTS, L. C., *Drama and Society in the Age of Jonson* (London: Chatto & Windus, 1937).

KOLBE, F. C., *The National Crisis* (Pretoria: Wallachs, 1915).

—— *Shakespeare's Way: A Psychological Study* (Cambridge, 1930).

KOLODNY, ANNETTE, 'Dancing through the Minefield: Some Observations on the Theory, Practice and Politics of Feminist Literary Criticism', in Dale Spender (ed.), *Men's Studies Modified: The Impact of Feminism on the Academic Disciplines* (New York: Pergamon Press, 1981).

KRIEL, I. J., 'English Teaching in South African Schools', *Trek*, 14/10 (1950), 25–7.

LACLAU, ERNESTO, 'Socialism Goes off the Beaten Track', *Work in Progress*, 90 (July–Aug. 1993), 33–6.

LAING, STUART, 'The Production of Literature', in Alan Sinfield (ed.), *Society and Literature 1945–1970* (London: Methuen, 1983).

LANGAN, MARY, and BILL SCHWARZ (eds.), *Crises in the British State* (London: Hutchinson, 1985).

LEAVIS, F. R., *For Continuity* (Cambridge: Cambridge University Press, 1933).

LEGASSICK, MARTIN, 'The Frontier Tradition in South African Historiography', in Marks and Atmore (eds.), *Economy and Society in Pre-industrial South Africa*.

—— 'The Record of British Firms in South Africa: In the Context of Political Economy', *South African Labour Bulletin*, 2/1 (1975), 7–36.

—— 'The State, Racism and the Rise of Capitalism in the Nineteenth-Century Cape Colony', *South African Historical Journal*, 28 (1993), 329–68.

LEMMER, ANDRÉ, 'ESL Shakespeare in Schools and Colleges', *NESLATT Journal*, 4 (1989), 22–7.

—— 'Upgrading the Study of Shakespeare in Southern African Secondary Schools: An Interim Report on the Schools' Text Project', *Shakespeare in Southern Africa*, 2 (1988), 67–77.

LENIN, V. I., *Imperialism, the Highest Stage of Capitalism* (Moscow: Progress Publishers, 1917).

LENZ, CAROLYN, GAYLE GREENE, and CAROL THOMAS NEELY (eds.), *The Woman's Part: Feminist Criticism of Shakespeare* (Urbana, Ill.: University of Illinois Press, 1980).

LEWIN ROBINSON, A. M., 'Catalogue of Theses and Dissertations Accepted for Degrees by the South African Universities' (Cape Town, 1943).

—— *None Daring to Make us Afraid* (Cape Town: Maskew Miller, 1962).

LEWIS, GAVIN, *Between the Wire and the Wall: A History of South African 'Coloured' Politics* (Cape Town: David Philip, 1987).

LEYS, COLIN, *Politics in Britain* (London: Verso, 1983).

'Literature, Science, and Art', *Cape of Good Hope Literary Magazine*, 1/1 (1847), 102–10; 1/4 (1847), 463–70.

LOCKETT, CECILY, 'Feminism(s) and Writing in English in South Africa', *Current Writing*, 2/1 (1990), 1–21.

LODGE, TOM, *Black Politics in South Africa since 1945* (Johannesburg: Ravan, 1983).

LONGHURST, DEREK, 'Reproducing a National Culture: Shakespeare in Education', *Red Letters*, 11 (1982), 3–14.

LOOMBA, ANIA, 'Dead Women Tell No Tales: Issues of Female Subjectivity, Subaltern Agency and Tradition in Colonial and Postcolonial Writings on Widow Immolation in India', *History Workshop*, 36 (1993), 209–27.

—— *Gender, Race, Renaissance Drama* (Manchester: Manchester University Press, 1989).

LYONS, CHARLES H., 'The Educable African: British Thought and Action 1835–1865', V. M. Battle and C. H. Lyons (eds.), *Essays in the History of African Education* (New York: Teachers College Press, 1970).

MABIN, ALAN, 'The Underdevelopment of the Western Cape 1850–1900', in James and Simons (eds.), *The Angry Divide*.

McCABE, COLIN (ed.), *Broken English* (Manchester: Manchester University Press, 1988).

McKAY, NELLIE, 'Reflections on Black Women Writers: Revising the Literary Canon', in Christie Farnham (ed.), *The Impact of Feminist Research in the Academy* (Bloomington: Indiana University Press, 1987).

MACKENZIE, JOHN M., *Propaganda and Empire* (Manchester: Manchester University Press, 1984).

MACKIE, W. S., *A Book of English Verse for South African Readers* (London: Macmillan, 1935).

—— Preface, in *Symposium on Practical Criticism* (Cape Town: University of Cape Town, 1948).

—— *Shakespeare's Language: And How Far it can be Investigated with the Help of the 'New English Dictionary'* (repr. Cambridge: Cambridge University Press, 1936).

MACLURE, S. J., *Educational Documents 1816 to the Present Day*, 4th edn. (London: Methuen, 1979).

MAGUBANE, BERNARD, *The Political Economy of Race and Class in South Africa* (New York: Monthly Review Press, 1980).

MAKGABUTLANE, SOL, 'The Pied Piper', *Tribute* (June 1990), 20–7.

MALHERBE, E. G., *Education in South Africa* (Cape Town: Juta, 1925).

MANGAN, J. A., *The Games Ethic and Imperialism: Aspects of the Diffusion of an Ideal* (New York: Viking, 1986).

MAQAGI, SISI, 'Who Theorises?', *Current Writing*, 2/1 (1990), 22–5.

MARKS, S., and A. ATMORE (eds.), *Economy and Society in Preindustrial South Africa* (London: Longman, 1980).

—— and RICHARD RATHBONE, Introduction, in S. Marks and Richard Rathbone (eds.), *Industrialisation and Social Change in South Africa: African Class Formation, Culture and Consciousness 1870–1930* (London: Longman, 1982).

—— and STANLEY TRAPIDO, 'Lord Milner and the South African State', *History Workshop*, 8 (Autumn 1979), 50–80.

MARSH, D. R. C., *The Recurring Miracle* (Pietermaritzburg: University of Natal Press, 1962).

MARX, KARL, 'The British Rule in India', in *On Colonialism* (Moscow: Progress, 1959).

—— *The Eighteenth Brumaire of Louis Bonaparte*, in *Surveys from Exile*, ed. David Fernbach (Harmondsworth: Penguin, 1973).

—— 'The Future Result of the British Rule in India', in *On Colonialism* (Moscow: Progress, 1959).

—— *The Grundrisse: Foundations of the Critique of Political Economy* (Harmondsworth: Pelican, 1973).

—— 'Marx to the Editorial Board of the *Otechestvenniye Zapiski*', in *Marx–Engels Selected Correspondence* (Moscow: Progress, 1955).

—— 'Marx to V. I. Zasulich in St Petersburg', in *Marx–Engels Selected Correspondence* (Moscow: Progress, 1955).

—— and FRIEDRICH ENGELS, *The German Ideology*, ed. Chris Arthur (London: Lawrence & Wishart, 1970).

MARZO, PATRICIA BEATRICE, 'An Investigation into the Nature and Function of Prescribed Literature in Schools from 1945–1980', MA thesis, Rhodes University, 1981.

MATTHEWS, Z. K., *Freedom for my People* (Cape Town: David Philip, 1981).

Maynardville Tenth Anniversary Programme (Cape Town, 1964).

MEMMI, ALBERT, *The Colonizer and the Colonized*, intro. Liam O'Dowd (London: Earthscan, 1990).

MERRIMAN, NATHANIEL JAMES, *On the Study of Shakespeare* (Grahamstown: General Institute, 1857).

—— *Shakespeare as Bearing on English History* (Grahamstown: General Institute, 1858).

MICHAEL, IAN, *The Teaching of English from the Sixteenth Century to 1870* (Cambridge: Cambridge University Press, 1987).

MILL, JOHN STUART, *Mill's Essays on Literature and Society*, ed. J. B. Schneewind (London: Collier, 1965).

MILLER, M. M., T. TYFIELD, and M. M. KRIGE, 'The English Literature Course', *Educational News of South Africa*, Dec. 1937, 264–6.

MILLIGAN, A., 'A Shakespearean Study: Lady Macbeth', *African Monthly*, 2/7 (1907), 21–32.

MODISANE, BLOKE, *Blame me on History* (Craighall: AD Donker, 1986).

—— 'The Situation', *Black Orpheus*, 12 (1964), 10–16.

MOHANTY, CHANDRA TALPADE, 'Under Western Eyes: Feminist Scholarship and Colonial Discourses', *Boundary 2*, 12/3–13/1 (1984), 333–57.

MOLTENO, FRANK, 'The Historical Foundations of the Schooling of Black South Africans', in Kallaway (ed.), *Apartheid and Education*.

MONTROSE, LOUIS, 'Renaissance Literary Studies and the Subject of History', *English Literary Renaissance*, 16 (1986), 5–12.

MORTON, C., 'A Case against Shakespeare', *Crux*, 15/3 (1981), 33–5.

MOSS, GLENN, and INGRID OBERY (eds.), *South African Review 5* (Johannesburg: Ravan Press, 1989).

MOSTERT, NOEL, *Frontiers: The Epic of South Africa's Creation and the Tragedy of the Xhosa People* (London: Jonathan Cape, 1992).

MPHAHLELE, EZEKIEL, *The African Image* (London: Faber & Faber, 1962).

—— 'Negro Poet: Trumpet at his Lips', *Fighting Talk*, 15/11 (1961), 12–13.

—— 'Prometheus in Chains: The Fate of English in South Africa', *English Academy Review*, 2/1 (1984), 89–104.

MUIR, KENNETH, 'Changing Interpretations of Shakespeare', in *The Pelican Guide to English Literature*, ii: *The Age of Shakespeare* (Harmondsworth: Penguin, 1955).

Muir Report. See *Special Reports on Educational Subjects*.

MULHERN, FRANCIS, *The Moment of Scrutiny* (London: Verso, 1981).

MULLINEUX, PETER NEWTON, 'An Examination of the Use of the Contextual Question in Examining Shakespeare's Plays at the Standard Ten Level in Cape Education Department Schools', MA thesis, Rhodes University, 1988.

NAIRN, TOM, *The Break-up of Britain*, 2nd edn. (London: Verso, 1981).

NASSON, BILL, 'Opposition Politics and Ideology in the Western Cape', in Moss and Obery (eds.), *South African Review 5*.

—— 'Perspectives on Education in South Africa', in Sandra Burman and Pamela Reynolds (eds.), *Growing Up in a Divided Society: The Contexts of Childhood in South Africa* (Johannesburg: Ravan Press, 1986).

—— 'Redefining Inequality: Education Reform and the State in Contemporary South Africa', in Nasson and Samuel (eds.), *Education*.

NASSON, BILL, and JOHN SAMUEL (eds.), *Education: From Poverty to Liberty* (Cape Town: David Philip, 1990).

NATIONAL EDUCATION CRISIS COMMITTEE, 'Towards a Language Policy for a Post-apartheid South Africa', in *Readings from a Workshop Held in Harare from 21–24 March 1990* (Harare: ANC, 1990).

NATTRASS, N., and E. ARDINGTON (eds.), *The Political Economy of South Africa* (Oxford: Oxford University Press, 1990).

NDEBELE, NJABULO, *Rediscovery of the Ordinary* (Johannesburg: COSAW, 1991).

Newbolt Report. See *The Teaching of English in England*.

NEWMAN, G., 'The Fairy-Lore in *A Midsummer Night's Dream*', *Bluestocking*, 5/2 (May 1935), 1–6.

'The New Syllabus in English', *Educational News*, 26/5 (May 1916), 69–71.

NGUGI WA THIONG'O, *Homecoming* (London: Heinemann, 1972).

—— *Writers in Politics* (London: Heinemann, 1981).

NIXON, ROB, 'Caribbean and African Appropriations of *The Tempest*', *Critical Inquiry*, 13 (Spring 1987), 557–78.

NKOMO, MOKUBUNG, 'Foreign Policy and Scholarship Programmes for Black South Africans: Philanthropy, Realism, or Winning Hearts and Minds?', in Nkomo (ed.), *Pedagogy of Domination*.

—— (ed.), *Pedagogy of Domination* (Trenton: Africa World Press, 1990).

NKRUMAH, KWAME, *Class Struggle in Africa* (London: Panaf, 1970).

NOBLE, RODERICK (ed.), *The Cape and its People and Other Essays* (Cape Town: J. C. Juta, 1869).

'On the Sources of Shakespeare's Plots', *Cape of Good Hope Literary Magazine*, 2/10 (1848), 571–92.

ORKIN, MARTIN, *Drama and the South African State* (Manchester: Manchester University Press, 1991).

—— 'Holofernes and the Transvaal Senior Schools Certificate', *Crux*, 16/3 (1982), 27–36.

—— *Shakespeare against Apartheid* (Craighall: AD Donker, 1987).

ORWELL, GEORGE, 'The Frontiers of Art and Propaganda', in *The Collected Essays, Journalism and Letters of George Orwell*, ii, ed. Sonia Orwell and Ian Angus (Harmondsworth: Penguin, 1970).

—— *The Lion and the Unicorn*, in *The Collected Essays, Journalism and Letters of George Orwell*, ii, ed. Sonia Orwell and Ian Angus (Harmondsworth: Penguin, 1970).

OWEN, ROGER, and BOB SUTCLIFFE (eds.), *Studies in the Theory of Imperialism* (London: Longman, 1972).

PALMER, D. J., *The Rise of English Studies* (London: Oxford University Press, 1965).

PARRY, BENITA, 'Problems in Current Theories of Colonial Discourse', *Oxford Literary Review*, 9 (1987), 27–58.

PARTRIDGE, A. C., 'English Scholarship: A Transmutation of Species', *English Studies in Africa*, 1/1 (1958), 1–9.

—— *The Humanities and English Studies* (Johannesburg: University of Witwatersrand Press, 1956).

PATON, ALAN, *Cry, the Beloved Country* (Harmondsworth: Penguin, 1958).

PELLS, E. G., *The Story of Education in South Africa* (Cape Town: J. C. Juta, 1938).

PENRITH, MARY CAROLINE, 'A Historical and Critical Account of the Teaching of English Language and Literature in English-Medium Universities in South Africa, with Particular Reference to the University of Cape Town and the South African College', MA thesis, University of Cape Town, 1972.

PLAATJE, SOL, 'A South African's Homage', in Gollancz (ed.), *A Book of Homage to Shakespeare*.

—— *Boer War Diary*, ed. John Comaroff (London: Macmillan, 1973).

—— *Mhudi* (London: Heinemann, 1978).

—— *Native Life in South Africa* (Harlow: Longman, 1987).

'Poetry', *Cape of Good Hope Literary Gazette*, 1/2 (July 1830), 23.

'Popular Literature', *Cape Town Mirror*, 1/1 (5 Sept. 1848), 3.

PORTER, CAROLYN, 'History and Literature: "After the New Historicism"', *New Literary History*, 21 (1990), 253–72.

POSEL, DEBORAH, *The Making of Apartheid 1948–1961* (Oxford: Oxford University Press, 1991).

POTTER, ALEX, 'The Role of So-called "English" Departments in English Studies in South Africa', *Journal for Language Teaching*, 21/2 (1987), 1–7.

Preliminary Report on the State of Education in the Colony of the Cape of Good Hope, by Donald Ross MA, FRSE (Inspector-General of Colleges and Schools) (the Ross Report) (Cape Town: Cape of Good Hope, 1883).

'Proposed Syllabus in English as a First Language', *Education Gazette*, 50/1 (Apr. 1951), 759–64.

QUILLER COUCH, SIR ARTHUR, *Historical Tales from Shakespeare* (London: Edward Arnold, 1899).

QUINCE, WILLIAM ROWAN, 'Shakespeare in South Africa', Ph.D. thesis, University of Southern Illinois, 1987.

RABKIN, DAVID, '*Drum* Magazine 1951–1961: And the Works of Black South African Writers Associated with It', Ph.D. thesis, University of Leeds, 1975.

RALEIGH, SIR WALTER, *Shakespeare's England* (Oxford: Clarendon Press, 1916).

RANDALL, PETER, *Little England in the Veld* (Johannesburg: Ravan Press, 1982).

REDFERN LOADES, H., 'The English High School Syllabus', *Educational News*, 26/10 (Oct. 1916), 160.

—— 'The Teaching of English', *Educational News*, 26/12 (Dec. 1916), 194–5.

REID, JANE, *English Literature in South African Senior Schools: A Critique of Set Books* (Cape Town: Centre for African Studies, 1982).

Report of the Education Commission (Cape Town: Cape of Good Hope, 1912).

Report of the Schools Inquiry Commission 1865–6 (the Taunton Report), British Parliamentary Papers (General Education), 20 (London, 1868).

Report of the Superintendent General of Education for the Year Ended 31 December 1930 (Cape Town: Unie-Volkspers Beperk, 1931).

Report of the Superintendent General of Education for the Year Ended 31 December 1939 (Cape Town: Cape of Good Hope–Unie-Volkspers Beperk, 1940).

Report of the University Commission (Cape Town: 1914).

RETAMAR, ROBERTO FERNANDEZ, 'Caliban. Notes towards a Discussion of Culture in our America', *Massachusetts Review*, 15 (Winter–Spring 1974), 7–72.

REYBURN, H. A., Prologue, *Critic*, 1/1 (Sept. 1932), 1–2.

RICH, ADRIENNE, 'Notes towards a Politics of Location', in *Blood, Bread and Poetry: Selected Prose 1979–1985* (New York: Norton, 1986).

RICH, PAUL, *White Power and the Liberal Conscience* (Johannesburg: Ravan, 1984).

RITCHIE, W., *The History of the South African College 1829–1918*, 2 vols. (Cape Town: Maskew Miller, 1918).

ROSMAN, DOREEN, *Evangelicals and Culture* (London: Croom Helm, 1984).

Ross Report. See *Preliminary Report on the State of Education . . .*

RYAN, RORY, 'Literary-Intellectual Behavior in South Africa', *Boundary 2*, 15/3 (Spring–Fall 1988), 283–304.

SACHS, ALBIE, 'Preparing Ourselves for Freedom', in Ingrid de Kock and Karen Press (eds.), *Spring is Rebellious* (Cape Town: Buchu Books, 1990).

SAID, EDWARD, *Beginnings: Intention and Method* (New York: Columbia University Press, 1985).

—— *Culture and Imperialism* (London: Chatto & Windus, 1993).

—— 'Intellectuals in the Post-colonial World', *Salmagundi*, 70–1 (Spring–Summer 1986), 44–81.

—— 'Opponents, Audiences, Constituencies and Community', *Critical Inquiry*, 9 (1982), 1–26.

—— *Orientalism* (Harmondsworth: Peregrine, 1985).

—— *The World, the Text and the Critic* (London: Faber, 1983).

SALES, JANE, *Mission Stations and the Colonial Communities of the Eastern Cape 1800–1852* (Cape Town: A. A. Balkema, 1975).

SAUL, J., and S. GELB, *The Crisis in South Africa*, rev. edn. (London: Zed, 1986).

SAUNDERS, CHRISTOPHER, *The Making of the South African Past* (Cape Town: David Philip, 1988).

SCHREINER, E., 'A Debt of Honour', *Bluestocking*, 1/3 (Apr. 1931), 4–5.

SCHREUDER, D. M., 'The Cultural Factor in Victorian Imperialism: A Case Study of the British "Civilising Mission"', *Journal of Imperial and Commonwealth History*, 4/3 (1976), 283–317.

—— *The Scramble for Southern Africa 1877–1895* (Cambridge: Cambridge University Press, 1980).

SEGAL, PHILIP, 'Practical Criticism and Critical Practice', in *Philip Segal: Essays and Lectures*, ed. Marcia Leveson (Cape Town: David Philip, 1973).

SEWELL, W. A., 'Shakespeare', *University of Cape Town Quarterly*, 14 (1931), 9–17.

'The Shakespeare Tercentenary', *Education Gazette*, 15/24 (27 Apr. 1916), 1022–3.

SHAKESPEARE, WILLIAM, *A Midsummer Night's Dream*, ed. P. de Munnik (Johannesburg: Voortrekkerpers, 1967).

—— *Hamlet*, ed. An Examiner under the Board of Intermediate Education (Dublin: M. H. Gill, 1920).

—— *Hamlet*, ed. John Hampden (London: Thomas Nelson, 1930).

—— *Othello*, ed. Guy Boas (London: Macmillan, 1934).

—— *Othello*, ed. Ram Gopal and P. R. Singarachari (Bangalore: Bright, 1928).

—— *Shakespeare for South African Schools: 'Macbeth'*, ed. J. L. du Plooy and V. H. Vaughan (London: Macmillan, 1960).

—— *Shakespeare's 'Julius Caesar'*, ed. Thomas Parry (London: Longmans, Green, 1882).

—— *Shakespeare's 'Othello'*, ed. Henry Roscoe (London, Swann Sonnenschein, 1883).

—— *Shakespeare's 'Tempest'*, ed. J. M. D. Meiklejohn (London: W. & R. Chambers, 1880).

—— *Shakespeare's 'The Tempest'*, ed. Revd D. Morris (London: William Collins, 1875).

—— *Shakespeare's Tragedy of 'Hamlet': A Study for Classes in English Literature*, ed. Lewis Carroll Maxy (Boston: Ginn, 1892).

—— *The Tempest*, ed. Edward Thompson (London: Macmillan, 1934).

—— *The Tempest*, ed. H. J. Oldendorff and H. Arguile (Cape Town: Maskew Miller, 1956).

SHAKESPEARE, WILLIAM, *The Tempest*, ed. I. S. Middleton and V. H. Vaughan (Johannesburg: Afrikaanse Persboekhandel, 1964).

——— *The Tempest*, ed. S. J. Newns (Cape Town: J. C. Juta, 1913).

Shakespeare Tercentenary Celebration (Cape Town, 1916).

Shakespeare's Tragedy of 'Hamlet, Prince of Denmark' (Rugby: Billington, 1870).

SHAYER, DAVID, *The Teaching of English in Schools 1900–1970* (London: Routledge & Kegan Paul, 1972).

SHEPHERD, R. H. W., *Lovedale, South Africa 1824–1955* (Lovedale: Lovedale Press, 1971).

SHERMAN, J., 'Cultural Despotism and the Shakespeare Treadmill: The Prosecution Rests', *Crux*, 19/3–4 (1985), 65–71.

——— 'No Literature for Anybody: A Stronger Case against Shakespeare', *Crux*, 18/2 (1984), 3–8.

SIMON, BRIAN, *Education and the Labour Movement 1870–1920* (London: Lawrence & Wishart, 1965).

SIMONS, H. J. and R. E., *Class and Colour in South Africa 1850–1950* (London: Penguin, 1969).

SIMPSON, DAVID, 'Literary Criticism and the Return to "History"', *Critical Inquiry*, 14 (Summer 1988), 721–47.

SINFIELD, ALAN, *Faultlines: Cultural Materialism and the Politics of Dissident Reading* (London: Oxford University Press, 1992).

——— 'Give an Account of Shakespeare and Education, Showing why you Think they are Effective and what you have Appreciated about Them. Support your Comments with Precise References', in Dollimore and Sinfield (eds.), *Political Shakespeare*.

——— 'Literary Theory and the Crisis in English Studies', *Critical Quarterly*, 3 (1983), 35–47.

——— *Literature, Politics and Culture in Postwar Britain* (Oxford: Basil Blackwell, 1989).

——— 'Tennyson and the Cultural Politics of Prophecy', *ELH* 57/1 (1990), 175–95.

SIVANANDAN, A., *Communities of Resistance: Writings on Black Struggles for Socialism* (London: Verso, 1990).

SKURA, MEREDITH ANNE, 'Discourse and the Individual: The Case of Colonialism in *The Tempest*', *Shakespeare Quarterly*, 40/1 (Spring 1989), 42–69.

SMIRNOV, A. A., *Shakespeare: A Marxist Interpretation* (New York: Critics, 1936).

SMITH, KEN, *The Changing Past* (Johannesburg: Southern Books, 1988).

SOLE, KELWYN, 'Class, Continuity and Change in Black South African Literature 1948–1960', in Belinda Bozzoli (ed.), *Labour, Townships and Protest* (Johannesburg: Ravan, 1979).

——— 'Footnote on Hofmeyr', *Work in Progress*, 2 (1977), 38–43.

—— 'Problems of Creative Writers in South Africa: A Response', *Work in Progress*, 1 (1977), 4–25.

—— 'Real Toads in Imaginary Gardens: A Response to David Attwell', *Pretexts*, 2/1 (1990), 86–93.

SOYINKA, WOLE, *Myth, Literature and the African World* (Cambridge: Cambridge University Press, 1976).

SPANOS, WILLIAM V., 'The Apollonian Investment of Modern Humanist Education: The Examples of Matthew Arnold, Irving Babbitt, and I. A. Richards', *Cultural Critique*, 1 (Fall 1985), 7–72.

Special Reports on Educational Subjects, v (the Muir Report) (London: Board of Education, 1901).

SPIVAK, GAYATRI CHAKRAVORTY, *In Other Worlds: Essays in Cultural Politics* (London: Routledge, 1988).

SPRIGGS, JOE, 'Doing Eng. Lit.', in Trevor Pateman (ed.), *Counter Course* (Harmondsworth: Penguin, 1972).

STOKES, ERIC, *The English Utilitarians and India* (Oxford: Oxford University Press, 1959).

STURGIS, JAMES, 'Anglicisation at the Cape of Good Hope in the Early Nineteenth Century', *Journal of Imperial and Commonwealth History*, 11/1 (Oct. 1982), 5–32.

SYKES, F. H., 'The Teaching of English', *Education Gazette*, 5/33 (7 June 1906), 790–1.

Taunton Report. See *Report of the Schools Inquiry Commission*.

TAYLOR, DORA, *The Role of Missionaries in Conquest* (Cumberwood: APDUSA, 1986).

TAYLOR, GARY, *Reinventing Shakespeare* (London: Hogarth Press, 1989).

The Teaching of English in England (the Newbolt Report) (London: Board of Education–HMSO, 1921).

TERREBLANCHE, S., and N. NATTRASS, 'A Periodization of the South African Economy from 1910', in Nattrass and Ardington (eds.), *The Political Economy of South Africa*.

THEMBA, CAN, 'Through Shakespeare's Africa', *New African*, 2/8 (21 Sept. 1963), 150–4.

THOMAS, ALBERT, '*The Good Woman of Setzuan*: Little Theatre Production a Fraud', *Citizen*, 3/5 (12 May 1958), 9.

THOMPSON, ANN, and HELEN WILCOX (eds.), *Teaching Women: Feminism and English Studies* (Manchester: Manchester University Press, 1989).

THOMPSON, E. P., *The Poverty of Theory and Other Essays* (New York: Monthly Review Press, 1978).

—— *The Making of the English Working Class*, rev. edn. (Harmondsworth: Penguin, 1968).

TRAPIDO, STANLEY, ' "The Friends of the Natives": Merchants, Peasants and the Political and Ideological Structure of Liberalism in the Cape 1854–1910', in Marks and Atmore (eds.), *Economy and Society in Pre-industrial South Africa*.

TROTTER, G., 'Education and the Economy', in Nattrass and Ardington (eds.), *The Political Economy of South Africa*.

UNION OF SOUTH AFRICA, DEPARTMENT OF BANTU EDUCATION, *English Second Language Examination*, Standard VI (1952).

UNIVERSITY OF BOPHUTHATSWANA INSTITUTE OF AFRICAN STUDIES, *A Collection of Solomon Plaatje Memorial Lectures* (Bophuthatswana: Centre for Development Analysis, 1993).

UNIVERSITY OF THE CAPE OF GOOD HOPE, *The Calendar of the University of the Cape of Good Hope for 1887–1888* (Cape Town: J. C. Juta, 1887).

—— *The Calendar of the University of the Cape of Good Hope for 1897–1898* (Cape Town: J. C. Juta, 1897).

—— *Examination Papers* (Cape Town: J. C. Juta, 1916).

University of London Calendar 1860 (London: University of London, 1860).

UNTERHALTER, ELAINE, 'Changing Aspects of Reformism in Bantu Education 1953–1989', in *Apartheid Education and Popular Struggles* Elaine Unterhalter *et al.* (eds.) (Johannesburg: Ravan Press, 1991).

UNTERSLAK, J., and D. RICCI, 'Shakespeare for Enjoyment and Instruction: An Alternative to Mr Joseph Sherman's Case against Shakespeare', *Crux*, 19/2 (1985), 51–5.

UYS, STANLEY, 'Nadine Gordimer's Worlds', *Fighting Talk*, 12/6 (1958), 15–16.

VAN DER HOVEN, ANTON, 'Planning the Future of English Studies in South Africa', *Theoria*, 68 (1986), 107–18.

VAN HELTEN, J. J., 'British Capital, the British State and Economic Investment in South Africa 1886–1914', *The Societies of Southern Africa in the Nineteenth and Twentieth Centuries*, 9 (1979), 1–17.

—— 'Milner and the Mind of Imperialism', *The Societies of Southern Africa in the Nineteenth and Twentieth Centuries*, 10 (1981), 42–57 (London: Institute of Commonwealth Studies Collected Seminar Papers).

VAN HEYNINGEN, CHRISTINA, 'Afrikaans Translations of Shakespeare', *Vista*, 1 (1950), 17–25.

—— 'Christian National Education', *Africa South*, 4/3 (1960), 50–6.

—— and A. W. VAN DER HORST, *English: Intelligent Reading and Good Writing* (Cape Town: Maskew Miller, 1938).

—— *On the Printed Page* (Cape Town: Maskew Miller, 1964).

VAN WYK SMITH, M., *What Literature?* (Grahamstown: Rhodes University, 1981).

VAUGHAN, MICHAEL, 'A Critique of the Dominant Ideas in Departments of English in the English-Speaking Universities of South Africa', *Critical Arts*, 3/2 (1984), 35–51.

VILAKAZI, B. W., To the Editor. *South African Outlook*, 1 July 1939, 166–7.

VISSER, NIC, 'The Critical Situation and the Situation of Criticism', *Critical Arts*, 3/2 (1984), 2–8.

—— 'South Africa: The Renaissance that Failed', *Journal of Commonwealth Literature*, 11/1 (1976), 42–57.

—— 'Towards a Political Culture', *Pretexts*, 2/1 (1990), 69–77.

—— (ed.), *English in Africa*, 4/2, Special issue on Herbert Dhlomo, (Sept. 1977).

VISWANATHAN, GAURI, *Masks of Conquest: Literary Study and British Rule in India* (New York: Columbia University Press, 1989).

—— 'Raymond Williams and British Colonialism', *Yale Journal of Criticism*, 4/2 (1991), 47–66.

VOSS, A. E., *Living in a Critical Community* (Pietermaritzburg: University of Natal Press, 1984).

WALKER, ERIC A., *The South African College and the University of Cape Town* (Cape Town: University of Cape Town, 1929).

WALLERSTEIN, IMMANUEL, 'The Three Stages of African Involvement in the World Economy', in C. W. Gutkind and Immanuel Wallerstein (eds.), *The Political Economy of Contemporary Africa* (London: Sage, 1976).

WATSON, R. W., 'The Teaching of English Literature in Secondary Schools, with Special Reference to South Africa', B.Ed. thesis, University of Cape Town, 1939.

WAYNE, DON E., 'Power, Politics and the Shakespearean Text: Recent Criticism in England and the United States', in Howard and O'Connor (eds.), *Shakespeare Reproduced*.

WIDDOWSON, PETER (ed.), *Re-reading English* (London: Methuen, 1982).

WILHELM, CHERRY, 'Trends in Recent English Fiction and Criticism in South Africa', *English in Africa*, 5/2 (1978), 17–27.

WILLAN, BRIAN, *Sol Plaatje: A Biography* (Johannesburg: Ravan, 1984).

—— 'Sol Plaatje, de Beers and an Old Tram Shed: Class Relations and Social Control in a South African Town 1918–1919', *Journal of Southern African Studies*, 4/2 (Apr. 1978), 195–215.

WILLIAMS, ELAINE, 'Guy Butler and South African Culture', MA thesis, University of Cape Town, 1989.

WILLIAMS, PATRICK, and LAURA CHRISMAN (eds.), *Colonial Discourse and Post-Colonial Theory: A Reader* (Brighton: Harvester Wheatsheaf, 1993).

WILLIAMS, RAYMOND, *Culture and Society 1780–1950* (Harmondsworth: Penguin, 1961).

WILLIAMS, RAYMOND, *Keywords*, 2nd edn. (London: Fontana, 1983).

—— *The Long Revolution* (Harmondsworth: Penguin, 1965).

—— *Marxism and Literature* (Oxford: Oxford University Press, 1977).

—— *Politics and Letters* (London: Verso, 1981).

—— 'The Uses of Cultural Theory', *New Left Review*, 158 (1986), 19–31.

—— *Writing in Society* (London: Verso, 1983).

WILLIAMSON, C., 'Imperial African Native Policy (in Relation to South Africa)', *Bluestocking*, 1/3 (Apr. 1931), 26–9.

WILLOUGHBY, G., 'Friends, Schoolchildren . . . Lend me your Ears!', *Weekly Mail*, 10/23 (10–16 June 1994), 31.

WILSON, RICHARD, and RICHARD DUTTON (eds.), *New Historicism and Renaissance Drama* (London: Longman, 1992).

WILSON KNIGHT, G., *The Imperial Theme*, 3rd edn. (London: Methuen, 1951).

WOLPE, HAROLD, *Race, Class and the Apartheid State* (London: James Curry, 1988).

WOODWARD, A. G., *Aspects of Literary Experience* (Johannesburg: University of Witwatersrand Press, 1966).

WRIGHT, LAWRENCE, Review of Martin Orkin, *Shakespeare against Apartheid*, *Shakespeare in Southern Africa*, 1 (1987), 72–4.

—— 'Shakespeare and the Bomber Pilot: A Reply to Colin Gardner', *Shakespeare in Southern Africa*, 2 (1988), 83–9.

WRIGHT, M. E., 'The English Literature Syllabus', *Educational News of South Africa*, Dec. 1937, 264.

WYNNE, ARNOLD, *The Growth of English Drama* (Oxford: Clarendon Press, 1914).

YOUNG, D. N., 'An Approach to the Teaching of Shakespeare's Plays', *Bantu Education Journal*, 14/6 (Aug. 1968), 30–3.

—— 'The Teaching of Shakespeare in the Classroom: II', *Bantu Education Journal*, 14/8 (Oct. 1968), 32–4.

YOUNG, ROBERT, *White Mythologies: Writing History and the West* (London: Routledge, 1990).

YUDELMAN, DAVID, *The Emergence of Modern South Africa* (Westport, Conn.: Greenwood Press, 1983).

ZANGWILL, ISRAEL, 'The Two Empires', in Gollancz (ed.), *A Book of Homage to Shakespeare*.

Index